CATCHING FIREFLIES

CATCHING FIREFLIES

Tony Rocca

CENTURY · LONDON

Published by Century in 2004

Century Books
The Random House Group Limited
20 Vauxhall Bridge Road, London SW1V 2SA

Random House Australia (Pty) Limited
20 Alfred Street, Milsons Point, Sydney,
New South Wales 2061, Australia

Random House New Zealand Limited
18 Poland Road, Glenfield,
Auckland 10, New Zealand

Random House (Pty) Limited
Endulini, 5a Jubilee Road, Parktown 2193, South Africa

The Random House Group Limited Reg. No. 954009
www.randomhouse.co.uk

A CIP catalogue record for this book is available from the British Library

Papers used by Random House are natural, recyclable products made from
wood grown in sustainable forests. The manufacturing processes conform to
the environmental regulations of the country of origin

ISBN 1 844 13594 2

Typeset by Palimpsest Book Production Ltd, Polmont, Stirlingshire
Printed and bound in Great Britain by
Mackays of Chatham plc, Chatham, Kent

For Mira, forever

To the many dear friends Mira and I have made in Tuscany, paramount among whom are Anelio, Fabiola, Vito, Franca, Giuliano, Alberto, Paolo, Baffo, Barba; our lawyers; the CIA; and the Man in the Rubber Dress.

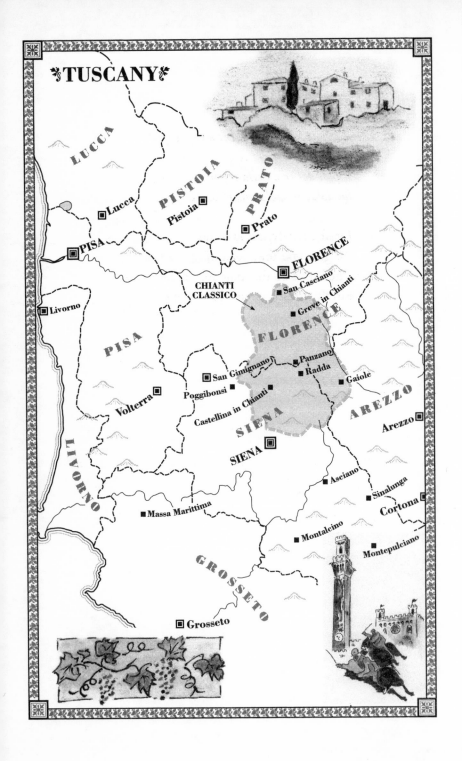

❊TUSCANY❊

LUCCA

PISTOIA

PRATO

Lucca

Pistoia ◙

Prato ◙

PISA

PISA ◙

FLORENCE

Livorno ■

FLORENCE ◙

CHIANTI CLASSICO

San Casciano ■

Greve in Chianti ■

FLORENCE

Panzano ■

San Gimignano ◙

Radda ■

Poggibonsi ◙

Gaiole ■

Volterra ◙

Castellina in Chianti ■

SIENA

AREZZO

Arezzo ◙

LIVORNO

SIENA

SIENA ◙

Asciano ■

Sinalunga ■

Cortona ◙

Massa Marittima ■

Montalcino ■

GROSSETO

Montepulciano ■

Grosseto ◙

Lucciola, lucciola, vieni da me;
ti darò il pane del re.
Il pan del re e della regina —
lucciola, lucciola vieni vicina!

Firefly, firefly, come to me;
I'll give you the bread of the king.
The bread of the king and of the queen —
Firefly, firefly, come close to me!

Contents

I

A Compromising Position

SIENA, 28 June 1990. We emerged from an ink-black doorway and blinked in the harsh backlight of sunshine on terracotta. In contrast to the good humour a radiant summer's morning normally induces in visitors to Tuscany's second city, any casual observer would certainly have seen worrying signs of trauma in our little group. We were four: myself and my wife, our accountant, and our putative partner in a business venture that had taken over our lives.

Benito, the accountant, was a lawyerly-looking man of impressive girth, tightly trimmed beard and booming voice: a big fellow in black silk Armani with damp patches under the armpits. He had a Mediterranean complexion and a habit of hitching his generous shoulder pads as he spoke his own brand of English that could be heard above the hubbub of the crowded piazza. 'I keep tellin' you, Tony. This ees *Eet*-aly!' he announced in the accent of a stage Italian as sweat made rivulets down his forehead. Patting the flow Pavarotti-style with a red bandana, he added: 'Where you think you are? Things take time 'ere, 'special in Siena where everything depend who you know.'

His delivery was not the only thing about him that was somewhat unusual. He was holding a smooth black briefcase in one hand and a bundle of documents in the other, along with the kerchief, and to our further discomfort we could see his attempts at synchronised gesticulations were beginning to attract attention.

'*Si, si si!*,' said Luca, our businessman friend, in *sotto voce* counterpoint. Despite his near-perfect English he was also clearly Italian, of a more athletic build with skin tones approaching mahogany resulting from his endless summers sailing the Amalfi coast. He was dressed for the part in requisite Fendi shades, navy blazer, slacks and a white open-neck Ralph Lauren polo calculated to display his shellac tan to best advantage. 'It's very difficult,' he concurred. 'This bank is the oldest and most conservative in the country. It is not happy doing business with foreigners.'

The root cause of our distress was a wreck of a property little more than 30 minutes from where we stood. It was in desperate need of love and care, with little roof, no windows, and in part no floors; just a ruin with a pervading sense of damp and neglect. We too were in limbo, suspended between dreams and reality and totally dependent on the bank, which had promised us a huge loan to restore the property and not delivered. We were almost bankrupt and it seemed as if our vision of a new life together was doomed.

We were a couple of Londoners (by adoption) who had succumbed to that seductive dream which these days increasingly captivates people trapped in the urban prison of modern life. We wanted to escape, to a haven of sunny contentment where the people are friendly, food comes fresh from an Italian kitchen and landscape and history compete pleasurably to torment the senses. We realised the goal could be illusory, that flight was not going to be easy and we would have much to learn. Also, that we would have to leave some baggage behind: quitting London after 25 years meant giving up jobs and careers as well as proximity to our families and the companionship of friends and colleagues. Moreover, as we were both in our mid-forties and too young to retire, our quest was a little more complex than simply looking for a new home. We hoped we could find a business venture to build up and enjoy together.

Mira had been a travel agent, and had plenty of experience of overcoming the challenges of living in a new country. From her eyes, black hair and olive-toned skin she could have passed for an Italian. However, her family was Jewish with deep roots in Iraq; they fled Baghdad during a pogrom after she was born and trudged through India, Palestine/Israel and Cyprus before winding up in London. She could switch effortlessly between English, French, Arabic, Greek, Hebrew and Spanish (though not, unfortunately, Italian). I, by contrast, was monoglot English, my greatest migratory undertaking having been from Manchester to London. But I could at least claim some Italian ancestry: my great-grandfather had emigrated to Victorian England from Liguria.

We had weighed up the expectations and likely disappointments a hundred times. The problems of the search for the right property; the challenge of dealing with a new land in a new language; the tensions of purchase and restoration on a limited budget. The hidden dangers. The fear of the unknown. The worry of city-dwellers facing country life. The cost. The negatives stacked up, but throughout it all Italy, the land of my forebears, beckoned.

And so, Siena.

* * *

Sixteen months had passed since we first started dealing with the Monte dei Paschi bank, an institution so old it helped to finance Columbus's first voyage to America (apparently the loan is still outstanding). It was an omnipotent moneylending establishment whose origins lay at the medieval core of Sienese life. As principal employer, patron of the arts and paternalistic public benefactor it was able to exploit a symbiotic relationship with its citizens and government that had spanned more than half a millennium. With half of its eight-man board of directors composed of city councillors it was fair to say the Monte dei Paschi was, in fact, Siena. Its tentacles of power and patronage reached into every cranny, and there was hardly a soul in either the city or province of which Siena was the capital who remained immune from its actions, good and bad.

The dilapidated farmhouse Mira and I had fallen in love with and set our hearts on bringing back to life was in the Chianti hills, the famous wine-producing region north of Siena. The beauty of those hills transcends time and visitors are transported back to the Renaissance in a tableau of vineyards, castles and old stone farmhouses surrounded by dark cypresses that stab the skyline.

We had spent almost all our savings on the purchase and getting the project started, and the little we had left had now evaporated after inordinate delays. We were in a rush to move ahead so we could start to earn our keep, but a paperchase of Olympian proportions had already eroded our dreams. Dilatory land registry searches, lawyers' meetings, architects' consultations and interviews with bank managers, town hall officials and provincial and regional bureaucrats had all left our Anglo-Saxon notion of timescale in tatters.

Initially, all had gone well. The bank had welcomed us in, studied our plan, and quickly agreed to consider a mortgage of

1,000,000,000 lire – one *billion* lire (nearly half a million pounds at the time).

'A billion lire?' I said, nervously. Mira, by far the more business-minded of us, sat po-faced in front of the local branch manager and appeared unfazed by the proposition although I knew her pulse was racing too. It sounded a frightening sum.

'*Si, un miliardo*. One thousand million lire,' said the bank manager, a weasel-like little man with eyes that kept darting to the CCTV monitor behind our heads as if it were spying on us. 'I assure you is no problem, will take only few month.'

'And in the meantime?' asked Mira, wishing like me that he would stop being so nervous. The sum was truly enormous in our circumstances.

'Please, do not preoccupy yourself with this matter. We make overdraft, to give you chance to start work straight'way.'

Well, a short-term overdraft made sense if we weren't going to remain idle for the immediate future. I leaned forward and spoke in Mira's ear: 'And who knows what "a few months" might mean in this crazy country? We have no control of that. The paperwork could take an eternity.'

'But how much is it going to cost?' she replied. '*Quanto costa, signore?* The interest rate?'

'*Ma signora!* Please do not worry,' replied the twitcher. 'We will make all the necessary calculations and when the time for the big loan comes we will adjust the interest rate down to that of the long-term mortgage. Any difference will be backdated and credited to your account.'

The true problem, as we innocents were only just beginning to realise, was that we were dealing with a monopolistic monster – a secretive organisation unencumbered with the transparent banking standards that are applicable in Britain. No matter how hard we tried to push the manager, the bank refused to fix or even specify interest rates or – more disquietingly – put anything in writing. (It was not unique in this, we were to discover. Years later the branch manager of another big Tuscan bank told us his head office had forbidden all written communication with clients, full stop.)

Time passed and 'a few months' turned into a year and four months. Our overdraft had been exhausted and renegotiated upwards three times, all the while on the promise that the major loan was imminent. We were powerless in the grip of a fearsome feudal machine, ignorant of each rack-up until later, when we read our bank statements and could only then discover how hard the screw had been turned. An initial interest rate of 15 per cent appeared good value in comparison with the rest of the horror story. The peak of the bank's usury hit the bell at 23 per cent.

It was useless protesting. As we were already well past the point of no return we simply had no alternative but to take more Monopoly money each time we passed Go. There was nothing in writing, just the unconvincing reassurance that things were proceeding as planned and delays were normal.

There had been no further news of progress until that day in summer 1990, which brought us to Siena and a meeting with the bank's lawyers and directors.

Our joy in arriving at this milestone was only slightly dulled by the length of time it took to find the address we had been given. Siena is a Gothic casket of palaces in which the bank has a major share, but instead of showing us a real jewel in a landmark setting it chose to direct us to a back street the width of a Fiat 500 behind the jazzy exuberance of Siena cathedral. Around the front, tourists by the busload were disgorging to gawp at its festooned façade of pinnacles, an overworked confection in black and white marble that has fascinated visitors for centuries. The doorway we wanted was considerably more humble, next to a souvenir shop stuffed with religious trinkets and ceramics and a sign that proclaimed WE SEND PACKAGES FLYING. Another notice announced that the Monte dei Paschi's offices were on the top floor of the same medieval building. We squeezed uneasily into a lift like a birdcage. Not for the first time, we wondered about the inadequacy of our Italian – just about basic O level despite Mira's absorbent linguistic capacities – and the enormity of the moment. Here we were, finally, on the brink of becoming borrowed billionaires and we had less gumption about how things worked or how to express ourselves than the average Italian five-year-old.

The meeting began with a reading of the contracts, which Italian law requires to be conducted out loud. However, the law makes no reference to the speed of this performance; it was recited at such a gallop we felt a rush of air in our ears. It hardly mattered, for even if it had been at less than warp speed our rudimentary linguistic skills did not include legalese, so we just nodded and considered ourselves lucky to catch one word in 30. The meaning was clear enough when the babble at last abated and Benito pressed a fountain pen into my hand. A billion lire! Having counted the noughts out twice to the right and then twice to the left, back in again, I signed, satisfied they were all there.

Neither of our trusted companions on that brilliant summer's day said anything particularly helpful during the signing. Benito smiled enigmatically like a male Mona Lisa and Luca merely seemed interested in the mahogany whorls on the boardroom table. The similarity of colour with his skintones was rather striking.

'Now,' I said cheerfully, 'when do we get to see the money?'

'But *signore*, this is just a preliminary procedure,' replied the senior of the three bank lawyers in surprisingly good English with hardly a trace of accent. 'I am sorry but you will have to wait a little longer before we arrive to the conclusion.'

It was explained that the document we had signed was the *compromesso*, a conditional contract. Only after signing the *atto*, the 'act' itself, would the deal be done and that could now take another laborious nine months. Already feeling pretty compromised, I then heard – or thought I heard, for my Italian really was seriously deficient – the dreaded word 'Mafia'. A worried glance from Mira told me that she had caught it too. I raised my eyebrows. Oh-oh, is this where the squeeze comes? I wondered. How much kickback is involved?

'Aha, yes!' said the First Vulture. 'Before anything else, Signor Rocca personally has to sign an anti-Mafia certificate.' So that was it. I gave a relieved smile and looked around the room, only to become alarmed again when I saw nobody smiling back. 'An anti-Mafia certificate?' I asked.

It was Benito who came to my rescue. Quietly and patiently – rather too quietly? – he explained that under the anti-corruption laws it was incumbent on anyone either lending or borrowing more than the equivalent of £20,000 to swear that it was neither coming from, nor going to, the Mob.

I took all this on board and frowned. Satisfying this obligation was all very fine for the Montegraspers (as we had already renamed the bank) with their huge history, impressive credentials and carefully fostered image of moral rectitude (though subsequent scandals were to demolish all that quite effectively). But to an Englishman with a patently Mafioso name like Rocca and a wife with flashing Italian – nay, Sicilian – eyes this posed a dilemma. I knew what was coming: I would have to satisfy the authorities I was who I said I was, and would not be able to. In those pre-European Union days only a document issued by the Italian Republic bearing my name and photograph, validated with the correct stamps, could be considered acceptable. I'd had some experience of this on a previous occasion when my British driving licence, passport, marriage certificate and even birth certificate, dredged out of the family archives, had been deemed inadequate. At the time, it meant I was rejected as a partner at the Co-op and lost the chance to buy Parmesan cheese and balsamic vinegar at a discount. The new consequences rather had the edge.

I have a fairly short fuse, but when I felt Mira's restraining hand on my arm I took a large breath and explained to the stern-faced lawyers that, strange as it may seem, we poor and under-privileged Britons are not endowed with any other form of ID except a social security number, which would hardly help in the case at hand. I knew the lawyers would be incredulous; like everyone else in Italy they had been brought up to believe civilisation would crumble, bereft of four fundamental pillars of life support. Didn't I have an ID card? No. A personal Tax Code? No. Well then, a Work Book recording my working history, stamped page by page by employers past and present? No. All right, OK, *bene* . . . how about a Family Book stating where I was living, and with whom, plus my children's and relatives' names? 'What?' I said, feigning shock. 'Most certainly not!' Even my own team, Benito and Luca, looked surprised at the revelation of the extent of individual freedom enjoyed in the UK's libertarian state. Surely nobody could be so unfettered, no society so respectful of personal privacy? But the men from Montegrasper were adamant. We Roccas were, most evidently, in trouble.

'OK, so what the devil do we do now?' I asked as the sun hit our faces and our foursome moved away from the corner of the city dominated by the world's oldest bank. Almost by gravitational pull we joined the tide of tourists flowing towards the Piazza del Campo along the narrow lane that is the Banchi di Sopra, from which historically the very word 'bank' derives.

It is truly a mysterious city, Siena. The strangest horse race in the world, the Palio, was about to be run and the air was already electric with anticipation. Passing a news kiosk, our disorientation and bewilderment grew as we caught sight of a newspaper billboard which appeared to read:

- VIPERS ARE FALLING FROM THE SKY!
- SNAKES ARE DROPPING FROM HELICOPTERS!
- CATERPILLAR IS FAVOURITE TO WIN THE PALIO!

2

Welcome to Paradise

UNTIL two years earlier the closest Mira or I had ever come to
Chianti involved the consumption of a not-so-glorious brew,
concealed in a straw-covered flask, in Parsons' Spaghetti Factory
on the Fulham Road. It never occurred to us that one day we
would be making the stuff, or that *it* would eventually come to
consume *us*. In the beginning, Mira didn't even drink. I was the
one doing the arm work, and like most journalists had a palate
so refined I could just about tell the difference between red wine
and white.

We had travelled a fair mile in our jobs. Before she started the
travel agency my beloved (whose name means Destiny in Greek)
had been co-ordinating all hotel contracts Thomson Holidays
held around the Mediterranean. I'd studied the art of warfare,
invasion and *coups d'état* as a reporter in Czechoslovakia, Israel,
Egypt, Greece and Cyprus. Holidays had been spent either with
the Club Med or with British friends at their *finca* in the Canaries
where they cultivated tourists, avocados and bananas with varying

degrees of success. In 1988 we abandoned England. We jumped; we weren't pushed. But losing my job was a helpful catalyst.

I was a veteran survivor of an epoch in publishing in which the word 'redundancy' came attached to the phrase 'new technology'. Half a dozen newspapers had sunk without trace in my many years in Fleet Street, with attendant loss of good well-paid jobs, but as always, there were office politics too. At the *Mail on Sunday* I had an unhappy, inglorious, period and found myself surplus to requirements after Sir David English, editor-in-chief of its sister *Daily Mail*, staged a takeover.

So much for job stability or loyalty. As a younger scribe I had worked for the *Daily Mail* for 10 years. I had moved on to *The Sunday Times*, stayed there 10 years (it's a weakness), then stepped forward smartly when Rupert Murdoch arrived seeking volunteers for redundancy. Next, I was recruited by Sir James Goldsmith's press gang to join *Now!* magazine as deputy news editor, and was rather hoping another 10 years of quiet hackdom might ensue. Instead the job lasted 10 minutes, *Now!* becoming *Then!* the very morning I joined. I picked up a year's pay in compensation and found myself leading the lunchtime news. 'All part of life's rich tapestry,' said Tony Shrimsley, the editor, handing me the cheque and patting me on the shoulder. I'd been there so little time I hadn't even found my way to the Gents'.

About the same time, Mira felt she had gone about as far as she wanted to with her business. She had started a travel agency in the City from scratch and the work was good, but after six brilliant years, building up a turnover from zero to £1 million a year, matters had reached that famous plateau where all small businesses get stuck. To move on she needed to expand, which in turn meant hiring new staff and accepting more responsibility. But the buzz she felt at the start had faded and she wasn't prepared to go that far.

With no children to encumber us we had buried ourselves in work and careers. Approaching middle age, we were in a rut, leading what had become typical humdrum lives: commuting to work, commuting home, spending high-pressured hours in between, wondering where all the money had gone, meeting perhaps once or twice a week by the freezer or at Sainsbury's. Relaxation meant watching *The Good Life* and *Fawlty Towers* and *It Ain't Half Hot Mum*. 'Quality time', as it is called today, hardly existed.

Mira told her surprised staff she was taking time off to look at ways of developing the business. Then one morning she and I managed to sneak away. A cab to Heathrow. Two business class tickets for Alitalia's 11.10 a.m. flight to Naples. And four hours later we were sitting in the back of a chauffeur-driven car, moving out of Naples Capodichino airport and into the busy traffic flow of the A3 autostrada heading south.

We were grateful for the air conditioning as the sun beat down on the black Mercedes, on the melting asphalt, on the slopes of Vesuvius and ruins of Pompeii to our left and on the Bay of Naples shimmering in a petrochemical haze on the right.

After an interesting drive, notable mainly for the way other road-users paid no heed to blind corners on overtaking, Neapolitan bravado once again triumphed over casualty statistics and we arrived unscathed in Sorrento. The small holiday town was bustling with pink, oversized pedestrians in bright beach clothes, the sight of which at last forced our driver to slow to walking pace and then nudge the limo through a clamorous wall of tourists and natives. Every one of the latter appeared to be selling something: ice cream, soft drinks, straw hats, T-shirts, sunglasses, sun lotion, postcards, Kodak film, vouchers for restaurants, boat tickets to Capri, embroidery and wood-inlay trinkets. At last two massive wrought-iron gates opened before us like a canal lock and we slid out of that loud and gaudy human tide and into another world.

A long paved driveway stretched invitingly before us to the merest suggestion of an ochre-coloured building, hiding in the distance. Fronds of palm trees, jacarandas and tall trees with lianas more typical of Africa than southern Europe formed a wondrous tunnel of shade in the blazing afternoon heat. The air was fragrant with floral scents tinged with citrus, and happy voices and distant splashing testified to a swimming pool some-where close by, hidden in the abundant undergrowth. Cicadas throbbed their Mediterranean chorus and the *chack chack chack* of a water sprinkler added its say. We looked at each other and smiled. Welcome to the Grand Hotel Poseidonia.

Our room with its private terrace looked out directly over the great curling sweep of bay with Naples in the background and brooding Vesuvius much to the fore. There were peeling frescos in the ceiling, red roses in the flower vase and a basket of fruit on the coffee table, courtesy of the management. Five minutes after we had been shown in, room service arrived with a bottle of chilled champagne. Welcome to paradise.

The hotel was old and crumbling in parts where earthquake damage 10 years earlier had left great fissures but the main section in which we found ourselves was perfectly intact, if somewhat in need of repair and decoration. Spectacular bursts of purple bougainvillea filled the cracks and gave the whole place that air of studied decay which endows Italian buildings of the *belle époque* with benign dignity. It stood alone on a high bluff above a marina buzzing with speedboats, yachts and hydrofoils that carved great white scars in the sea as they made their scheduled runs to Capri. To me they looked like bath toys far below, viewed from the cocktail terrace which projected out towards the bay with chipped marble busts of Roman emperors on its parapet. From this vantage point, a private lift was at the service of any guest who wished to descend to the port below. A special kind of hotel a million miles from the screaming world of the tabloids and travel agencies. Just the place to relax, take stock of the situation, plan a new life, set off on a new course.

It was Mira's secret, Mira's idea. She had known the hotel owner personally from earlier Thomson days and he had first described the Poseidonia when they met at an ABTA convention. This was far above the package holiday level her company was interested in but she filed the information anyway, sure of being able to put it to good use one day. Hence the Mercedes, roses and champagne: the VIP treatment, courtesy of sun-bronzed Signor Luca Mariani, hotelier, businessman, wealthy Neapolitan and distant relative of The Great Caruso (he had even named a Caruso Suite in his honour).

Luca kept a discreet distance after a first polite hello, leaving us alone to unwind and enjoy the hotel and its surroundings, its gilded salons, three restaurants, gorgeous pool with swim-up bar, lemon groves, and servants in attendance to satisfy every demand. Finally on our fourth day he invited us to join him on his yacht for a trip down the stunning Amalfi coast, with its towns like Positano clambering down vertiginous slopes to the sea. It was a lovely sail. We talked a lot about our lives, and how fate had dealt us a rather curious hand. He talked a lot about himself, the hotel, and – ever the entrepreneur – about how he was always hoping one day to be able to open a new business in Chianti, 500 kilometres to the north. 'My dream,' he said, 'is to have an *agriturismo.*'

'A what?' we asked.

'An *agriturismo*. A kind of farm hotel. More particularly, a wine hotel, without the hassle of having to apply for hotel permits.'

This sounded good.

'*Si, si*. It's possible anyone with an old farmhouse can rent part of his property to tourists and this way get extra money to support himself beyond what he gets from *agricultura*, from his grapes. No, not Bed and Breakfast. You must understand. You English, you had your Industrial Revolution a long time ago, the time of the Queen Victoria. Here in Italy our revolution happened after World War Two. Till then our agricultural sector was very important and dependent totally on a system called *mezzadria*.'

We looked blank. 'It's very difficult to explain,' he continued. 'The farmworkers were peasants who worked for landowners free of charge in exchange for free lodging and half the crop, which is meaning of *mezzo*.'

'Sharecropping!' exclaimed Mira.

'*Si, si*. Cropsharing. It finished after the war, because Italy was in *crisi*, broke, and new industry had to be started if the country was to survive.'

The workforce gravitated to the industrial cities of the north, lured by the prospect of well-paid work in factories such as Fiat or Olivetti or jobs in the fledgling fashion industry. That was why, he said, there were no farm workers left in rural areas such as Tuscany where it was reckoned that by the mid 1960s as many as 60,000 farmhouses stood empty.

Luca paused to top up our glasses of chilled Greco di Tufo, the dry and nutty local wine he said came from the South's best native white grape. 'This is where it gets interesting,' he said. We took another slurp and started to feel heady.

At first, he explained, there had been a rush of well-heeled foreigners eager to take advantage of the rock-bottom prices which were all that the owners of such properties could hope to achieve 'for what in real terms were damp old ruins with zero comfort – no water, no power, no bathrooms. Nothing!' Then the government acted, and in a bid to stem the exodus it introduced *agriturismo* laws giving farm-owners tax breaks and planning privileges that could short-cut the usually lengthy and tedious business of hotel permits. 'There are still places that sing out for buying,' said Luca as he got more excited by the prospect and began to trip up on his idiomatic English. 'If you 'ave the right property in the right place it could be good way of doing business as well as provide you with interesting lifestyle. I dream one day I will find something and make it into apartments for tourists. This is the way of the future in Tuscany. Demand is rising every year. It is fashionable. It is very profitable!'

He said he was going to help some Chianti friends pick their grapes that year at harvest time and during his stay would look around for a likely place to buy. 'Why don't you come and give a hand too?' he said, grabbing my arm so hard he almost knocked me overboard in his excitement. 'If you 'ave some funds to invest, you might even think of doing something like this yourselves. Who knows, we might even join our forces and make business together if we find a right place!'

The idea sounded enchanting. 'Why not?' we said in unison, raising our refilled glasses for a toast. We were hooked.

Only years later did we read in the Michelin Guide that Sorrento was where Ulysses resisted the call of the sirens, plugging his crew's ears with wax and making them lash him to the mast of his ship.

3

Early Pickings

THERE were ten of us toiling in the vineyard that October. *Vai!* Go! *Ferma!* Whoa! – we shouted along with Luca and the rest of the gang as the fruits of our labour stacked up behind a Lamborghini tractor. Autumn had turned the Chianti fields ochre, russet and copper after the hot, dry summer had brought the grapes to their luscious fat prime. Then, bathed in late sunlight, big black juicy bunches surrendered to our secateurs as fleeing puffs of cloud scudded across the horizon like artillery smoke. On the wind, too, came church bells tolling across a tapestry only partly changed in the half-millennium since the Mona Lisa smiled at it, just down the road.

Truly, it was a discovery for us. The 1988 Chianti harvest fully satisfied the foreigner's fantasy of Eden, an impression the world's wine buffs unconsciously endorsed by the exotic notes they claimed to be able to detect in the finished product: of mint, lovage, cloves, curry powder, blackcurrants, prunes and chocolate. We did smile about that as we tramped the Chianti Classico-to-be under our green wellies in the back of an old truck at the start of its long journey from purple juice to fine wine.

Thanks to Luca we had joined a group as diverse as Italy itself: English, Scottish, American and Italian, all friends in common with our host and veteran Lambo driver, Bruno, a Genovese aristocrat and former cruise ship captain known to everyone as Il Comandante. Though diminished in rank to *contadino* – peasant farmworker – and confined in retirement to plotting a course through the twists and turns of his private ocean of vines, he was still a commanding figure even if the most we ever saw of it was his bald and bearded head floating majestically above the waves of greenery like Mao crossing the Yellow River.

We had to wait a long time for the harvest to begin. Not only was it jointly dependent on the weather and ripeness of the grapes; the lunar cycle and atmospherics also had to be weighed in the balance. A dash of folklore added a further restrictive note: an old proverb, designed to ward off the evil eye, which Bruno's wife Gina assured us had been handed down from generation to generation of superstitious sharecropping farmers.

> '*Né di Venere, né di Marte, né si sposa, né si parte;*
> *Né si da principio all'arte!*'

she recited in Tuscan dialect. It was a warning not to get married or take a trip or start new work on a Friday or Tuesday.

The Comandante was restless. Deprived of a bridge to pace or weather satellites to guide him, he was restricted to the dining table where a well-tapped barometer and moon charts helped him plot our attack on his 10 acres. He was scanning the horizon for a clear period of four days to enable us to pick in seven-hour shifts that would help fill Italy's national wine lake, already so deep it accounted for 20 per cent of world production.

For the harvest to succeed the moon had to be waxing, according to ancient lore which said that helped grapes to ripen. Yet if we started picking too soon the all-important sugar content, which converts to alcohol, would be low and that would make the must sour. On the other hand, if we left the picking too late and the weather turned warm the grapes would overripen. Picking in the rain was not only undesirable, it was unthinkable; apart from our personal discomfort, the vines would soak up water, further diluting sugar content.

It all became a bit '*allucinante*' – staggering – a word we were later to hear applied to many things Italian, especially bureaucracy and the contradictory ways new laws and regulations had of creating crises and sowing confusion among the (understandably paranoid) citizenry. It had all seemed so different, sipping chilled wine on Luca's yacht, bobbing gently in the Amalfitana swell and listening to his tales of rustic life and new opportunity. 'If this is what it means I certainly don't want to get involved in making wine,' I said to Mira.

In the end, a huge high pressure weather system moving in from the Atlantic concentrated all our minds, resolving all questions. On a Wednesday, we were glad to note. By then Bruno's impromptu headquarters had become Captain's Table for every meal, the table itself barely visible beneath lashings of Tuscan food and unlimited quantities of the previous year's vino. The old sea dog entertained us with Chianti yarns, of village life and peasant customs and traditions.

Bruno said the Italian flag had flown over Chianti for a relatively short time. Way back in history, two warring tribes, the Guelphs and Ghibellines, fought bitter battles over it for generations as each of two city states, Florence and Siena, sought to impose dominance. Castles, forts, keeps and entire fortified villages echoed to the whizz of cannon balls and clash of arms for over 400 years.

It hit me that Chianti could not have changed much through the centuries. I could just see Leonardo painting *La Gioconda* up the road past the Agip station. Machiavelli's taverna still existed in its original guise. The landscape had been modelled by generations of man in perfect harmony with nature. Here indeed was something worth cherishing, a desirable lifestyle worth striving for. More wine flowed as the Comandante passed sweet *vin santo* and *cantucci* almond biscuits around the table.

Mira's most recent gardening experience concerned our window boxes in London but she took to the harvest as to the manner born. However, I played the role of lapsed journalist better than *contadino*. Up to that point, to me, 'cuttings' had meant newspaper clippings. Working the smooth modern hillside using the best Wilkinson Sword secateurs I could bag from Bruno's kit, I was only too aware of my inadequacies as I tried to establish my grape-picking technique, toiling up the long banks with my weight braced downhill, filling plastic basket after plastic basket to be decanted into a trailer hauled by the smoking, venerable Lamborghini.

It was a sticky business. As the others raced ahead I rather dawdled, lost in contemplation of the grapes.

First there was the *capo dei capi* of the grape world, Sangiovese, Blood of Jupiter, corpulent and dark-skinned. His corkscrewed stalks, reluctant to unclench their knotted hold, surrendered only after a struggle, giving way finally with a squirt of rich, purple juice over my arms and chest. Then came his *consigliere* Canaiolo Nero, another heavy, just as perverse if mildly more fragrant, and ever eager to see me juiced. Bringing up the rear came Malvasia and Trebbiano – one sad, green and unappetising, the other packing nasty surprises in the form of whiplash vines that flew in the face with a painful sting. Definitely a story to recount at El Vino's should I ever survive.

You get to chat a lot while picking grapes. Picking with Harry, a history professor from upstate New York, I learned that the Etruscans had been first on the scene in what they called 'Clante'. The Romans came next: legionnaires returning from the Punic Wars and garrison duties in faraway Britannia were given land in lieu of pay and set about building roads and stone-walled terraces where they could turn swords into ploughshares and spread their knowledge of viticulture. 'Clante' morphed into something a little softer on the tongue: Chianti, synonymous with a dry red wine, later sold exclusively in wicker flasks that were often valued more for their use as candleholders or lamp-stands than for the distinction of their contents.

How a place like that later came to be endowed with so genteel a name as Chiantishire was beyond me, but it was easy to under-stand the potent appeal it held for the first British settlers in the 1960s and 1970s, when new autostradas made the area accessible and those abandoned farmhouses could be snapped up for a song. I remembered reading how a converted Chianti farmhouse became *de rigueur* as a secondary home for the upper classes. And I supposed Bruno had a point when he said that if it hadn't been for them the area would not have survived. For as they attacked the dilapidation they brought work and wealth and a change to everyday life. Now property was no longer so cheap.

It was the optimism of it all that we remember best about our first direct experience in the vineyards. That magical light must have kindled something, awakening deep and unsuspected yearn-ings within our souls and possibly disturbing dormant genes. Mira was reminded of her childhood, growing up in Cyprus and the Middle East with medlars and mulberries and perpetual sunshine;

I was thrown into reflection about my own Anglo-Italian roots. The village my great-grandfather had forsaken in favour of a tough immigrant life in Victorian England can't have been very different from the Chianti villages all around us, and I doubt if he went there speaking any English. I identified so strongly with Italy: there was passion there, something we had not experienced at all in our grey lives in rainy England where conversation increasingly turned on company cars and expense account dining. Seated around Bruno and Gina's happy table after the day's hard work, enjoying good stories, good Chianti food and copious amounts of eponymous wine, the lifestyle of the latter-day *contadino* suddenly appeared compellingly desirable, something worth all manner of sacrifice and struggle to emulate.

I can't remember what it was, precisely, that caused us to give up everything and go for it. It could have been the lovely sight of the harvest moon rising over the crenellated skyline of Radda as we packed the last load of grapes off to the co-operative winery to make the vintage we would be drinking in a year's time. Or maybe it was the *Daily Telegraph* I bought in the village one day, confirming our prejudice with a reference to Chianti exuding 'the kind of peacefulness that casts a faint shadow of content across the future'.

Whatever it was, the spell was complete. The question was, could we afford it? Could we work with Luca, using his professional skill as a hotelier? And what kind of property could we afford, given the disastrous effect on prices and demand of the intervening years since the 1960s boom? For the journalist responsible for the 'shadow of content' article had added an ominous rider. 'About the only stones that have not been restored in Chianti are the piles of roadside chippings left by the maintenance men,' she wrote. 'Left long enough, one suspects even they would be turned into holiday homes.'

4

A Long Hill Far Away

❧

THREE months had passed. We had come a long way since hugging Gina and the Comandante goodbye one warm moonlit night in October. Then, we were full of the satisfactory glow a good harvest can bestow. Mira had put her business up for sale the moment we returned to England, and it had been snapped up by a large conglomerate. We had put our flat on the market and were hoping a sale was imminent. We were elated. But Luca had retreated to his sunny south, attending to urgent renovations at the Poseidonia, and we had not heard so much as a peep out of him regarding likely properties for our venture. How were we to set about finding our dream property?

We were not quite alone in the quest. Prior to our departure, Bruno had driven us to a nearby village to meet an elderly lady whom he introduced as Auntie Barbara. Bruno had spoken of her house-finding capacities in almost reverent tones. She had Chianti covered by a personal grapevine of contacts that ensured that should anything move on the local real estate scene she would be the first to know. Everyone knew and loved Auntie Barbara.

Well into her late seventies, Auntie B. was of redoubtable English memsahib stock. She greeted us from a wheelchair, surrounded by a menagerie of cats and a dog named Brigadier who also appeared to have lost the use of his legs, for the rear half of his torso was attached to what I can only describe as a canine skateboard. It was clear she had been a beauty in her day and on her mantelpiece was something to prove it: a sepia photograph of her as a Bluebell Girl at the Paris Lido. If I remembered correctly, these were girls whose legs were too long for them to have been ballet dancers.

The next piece of information was equally unsettling. The house we were sitting in had been Gestapo headquarters during the war. An interrogation followed, with our inquisitor appearing to scrutinise our credentials to see whether we were going to be suitable people for Chianti, checking whether the social fit were right. It was conducted subtly and skilfully, the softening-up process greatly helped by liberal applications of gin and tonic rather than thumbscrews, any perceived threat coming from nothing more sinister than the 14 (I counted them) mousers perched about us, flexing their claws on bookshelves.

Within half an hour she knew everything there was to know: our background, available capital, motive, desires, likes, dislikes, business experience. Did we know anything about hotel life? Had we ever done any home conversions? Were we capable of hard physical work? Did we have any ambitions of making wine or olive oil? Soon we were trading intimacies like old friends. It was not so much that we had appointed her as our estate agent; more as though she had graciously accepted us as clients.

Clearly we were acceptable, for after an appropriate pause the conversation took an altogether different tack and Auntie B. went into sales mode, proposing several properties which she thought might be suitable for us. The list sounded magical, mantra-like; a roll-call of Tuscan castles, abbeys, towers, villas and farms that lulled us with the romance of their names, nearly all *monte*-somethings, or something-*iglianos*. The price tag that came attached to each one was equally fanciful and beyond reach. But a bank loan would be no problem, she said. There was one bank in particular, the Monte dei Paschi di Siena, which looked kindly on applications concerning the restoration of old properties and was very big in the region.

We were back in London when we next heard from her. We were watching TV again when the phone rang one evening: Barbara, to say she had heard some exciting news from her most treasured and trusted source, Fonzino, the village postman. He had just called to say that a beautiful property, Collelungo, was up for sale. She assured us it was ideal for our *agriturismo* dreams even though it seemed intimidatingly big: the name meant 'Long Hill' and it covered 200 acres, had 30 acres of vineyards (still an undervalued asset then), some olive groves and plenty of woodland. It had a farmstead at its heart that could easily be turned into apartments. She had walked over every centimetre of it herself, she said, and knew it intimately. She omitted to say when, precisely, and we were too polite to ask how long she had been confined to her wheelchair. But, as Luca had not come up with anything better and the asking price of 650 million lire (£280,000, by our calculations) seemed marginally less outrageous than her other quotes, we felt it was worth at least a look.

'How big's an acre?' I asked Mira as my eyes glazed over and we reached for the reference books. 'Big,' she said. 'Have you forgotten, Bruno's vineyards covered 10?' Two hundred acres, we discovered on further investigation, were equivalent to a third of Hyde Park.

* * *

Our Renault's tyres scrunched across icy tracks as we turned off the main highway and onto one of the rough unmade roads that wriggle like ribbons across the Chianti hills, giving access to scattered houses and wine farms and an Italy snugly hidden from the hustle of the tourist pavilions. These dirt tracks – 'white roads' as they are called – penetrate a world where there is scarcely a telephone pole, electricity cable or road sign and get their name from the dust kicked up in summer by anyone travelling down them. Only they were truly white now with frost, and a cold mist clung to the valley.

We turned again and the white road vanished once more into what seemed like thick forest. Pressing on, we were able to follow young cypresses lining the route, but mature oaks still bearing rusty dead leaves crisp with frost made an impenetrable wall on both sides closing in behind us. At last, after what seemed like miles, we entered what had once been a fine avenue of grand cypresses and timidly came to a halt at a small hand-painted sign nailed to an ancient oak. We could just make out the name, in flaking green paint: CO LE NGO.

We were hushed as we got out of the car. Suddenly there was a shaft of sunshine and we realised we were on top of a hill and had left the fog behind. Ahead stretched a view across green-brown hills that folded into the horizon in wave after wave of deep forest. Dormant vineyards awaiting winter pruning raced away in every direction, their long vine tendrils designed by Salvador Dalí. A carpet of acorns crunched beneath our feet and we looked up to see the protective canopy formed by two massive oaks guarding the property. But the sight in the fore-ground was not encouraging.

Directly in front of us were Collelungo's two stone farmhouses, set facing each other across a small piece of steeply descending and overgrown land. There were tumbledown outbuildings and what appeared to have been at one stage a stone barn.

The roof of the building on the left had collapsed. Broken shutters dangled from window ledges where washing undoubtedly once hung. Sparrows swooped through window spaces that had tattered patches of yellow plastic in places not covered with shards of glass. The floor separating a cattle stall, downstairs, from the farmworkers' living quarters upstairs had given way beneath the weight of debris piled on top: fallen tiles, bricks, masonry, a bathtub and other detritus. From this 14th-century heart of the property rafters stuck out in mid-air like the ribs of a shipwrecked galleon. An oak beam reminded me of something I had once seen on a visit to Nelson's *Victory* – ancient, massive, apparently the building's sole means of support but so riddled with rot it was of no more use than a Crunchie bar. Patches of plasterwork mixed with what looked suspiciously like dung had turned the metre-thick walls an unusual colour, and a pervading smell of animal hung everywhere. It was, to say the least, interesting. As Chianti farmhouses went, this was about as ruined as they got.

The building on the right was marginally better, smelling powerfully only of neglect. Here the last of the peasant workers had been able to eke out an existence behind doors that closed and casements that held their glazing, if only just. But the fittings were primitive and insanitary. A composition floor of black, brown and white chip tile had been laid in a bid to upgrade the 18th-century living accommodation to the G-Plan standards of the 1960s. A quarter of a century later, alas, it merely served to accentuate the sadness of the scene.

What Mira and I were looking at was evidence of flight. The remains before us bore a tenuous similarity to the ruins of Pompeii we had visited only months earlier on our trip to the south. As the ancients fled the rolling lava of Vesuvius, so had the old farmworkers abandoned the countryside in the years following the Second World War as the surge of progress overwhelmed Italy, transforming an agricultural nation into one of the elite of the industrialised world. The flight from the land and the country's consequent mass urbanisation hit with volcanic force, and proof of hasty evacuation was plain to see. It lay in the deserted, filthy pigsty that now had mature acacias growing through its roof; in the empty Agip oil drums strewn helter-skelter everywhere; in the abandoned cellars below the living quarters full of barrels, bottles, flasks and demijohns. We brushed past the trunk of an ugly almond tree whose roots had invaded the front of the second house, and entered a chicken coop so mouldy with rising damp the animal rights people would have had it condemned. The front door screeched like a live thing when we pushed it open. As the wind blew, a scatter of labels eddied around us in little whirlpools that the river of life had left behind in its rush to better things.

My first thought was to make my excuses and leave, a reasonable reaction in most mentally stable people. But the glint in Mira's eye told me something else. I felt it too. Here, on the threshold of Europe's greatest cultural, artistic and architectural treasures, in what, nearly 300 years ago, Cosimo de' Medici, the Grand Duke of Tuscany, declared as the world's first official grape-growing area, we had found what we had been looking for. We had fallen in love with the place.

Building One had ancient stone steps sweeping up to a pretty Tuscan loggia, a delicate architectural structure covered in pantiles which must have been beautiful in its original form. Building Two also had possibilities. It was solidly built, and although it was of later origin we could see, even with our amateur eye, that some half-hidden features lay masked.

There was no other sound except birdsong that fine January morning, no movement except the ripple of silver leaves caught in a little breeze filtering through the olive grove and a flick of a lizard's tail as it vanished behind the rock on which we had caught it basking in the surprisingly hot sunlight. The houses seemed to be holding their breath.

The whole spot was impossibly romantic. There was a spirit of place, a feeling of belonging, a soul. We found the size of it intimidating. We knew we could not afford it alone and that we would have to borrow heavily in order to fund the repair work. Luca had made it clear that his other commitments meant he could only come in with a pledge of about a third of the seed money required. But if we joined forces as he had originally suggested we could form a company with him holding a third of the shares to our two thirds, make a business plan and approach the Monte dei Paschi for some major backing.

Hugh Johnson described Chianti as something coming 'as near to the Roman poet's idea of gentlemanly country life as anywhere on earth'. Yes, we were under that influence all right, though not entirely unaware of the potential dangers we faced as well: the snakes and the scorpions, the possibility of power cuts and water crises. But as everywhere else in the world, even in this idyll there were yet darker forces at work – corruption, scandal, suspicion and even sabotage.

5

A Jump in the Dark

HAD we not been so ignorant of the workings of official Italy we might not have been so surprised when, only a week later, Luca called with some disturbing news. He couldn't come through with his share of the cash.

Luca had already explained that he was deeply committed to overseeing repairs at the Poseidonia, but now it transpired that he was trapped in a financial vice. Literally the day after we'd shaken on the idea of joining forces there had been a government announcement releasing blocked relief funds destined for earthquake victims. He had been waiting 10 years for this – a decade since major tremors had caused serious damage to properties around the Bay of Naples.

So much for his good news; now for the bad. Disaster relief funds came with a catch: for every lira coming from the government the beneficiary had to put up one lira, and in order to qualify, repairs had to begin by the spring.

'My friends, I am sorry,' he said on the phone. 'I have no time to give to Tuscany right now, and the money I have to ask you to wait for. This opportunity to repair the hotel cannot be missed.'

This left us with a big decision to take. We could make the purchase alone but it would make a huge hole in our savings. We would have to take on bigger debts. Or we could pull out; it still wasn't too late.

We had a meeting planned, a few weeks later, in a notary's office in Siena on the Banchi di Sopra. We all duly gathered – Luca, Benito, Auntie Barbara and Brigadier included. Even on that morning in February it was warm enough for the windows to be open and the sounds of the city – a police siren, a tolling bell and fluttering pigeon wings – fought a losing battle against the noise that was coming from within. Everyone was trying to be heard at once, with the exception of Mira and me, who were by the window searching for some fresh air. Somehow I had managed to shut out the din and was lost in personal reverie, staring at the Hotel Continental directly across the street.

My very first encounter with Siena had almost been my last. It had happened a good many years earlier, and I had reason to remember it well for it almost killed me.

I was 14 at the time, staying with my parents at the Continental on our first Italian holiday. I was especially thrilled to be visiting the city just at the right moment to catch the Palio, which only takes place twice a year. Once again the ancient stones of the Campo were going to thunder for 90 seconds as 10 nags galloped clockwise around the great scallop-shaped piazza, ridden bareback by grown men armed with metal helmets and whips made from calf phalluses which they had to wield remorselessly, both on their mounts and on each other.

Schoolboys tend to like that kind of thing. Boys my age were tossing flags on poles and playing catch with them. The city's streets were filled with players in a medieval costume drama the like of which I had never thought possible. Like soccer fans, they wore the colours of their particular team – gaudy silk favours with bizarre printed images of giraffes and elephants, tortoises, panthers, owls, caterpillars, and many more creatures. These were the symbols of the various *contrade*, or city wards, that compete in the race. The symbols themselves have survived since the 13th century when real animals used to represent them.

It was the Campo that I remember best, and the Torre del Mangia that casts its shadow like a huge sundial across it. It still amazes visitors, soaring to the sky, asserting its authority over the city and surroundings for mile upon mile. I remember climbing its 503 steps – of course I counted them – to the very top where I felt I could dominate all of Tuscany, so vast was the panorama. I could look north and imagine fighting the Florentine armies camped out in their castles that dotted the Monte del Chianti, the beautiful hills where Castellina and Radda and Gaiole and lesser hamlets nestled amid the vineyards. When I dropped my gaze to the ant heap below I saw how cleverly the majestic palaces built by the city's noble families encircle the piazza to protect it. Running from it, spiralling streets and alleys strung with washing took on the look of something I had seen in biology class: a fossil, perhaps, or the model my schoolroom had of the workings of the inner ear. The streets and buildings were so tall and thin and so uniform of colour, the Burnt Sienna of my Winsor & Newton paintbox, that the meaning of 'terracotta' came home in a flash: the old city was made of baked clay.

It was from there that I saw the Palio horses being led into the piazza for the first of what would be six trial races before the event itself, three days later. The sound of drumming filled the city, summoning people to the spot, right there, where three hills converged, the beat as compelling as any that had sounded for centuries through its labyrinthine passageways – a sound unchanged by time. Primordial. Arousing. Exciting.

That night at the hotel I was so overexcited that I almost defenestrated myself. I sleepwalked right to the sill of our open fourth-floor window before the throb of drumming and the noise of the crowd outside jolted me awake.

I felt a sharp dig in my ribs. It was Benito, brandishing a pen: the cue to bring out our Eurocheques and jump. Mira gave a little laugh at the surprised look on my face. She knew where I had been.

'Well, go on then, sign it,' she said. And I obliged, with difficulty.

Writing large sums of money in the cramped space on a cheque normally made my hand go into contractions even when the amount was in sterling. Having to write the millions of lire expressed as one word, in Italian, on our little Eurocheque felt even more hazardous. I checked all my zeros to make sure we weren't paying billions of lire by mistake. Not that we had any.

The Hotel Continental lay around the corner from Piazza Salimbeni where the Monte dei Paschi bank had its headquarters in all its glory. It completely filled the square with its ornate *palazzo*, considered to be so impregnable it was even nicknamed their fortress, the 'Rocca Salimbeni'. That's the meaning of our name, *rocca*.

That other name, Salimbeni, seemed propitious. I looked it up and discovered it originally belonged to a rich businessman who paid for German horsemen to lead the city's Ghibellines to victory over the Florentine Guelphs at the battle of Montaperti in 1260. (The Palio has been run ever since in celebration: to the Sienese it forms an umbilical link with each citizen's heritage, and is surrounded by a cloak of intrigue that envelopes daily life. As we were to discover, it infiltrates every conversation, touches every business deal and perpetuates the mutual loathing of the Sienese and Florentines which is still felt even today.)

Mira and I were introduced to old Salimbeni, figuratively speaking, by another Sienese businessman, Leonardo Pascucci Pepi, whose name was subsequently to enter Sienese history for quite another reason. The scion of one of Siena's most famous families, Signor Pepi was heir to the old spice merchants who first brought cinnamon and cloves to Europe and a strong candied fruit cake, *panforte*, rich in vitamins and cholesterol, to the world. He was also owner of CO LE NGO, the object of our desires.

Thankfully he spoke good English, so our dealings had been brief, to the point, and seemed straightforward enough. Once a price had been established – unfortunately, the asking price – we wanted to see the land survey map, showing the property in relation to its surroundings. The spice king spread across his desk a sheet of official paper the size of a tablecloth, with a design on it describing an outline roughly the shape of America divided into parcels of land like US states.

Yes, we said, but where precisely was the property? 'Why, all of it,' he replied.

'Do we have to have the vineyards? Can't we just buy the houses and leave the land?'

'I'm sorry, no. It would not be permitted to break up the *patrimonio* – in English I think you say estate, or heritage.'

Trying not to show too much ignorance we asked what we had to do to acquire it. Pepi explained that he had registered a limited liability company in the name of Salimbeni, after the Sienese hero. It was a company that had never traded; an empty box which he proposed selling us for the price of Collelungo. That done, a second manoeuvre would take place whereby

Collelungo would be tipped into the empty box, with no further payment to himself. By this sleight of hand – perfectly legal, Benito admiringly admitted – we would pay a transfer tax of 1 per cent on the deal instead of 19 per cent in VAT.

Benito just smiled inscrutably. Far from the joke figure he had first appeared – roly-poly in frame, comic opera in speech and manner – he turned out to be a formidable accountant, business adviser and staunch ally. He'd been born in 1937, the year Mussolini and Hitler formed the Rome–Berlin axis, to a mother with Fascist sympathies and it must have caused him great regret that she had stuck him with such a name. We quickly warmed to him and even grew to understand his fractured English and odd vocabulary, but his repertoire of mysterious private utterances always left us amused. If either of us asked us how he was he would reply: 'Very bad.' Or, to the question 'Any news?' he would say: '*Enny* news!' Meaning no news. For an educated and intelligent man his choice of phrase could also take us by surprise. 'The Sienese? They eat dogs,' said this most convivial and civilised person when we asked him to be our consultant and come to meet Pepi. 'Everything special in Siena where traffic impossible and you have to park in the bush.' For a Florentine there was something uniquely troubling about doing business in Siena.

'What we do?' asked Benito, hiking his shoulder pads. The question was obviously rhetorical. 'We do two things. First we ask for an assessment on the property. That is how you say, an official valuation made by an officer of the court. We make sure the price is fair for the market, that nobody can come later and accuse us of complicity in asset-*stree*ping.' Mira and I looked at each other. We would never have thought of that. 'Second thing, we ask Monte dei Paschi for mortgage terms.'

The valuation had come through OK, as expected, and the bank was on our side. We thought we were home and dry.

Suddenly a ripple of clapping broke my concentration. We had done it! The ruin was ours. Now all we had to do was sell the London flat, secure that financing, appoint an architect, choose a builder, get rid of the animal stink, move to cheap lodgings for the duration and take a crash course in Italian. How I wished the language had come as part of my family legacy. The only trace of anything Italian in me were my name and an overdeveloped taste for ice cream.

And ice cream was precisely what Mira and I were thinking of as we set off to celebrate the signing with a visit to Nannini's pastry shop, winding our way through the Banchi di Sopra with what seemed like the rest of Siena's business community and a stream of tourists even on a winter's day. Rarely more than 8 metres wide, with projecting roofs of medieval palaces almost touching to form a bridge four storeys overhead, the street was a cross between the Via Dolorosa and the Via Veneto, a point of high pilgrimage and even higher fashion through which a river of humanity constantly flowed.

Nannini's was one of Siena's oldest haunts, a temple to the gods of coffee, pastry and ice cream where business was conducted in rowdy chaos amid clattering crockery and air that managed to be simultaneously blue with tobacco smoke and white with steam from hissing Gaggias. No matter how hard we tried to understand, we could only catch about one word in 20. We saw Luca deep in conversation with Benito but it was like watching a silent film. Being unable to speak the language was a bad handicap. Being unable to hear it was hopeless.

'Cheers!' I said, raising a monster cornet of pistachio ice cream in salute.

'To us and Collelungo!' replied Mira, struggling to lift a huge cappuccino to return the toast.

6

Italian Lessons

THE immigrant in the family had been my great-grandfather Luigi, who left Italy for England when he was about 30 years old, in or around 1865. Luigi became Louis ('Looie') pretty quickly, but he could not shake off his nationality so easily; it took 25 years before he got his naturalisation papers and passport (which is my only heirloom, on the wall in front of me now). He had gravitated north-west to Manchester's 'Little Italy' which became our family home and base for an ice cream business proudly bearing our name, 'Est. 1872'.

When I was with the *Daily Mail* I once worked for a spell in America, with its large colonies of Italians in New York, Philadelphia, Chicago, Baltimore and Detroit, and friends were constantly surprised to hear that a country like England should also have its share of Italian immigrants from the 19th century. In fact, their presence in Britain pre-dated their arrival in America; records show there was little Italian immigration to the United States before 1870, by which time more than half the migrants leaving Europe were sailing from the port of Liverpool, only 35 miles from Manchester.

The greatest influx of Italians into Manchester took place between 1865 and the early years of the 20th century, so Great-grandpa was one of the first. The city was prospering at the heart of the cotton trade, the bales being shipped from America via Liverpool before being hauled off to Lancashire's spinning mills. It was the greatest industrial centre in the world and held a dynamic pull for thousands who uprooted themselves from the poverty of their rural villages in search of a better life in an unknown land. Many like Great-grandpa walked all the way through Switzerland and France to get there. Basically farming people used to a landscape of mountains and hills, they settled under leaden skies and a vastly different outlook of grime and brick, trading open country for narrow streets and the stink of huddled masses at close quarters.

The *contadini* gravitated to the Ancoats industrial area of the city, which had been an unhealthy and violent place in the early 19th century with its mills, back-to-back slum dwellings and high crime rate. But in the rows of mill-workers' houses, many of which were over a century old even then, they must have found advancement: these at least had separate kitchens, living rooms, bedrooms and outside privies. In 19th–century Italy the farming sector had only marginally progressed since the Middle Ages. For many peasants, housing consisted largely of huts, with straw roofs and no flooring. The more fortunate shared their home with the animals in *case coloniche* like Collelungo where humans occupied the first floor and the animals the ground. Bread or polenta were the staples, supplemented by beans, oil and a few other vegetables. Hygiene was non-existent; disease and physical deformity were commonplace, with malaria alone killing something like 2,500 people each year. There were 110,000 landless labourers in Tuscany at the time the Marquess of Salisbury, then British Prime Minister, was signing my ancestor's passport requesting and requiring in the name of Her (Victorian) Majesty 'all those whom it may concern to allow him to pass freely on the Continent without let or hindrance and to afford him every assistance and protection of which he may stand in need'. How grand that must have sounded and how proud he must have been.

The Rocca residence was No. 13 Great Ancoats Street (which strangely enough later became part of the *Daily Express* office where my dad got his first job – but that's another story). Great-grandpa's official occupation was listed as 'musician'; but then, the 1881 census of England and Wales shows that nearly a third of the immigrants were musicians. It seems amazing now, and incorrect, that they would walk the streets of Manchester and surrounding districts playing their barrel organs and hurdy-gurdies, some with monkeys in red waistcoats and hats, and a few with dancing bears.

The Italian colony grew, and began to outnumber the English and Irish families in the parish. Making and selling ice cream in the cellars of their little homes became a big industry – for some a brief living, for others like the Roccas a way of life.

Somewhere along the line, though, Louis's son, my grandpa, another Louis, became involved with a local soccer club – deeply so, considering he worked there for over 40 years in a non-sporting capacity. Back in 1902 when the club wanted to change its name from Newton Heath to something more territorially attractive he even suggested the name by which it is known today. He eventually became chief talent scout and is remembered for bringing a young chap called Matt Busby to the team. Would that he'd had some shares to pass on to his grandson. The name is Manchester United.

Mira and I had made an attempt at pilgrimage to the village old Luigi came from, south of Genoa near the border of Liguria and Tuscany, about a two-day cart ride from Castellina in the old days but just over two hours by car today. We were hoping to find some specific explanation for his departure at a time when 'Italy' was in quite an interesting condition: the fledgling Italian state had only just been created after the Risorgimento, the Reawakening, which led to revolt, insurrection and the proclamation of the Kingdom of Italy in 1861. (Florence became the nation's capital around the time he packed his bags.) But all we found was a quiet, untouristy collection of dwellings in the countryside with *contadini* tending their sheep and goats: an agricultural community based on the cultivation of corn and grapes – just a few scraggy vineyards hanging precipitously over the sea. Maybe old Luigi had been a winemaker originally as well as a musician? It would be nice to think so, and there was no indication to the contrary in the family annals. We couldn't take the research any further as we were thwarted by our lack of Italian. It was literally a dead end: all we found were several graves in the churchyard bearing the family name.

Being tongue-tied was getting to be a big liability. Amusing oneself with *Roots*-type diversions was one thing; when you had just parted with a cheque representing most of your *patrimonio* you were into a whole new ball game, as Grandfather Louis would certainly have understood. We would forever be foreign if we were able only to feel deep sentiments without finding a way to express them.

Everything that lay before us was new and strange and not a little disconcerting. We had no difficulty ridding our systems of the Iberian virus that confuses *burro* (Spanish for donkey) with *burro* (Italian for butter). We came to terms with *salida*

(Spanish for exit) being different from *salita* (Italian for bus entry). We conquered the shock of *vaatair* meaning water closet, *lidair* meaning leader of a country, *speekair* meaning TV announcer – rather, *teevu* announcer – or that cars were sold *full-optional* and that pop stations insisted on playing the *flash parade*. We studied our grammar books, adding new words to our growing lexicon every day. But just when we thought we were advancing, along came a Gotcha! phrase like *Juve merda!* (a comment about Juventus FC, not a racist slur), or *Dio c'è* (God exists). This became one of our favourites, written, we assumed, by devout taggers on almost every road sign, obliterating whatever warning lay beneath in order to hasten the reader's dispatch to the Pearly Gates. Only years later did we discover that it had less to do with divinity and more to do with the proximity of drugs.

The word 'jolly' seemed to enter Italian life at curiously frequent intervals. There is a hotel chain of this name, and we also saw it emblazoned on various other commercial properties and vehicles, notably tanker trucks with big hoses attached to their flanks, the better to clear blocked drains and empty sewage systems. 'JOLLY SPURGHI', we read, which drove us to the dictionary and the discovery that 'jolly' means joker and the other word came from the verb 'to purge'. The Jolly Purgers. Jolly good.

This came in useful later. Meanwhile our rapid learning curve took us on a rocket trajectory to the words for damp course, ventilated chimneys, load-bearing walls, beams, plaster, cement mixers and septic tanks. Handy words to liven any cocktail conversation. Such pleasures paled, however, in our struggle to integrate with the Tuscans themselves.

Behind the guidebook cliché of Tuscany as 'a sun-splashed region with a breathtaking landscape, robust food and wine, and people with a remarkable zest for living' (Fodor) lies another place called Tuscany. We were already discovering two Italies: the one of natural and artistic beauty, mandolins and monster ice creams, the other offering a darker side of paradise. In that one we had revolving-door governments with an average 10-month lifespan, a black economy and corruption from which presidents, prime ministers, Cabinet ministers and captains of industry were all cheerfully profiting; an Italy of organised crime; and, for anyone visiting for more than two suntanned weeks, totally dysfunctional bureaucracy. What we now had to cope with was the difference of the Tuscans from other Italians, the differences between Tuscans themselves and the differences between co-habitants even within the same city.

It beggared belief how ancient animosities could still fester through the centuries inside a Gothic city like Siena, with its complexities of the *contrada* 'system'. Although the Medicis put an end to its city statehood five centuries ago, it still thinks of itself as being culturally and spiritually aloof from the rest of Italy. Its citizens, we quickly discovered, are a tribal community living in 17 different *contrade*, their place of birth within the city's walls (which still stand) determining to which they owe allegiance. This bond is not to be underestimated. Should a Sienese woman have the misfortune to bear a child outside the city walls, no matter where, the father is likely to rush to her side and place a tray of earth from the *contrada* under her bed. (We actually witnessed this phenomenon at the Royal Free Hospital, Hampstead, when a Sienese friend gave birth.)

We were constantly being reminded of the passionate loyalty a Sienese develops for his or her *contrada* that functions as social club, welfare organisation and masonic lodge. It is womb-to-

tomb stuff every inch of the way in the extended family: one is born into the *contrada*, baptised in the *contrada* fountain, receives a *contrada* telegram when one graduates, has a *contrada* herald at one's wedding (when the bride can expect a bouquet from the *contrada*, made up of the *contrada* colours), and can even expect to go to one's grave with the *contrada* flag by one's side.

The secrets of the *contrada* remain secret, for the law of the *contrada* is based on the Sicilian principle of *omertà*: the conspiracy of silence. Alliances – for reasons good and bad – forged under these conditions are truly privileged. Perhaps surprisingly, the city works well in this fashion . . . if having the lowest crime rate in Italy is your yardstick.

The apogee is the Palio when emotional outpourings reach screaming pitch. During Palio days anything goes. Old scores can be settled without fear of official recrimination. Vendettas can be conducted between sworn enemies, such as the Caterpillar and the Giraffe *contrade* (each *contrada* has a traditional enemy and it is undesirable for two Sienese to fall in love across the gulf. Should they marry, during Palio days they retreat from each other to support their home *contrada*.) Events, especially betrayals, which occur then are never forgiven nor forgotten by the injured parties who have not only the right but the duty to take appropriate revenge in the future. The *crimes passionnels* sometimes never even make the papers.

We bore all this in mind when we met the Caterpillar man.

7

Creeping Along

❧

OUR new life down on the farm began with a company with a 700-year-old name that had never traded, a putative partner who seemed to be developing cold feet, an accountant who thought the Sienese had strange digestive habits and a very worrying hole in our budget.

When we bought our first house shortly after we were married in the early 1970s, organising a mortgage was a relatively straightforward affair. Both of us were earning good salaries and the Abbey National appeared very keen to clap us in golden handcuffs. With little fuss we signed the necessary papers, shook the branch manager's hand, and the rest was only painful if we looked at the bank statements too often. No sleepless nights. No worries about who to give a kickback to, how much to give and in what circumstances. Subsequent London house moves and negotiations for loans had proved equally simple.

Dealing with Siena was different. Pepi had mentioned the name of an architect we might consider using for the project and assured us Alfredo Faraoni was our man; if anyone could cut through the red tape that lay ahead, he could. He was a true Sienese, a leading figure in the Caterpillar *contrada* and had the right connections everywhere, including the Monte dei Paschi. This could be useful to speed up our loan, said Pepi.

We were aware that we would probably have to bribe someone somewhere along the line; we had read the books and seen the films. With most Italians, corruption was both involuntary and inevitable – or so the stories went. Everyone knew the wheels of commerce were greased by a *regalo* (gift), *tangente* (kick-back), or a basic *bustarella* (little packet, or bribe); these were the first Italian words we had learned from our eager tutor, Benito. But it seemed we were wrong. 'I would not recommend that you try,' said Pepi. 'You have to be very careful. Siena is a totally Communist province. People are proud. They would hate to have foreigners, even other Italians, thinking they can be bought. It would be seen to be patronising and condescending. If you don't get the right person it could have the completely wrong effect and you may never get your permits or loans.'

Signor Faraoni turned out to be an effete character who smoked thin cheroots through a Noël Coward cigarette holder which he held before him like the bowsprit of a yacht. He was an effeminate little man, dandily dressed, and we took an instant dislike to him. He spoke with a heavy Sienese accent which converted all hard 'c's' into aspirate 'h's' – '*casa*' becoming '*hasa*' for instance – which further complicated our lives. And we noticed two things that distinguished his office from other architects' studios we had seen: the general state of disarray and the extraordinary collection of caterpillars, some up to a foot long, made of wood, plastic, glass and metal that appeared to be crawling all over the Formica top of his desk. But if that was the way to get on, what did we care?

Faraoni was not in fact an architect but a *geometra*, or surveyor, which is a fair substitute in Italy for the type of work we were proposing. One of the main reasons for hiring him was that he was local – an odd qualification for a surveyor, but Auntie Barbara and Bruno had both warned us against engaging any professional from outside our province. Another Florentine like Benito, especially, would have been anathema.

Faraoni seemed very positive. We could get started on the project immediately without permits, he said, as long as it could be classed as remedial work – roof repairs, that kind of thing. He would take care of all the applications for planning permission meanwhile, and if the formal approach did not bring the desired results we could always take a risk and build whatever we wanted anyway. Such was the way of doing things in Italy. Mira and I lost him here a bit. Was he saying we could get away with *anything*? 'No, it has to be within reason,' he said, 'a window here, a door there. Sometimes the height, sometimes the size of a building. This is what we call *abusivo* but everyone does it, then you wait for a *condono* and pay a fine and that's it.'

'*Abusivo*?' '*Condono*?' We looked askance, but there was no further help coming from our man, so we had to turn to Benito later for explanation. He confirmed that building without benefit of a permit, 'abusively', had become rampant, aided and abetted by a parallel system that actually condoned wrongdoings: a bizarre Italian solution of amnesty. (Not so odd, really, considering how central a pillar of Roman Catholicism is the old confession/expiation/absolution routine.) It was all there. It meant you could confess your sin and be forgiven for building something without planning permission on eventual payment of a fine, which may not be due for many years. As a system it was totally self-defeating, for frantic building work would start the length of the land upon the merest whiff of a *condono*. Even without that whiff, illegal buildings sprang up without benefit of permits, the owner knowing that with luck and by the law of averages an amnesty would be declared and, for a premium, he would get his way. It was the building that was *abusivo*, not the owner. He would pay only a fraction of the fine he would otherwise have to face if prosecuted – and would have avoided the long wait normally associated with obtaining permission. 'We have village not far from Rome, who become famous as most *abusivo* town in Italy with 3,667 *condono* requests in one year,' Benito said. 'His population is 2,000.'

We considered the *condono* route and rejected it. With a high-profile project such as ours it was prudent for us, as foreigners, to tread softly. Our village, Castellina in Chianti, lay on the old hill road between Siena and Florence. It was small, everyone knew each other, and on Sundays we had already become a tourist attraction with a continuous flow of inquisitive locals passing by. We suspected that envious eyes might easily be cast our way and we did not want to run the risk of being reported for any misdemeanour, intentional or otherwise.

But Faraoni did seem to be able to offer some hope on the banking front. Yes, he said, he knew a certain Professore, *'un personaggio'*, who could help us fund the restoration of Collelungo quickly. Faraoni's key to the Montegrasper monolith lay deep within its corridors of power, a fellow member of the Caterpillar *contrada*, a man of trust and great influence. And so, concurrent with our approach to the Monte dei Paschi through the front door we plugged into the old boy network around the back. Or more specifically in this case, the old Caterpillar connection.

Italy's major political corruption scandals had yet to erupt when we first met Professore X, The Caterpillar. At his insistence this was not in his office but in the bank's lobby – and solo, without the presence of advisers, which struck us as odd. We were far from happy not to have Benito along. Why wouldn't the Professore see us in his office? Faraoni said he was a senior executive at the bank, very well placed in a property and mortgage division that dated from the 15th century when the Monte dei Paschi was the municipal pawnshop. We, to our great surprise, were new owners of a property which provided abundant collateral for an open deal and having decided not to build anything *abusivo* we had absolutely nothing to hide. But Faraoni was adamant: we were to be present with him alone in the lobby of the bank headquarters in Piazza Salimbeni and wait. Which is what we did, in an ambience that owed as much to Ancient Rome as to the stock exchange.

'Meestair and Meesis Rocca?'

'*Si!* Er, yes!'

The man who could be about to control our destiny was as bald as Kojak but smaller, more like a shrivelled Yul Brynner. Less immediately obvious was his dental work: he had a front tooth on a palate that became dislodged with troubling regularity and shot out at unexpected moments like the bird from a cuckoo clock. Once I was aware of it I was transfixed, anticipating its appearance in studied fascination.

The Caterpillar's wobbly incisor lay inactive and under control until excitement got the better of him on his second or third sentence – in surprisingly excellent English. I gave an involuntary jump as it flicked out like a lizard's tongue soon after our handshake.

'I never invite customers to my office for fear of being accused of favouritism,' said the Professore, tucking away the offending palate and contriving to smile. He also neatly tucked away the gift of vintage French claret we had brought along at Faraoni's suggestion (insistence, actually).

'*Allora?*' I replied, using one of my brave new words and shrugging Italian-style as I was learning to shrug. He seemed ill at ease and shooed us out of the echoing entrance hall forthwith. Not for us the comfort of the confessional, the intimacy of the interview room, the privacy normally accorded matters of such great weight.

'*Andiamo da Nannini!*' said this Kojak-Brynner-Caterpillar. And with that we set off with what seemed like the rest of Siena's business community for what was rapidly becoming our favourite cake shop, line astern behind Caterpillar Faraoni – a caterpillar conga worming its way through the bustling Banchi di Sopra, choked with locals and tourists. Finally, in a setting that could have graced a Fellini film – that hiss and babble and clatter of coffee cups – we just drank coffee and tried to look intelligent whenever the two Sienese looked our way. Not hearing a word, not understanding a word, not saying a word. Hear no evil, see no evil, speak no evil down among the Caterpillars. It gave me the creeps.

Benito turned catatonic when we told him about our meeting. 'I have in my hands many newspaper stories regarding the matter of banking corruption,' he said. 'I am sorry but I cannot help. I can only suggest you a good lawyer in Firenze.'

I was, frankly, getting pretty anxious. I hadn't managed to get a good night's sleep after that rum do at Nannini's, after which we heard nothing (because, as it turned out, the ceiling was about to fall in on Signor Pepi and on the bank's top executives too). The episode seemed forgotten and was never referred to again by Faraoni in our subsequent, and brief, dealings. Then one day we managed to break through the impasse created by the lack of documents to back up my anti-Mafia declaration.

The mentality that says if you haven't got the right piece of paper you don't exist is so typical of a people who are Olympic gold medallists at bureaucracy. But what is endearing about the Italians is their ability to find a way out of the dead-ends they create for themselves: show them a law and they will instantly find a way to circumvent it. The law itself is patently a good thing, they will argue; it is merely its enforcement that is undesirable. Therefore laws exist but they do not produce the desired results. Or as Benito put it: the law is an '*asino*'. 'You make income tax declaration: not to do is penal offence. But if you don't pay is no penal offence – so nobody pay!' That was our accountant speaking.

We were saved by the same native ingenuity that created the confusion in the first place. After much deliberation the bank's lawyers agreed that circumvention was both possible and legal in my case. As I did not have the required documents, being a foreigner, therefore, quite logically, they should not be expected of me. A simple sworn statement, or auto-declaration, would suffice.

Concluding my affairs with the underworld in this way came as no small relief and meant we were going ahead with the orthodox mortgage application. No longer did we risk being in the clutches of the *contrada*. Coincidentally, it was about then that another worrying loose end was also resolved: the little matter of the flying vipers. It seemed like such a good story Mira was amazed I had not thought to follow it up immediately and write about it, but quite frankly I was enjoying my retirement from journalism. That I had not nosed around to discover more, like the old news ferret I used to be, was symptomatic of my withdrawal. And the weight of other matters on my mind.

Bumping into Pepi by accident one day we discovered an erudite and reliable Sienese source to educate us on the subject.

And what he said undoubtedly put things in perspective even if it did leave some nagging doubts about certain people's sanity.

As we already knew, the Tuscan countryside had its quota of grass snakes and adders as well as nasty black vipers (the locals call all of them, collectively, *'viperi'*). Siena had a pharmaceutical firm, SCOLA, which used snake venom to manufacture medical products, mainly for anaesthetics. The vipers had been taken to SCOLA to have their venom extracted. It turned out that the newspaper story behind the billboard headline detailed the problems of redistributing them. In earlier times they would simply have been killed, but in a more enlightened era, no doubt fearing the wrath of reptile rights activists, the company had decided to return them to their natural habitat as humanely as possible. As a public service the Carabinieri had provided a helicopter to scatter them evenly around the province, dropping them from treetop height, so that everyone got their fair share.

The scaffolding went up. A crane emerged from nowhere and was assembled, Lego-style, in next to no time. Our builder Massimo (a Faraoni recommendation) and his team of three fellow Neapolitan workmen swung into action. They could have been from Ruins 'R' Us. In the space of a few weeks they managed to turn a scene of simple dereliction into one of near-total destruction. I kept being reminded of the Vietnam village that was razed on orders of the American general who said he had to destroy it in order to save it.

We had to go on squeezing that overdraft that was costing a fortune. We simply had to press on. We couldn't continue to have money tied up with nothing coming in. There was a plumber, an electrician and a carpenter to appoint; the *comune* (our local council), the *provincia* and *regione* to approach for building permits; and a development plan to prepare for approval by the *Belle Arte*, or fine arts commission, guardians of Italy's heritage. In addition we had to contact the health authority (USL); the environmental authority (IRPAT); the electricity people (ENEL); the phone company (SIP); the chamber of commerce (CCIAA); the road authority (ANAS), the water authority, forestry authority and the fire brigade (in relation to the LPG tank we wanted to bury in the grounds, ASAP). Acronym-itis was setting in.

Our working environment was rather original. The hotel we were staying at had only one phone and it was constantly in use, so we had to make all our calls from the main bar in the village. It doubled as our office; we held all our meetings there. In winter it served as a cinema, specialising in Kung Fu films, as well as amusement arcade and public lavatory. It was remarkable for two elements one does not normally associate with *la dolce vita*: the stink of pee and the noise of the slot machines.

We were familiar with the wayward nature of Italian payphones; how you had to juggle tokens and 200-lire pieces to feed the mechanism's insatiable appetite. But in this case, making a call required supplementary efforts: cupping an ear to drown the clang of the pinballs and Bruce Lee as well as blocking your nose to avoid the smell. The ability to stand on one leg also helped, in order to kick the door of the Gents' shut with the other. It had a habit of swinging open towards the caller in a slowly widening arc – predictably, just as you got through to your number after several failed attempts. It was our only link with the outside world. We even made our Sunday calls from there to reassure worried old folk in England that all was '*splendido*'.

The vines were another concern. In latter years Pepi had rented the whole lot out to a local winemaker as an excuse to get rid of his sitting tenants at Collelungo – the *contadini* family called Migliorini whom (we later discovered) he had unceremoniously booted out in order to ease its sale. From my viewpoint I didn't even want to tackle finding a new producer who might pay more. So after talking it over with Mira we simply renewed the contract. 'That's one thing less to worry about,' I told her.

The cement mixer churned, the crane jib swung, the Neapolitans sang love songs. We found ourselves unexpectedly busy. We had thought that by appointing a surveyor and paying professional-scale fees (Faraoni had insisted on having 50 per cent up front) we would receive something more than just designs and a list of places where we could get our supplies. But we were on our own. From our modest digs in Castellina, where we had wisely negotiated a long-term rate, we made endless sorties in search of the right stuff. The long days were exhausting, and when it came to picking the correct terracotta the choice was so vast we almost gave up. Roof tiles had to be a mixture of old and new, the new ones given a patina of age to make them look right; floor tiles had to be glazed because pure terracotta stained easily and would need regular waxing; half-bricks from which a series of new steps and pathways could be built had to be just the right thickness.

All these specifications were to suit Faraoni, the master aesthete, a man not easily deflected. Who was working for whom was a good question. We found out later that he got kickbacks from our purchases, which he made us make far too early in the project – 600 square metres of tiles before we even had a permit, for instance, when we could ill afford it. He insisted we keep our conversations with Massimo, his builder, to the minimum, 'to avoid confusion,' he said.

On our site visits Mira started planning the garden, visualising terraces, walkways, and bowers where wisteria might one day thrive. Even I caught the mood of optimism and rather recklessly started strimming the knee-high grass to keep my mind from thoughts about throttling our *geometra*. This turned out to be a disaster because the strimmer leaked petrol down my back and I was exhausted after 15 minutes. That was when we met our first neighbour, a lovely toothless Tuscan called (we thought) Cheeso – actually 'Ciso, short for Narciso, or Narcissus – who came to our rescue with a broad grin and a present of rose bushes dug up from his own garden. A former sharecropper, he was busy saving up enough money to buy his farmhouse from his landlord, even though everyone else seemed to be too anxious to leave theirs to rot.

Cheeso made short shrift of the jungle, cackling like mad to himself as he strimmed thisaway and that. We couldn't see what was so funny.

'Hey Cheeso, what's the joke?' Mira shouted above the din of the two-stroke as he swished professionally under the cypresses.

'Ha! I planted these trees 40 years ago!' he yelled with a huge grin.

Our bank balance (what was left of it) dwindled. New timbers and rafters and insulation material arrived. A new roof went up – as Faraoni said, repair work for which we did not need a permit. We started to feel that at last, things were coming right. The two-year goal we had set ourselves for the rebuilding operation seemed attainable. We even went ahead and ordered stationery, choosing as our proud logo one of the beautiful old oak trees standing at the entrance to the property.

But still Monte dei Paschi financing was nowhere in sight. The local bank manager (The Weasel), pleading ignorance of head office dealings, pressed us to take a further overdraft on the basis that he had been told unofficially that our mortgage would be approved. We were running into serious money problems despite trying to keep costs to a minimum. We could scarcely do anything but accept.

And then Pepi went bankrupt.

8

No Place Like Home

❧

THE *panforte* families are the snobbish elite of Siena, which despite its Gothic grandeur is a resolutely working-class city of only 70,000 souls. So when Pepi's empire crashed, in certain quarters the news was considered hardly less traumatic than the fall of the Republic of Siena in 1559 when the city became subsumed into the Tuscan dukedom. For the higher echelons, bankruptcy of one of their number was a disgrace, a humiliation hard to reconcile. Many went into denial, pretending it hadn't happened. Others shrugged and appeared genuinely sorry that he had fallen off his high horse – which was appropriate as it was nags, not sticky cake, that had brought about his downfall. The racehorses he owned, in addition to his properties and businesses, were a constant drain on his resources. (He had ventured into blood-stock when he took over the company from his dad.) The Monte dei Paschi foreclosed, throwing out of work hundreds whose families had for generations considered the Pepi bakery as secure as the city walls themselves. They did not immediately know that the disaster had nothing to do with the quality of their product, which remained excellent if over-rich, or that the sale of Collelungo had bought their *padrone* only a brief reprieve. We were sorry for Pepi and for his wife, who suffered from Parkinson's disease; sorry, too, for his father, Don Vito, who was the last person ever to have made wine commercially from grapes grown at Collelungo. That was in the 1960s when the place was a vibrant hub. Up to 20 people lived there, and the produce was carted off to be mixed with grapes from other farms belonging to the Pepis, who sold the result to supermarkets.

We should also have been sorry for ourselves. For when Benito next spoke to us he wasted no time in spelling out the full implications. "Orrible news,' he said. 'Now we too can expect inquiry.' But why? we asked. 'Because in Italy the court has right to investigate all business of bankrupt for two year before bankruptcy. You have same in England, no? Is possible asset *stree*ping.'

'But hold on. You insisted on having a court-approved valuation! We can show that he wasn't asset-stripping,' we protested. 'We bought it at a fair price!'

'Listen,' he said, 'this is Italy. You no unnerstand.'

The Monte dei Paschi did. In spite of our signed contract and our having followed their requirements to the letter, Faraoni told us it was pulling out of our deal and recalling its overdraft. Soon after that, Italy's Communist Party reinvented itself and came up with a new name, the Refounded Communists, and a new logo. It chose an oak tree – just like the one standing proudly at the entrance to our property and on our letterhead.

It was about this time that the new owners of Collelungo began to consider that they might have made a mistake.

Until recently the Migliorini family had made their home in the second building, the one that had the benefit of a roof.

Following instructions, Massimo and his squad had created a small living space for us in the middle of this mess so we could move from the hotel and save money. It was a parody of the Tuscan dream with rubble everywhere, rain coming through the roof and nowhere immune to cold draughts.

We had a bedroom, a kitchen where we could cook, open-plan with a living room with a fireplace, a bathroom with a tub and WC, running water, electricity and – at last – a telephone of our own. The bedroom was OK despite having only half a floor and a Force Eight gale blowing into it from the empty space below, presently without any glass in its windows, via the hole under the bed. The kitchen was really a makeshift hob attached to a cylinder of camping gas, but we had a fridge. The living room was an enormous, cold volume and the big Tuscan fire-place, grand enough to walk into, demanded an enormous amount of chopped wood to provide the merest hint of warmth. The WC was connected to an individual septic tank which the boys had planted directly beneath our bedroom window. The water ran cold; it had been piped in by garlanding lengths of PVC tubing outside and running it through these loops by gravity from an old concrete tank up the hill. The electricity cable, simi-larly, looked like a Christmas decoration running through the air from the building site junction box, nailed to an upright plank. Inside, wiring ran down the walls in parallel lines to a big porce-lain switch from which sparks flew at frighteningly frequent intervals when it rained. At least the telephone worked, most of the time. The line crackled promisingly when an engineer from SIP, the state telecom agency, tested it and said it needed working on: the old-fashioned conductor outside was cracked and obso-lete. The phone came complete with an ancient timer that clocked up the units with a loud click, starting from the second you finished dialling and well before anybody could pick up the call.

Even when we got through there was no guarantee that we could be heard. One day, Mira's mother in London was so fed up with the echo on the line that she called BT to complain. Only she didn't tell us, and out of the blue I received a phone call that was to result in the most bizarre conversation I suppose a Tuscan farmhouse has ever been party to.

'Hello?' said a Cockney voice. 'Is that Siena 740 . . . ?'

Reassured that he had the right number he introduced himself as a BT engineer, wanting to check the quality of the line. 'There's been a complaint, you see. We have to check these things out. Know what I mean?'

'How can I help?' I asked, amazed that the British Telecom of blessed memory had become so consumer conscious.

'Well, could you say something so I can put the mikes on the line and we'll see where that gets us?'

The problem is, unless you are a thespian and can remember some famous lines you tend to dry up when ordered to 'say something', especially if you know it is being recorded. 'Sure, like what?' I asked, and a couple of minutes later found myself reciting tongue-twisters and nursery rhymes to a grown man I did not know half a continent away.

'Around the rugged rocks,' he prompted from London.

'The ragged rascal ran,' I replied from Tuscany.

'Peter Piper' '. . . picked a peck of pickled peppers.'

He seemed to like what he heard and was almost happy to tell me that there was indeed a lot of interference causing echoes. Thus encouraged, I launched into 'Mary had a little lamb' – at which point Mira came into the room and thought I'd gone potty.

It wasn't that the walls were all damp, or the roof all that badly in need of repair, or the evidence of active rodent life all that conspicuous. It was just, somehow, not quite the epitome of Tuscan bliss we had in mind when we left our snug, modern apartment in London with its piped TV, porterage, central heating and constant hot water.

That first winter was the worst. The penetrating cold and damp seemed to bore its way into the thick stone walls and hang in there, exuding icy malice. The windows were rattletrap frameworks, hastily nailed together and held in place with quick-fix cement; consequently they made great conduits for draughts. We invested in a Japanese paraffin heater, a powerful survival tool which we had occasion to bless many times.

All around us, the world was turning negative. The Gulf War was blazing across television screens in rival bars around the snow-dusted Campo, where the whinnying and shouting of the Palio were but a distant memory. Awash with a tide of humanity in summer, it was now flecked with only a sprinkling of tourists, Japanese mainly, little Lowryesque figures bent to the east wind, condom-wrapped in plastic macs. The Sienese, being a closed community, seemed unconcerned by Operation Desert Storm. The billboards that had once screamed about flying vipers were displaying hysterical typography again, but this time the subject matter was merely hamburgers. McDonald's were at the city gates, demanding to be let in. Medieval greatness was about to be breached, by golden arches rather than Florentine cavalry.

We boiled our pasta and coffee on the primitive stove and crouched around the fire embers listening to crackly BBC World Service reports of cruise missiles falling on Baghdad. The elements didn't help. We experienced a succession of storms that seemed determined to tear the farm from the ground. Gales sent tiles flying from the roof, put our guttering in perpetual motion, rattled the window panes and battered the walls with earthquake force. More than once we could have sworn we saw something structural move. Nothing moved on the Monte dei Paschi front, however. The bank had gone completely quiet, deserting us and refusing to correspond with us. We only had our surveyor's word for their decision to abrogate the agreement, never once receiving an explanation, either verbally or in writing, official or otherwise. The Weasel declined to see us. Benito tried phoning the lawyers and was stonewalled. Silence. It was as though we did not exist.

Thunder, lightning, rain, hail and snow hit us with equal vengeance, and sorties to gather wood for the fire became Outward Bound adventures. Then one night the mercury started to drop. Our dangling water pipe froze. We went to bed early at 9 p.m. carrying two hot-water bottles each and wearing ski hats and gloves and sweaters over the long-johns and sweatshirts we had adopted in place of pyjamas. So clad, we were sitting up reading with our teeth chattering when a giant crash of thunder and a flash to equal anything seen in Baghdad caused our solitary light bulb to fail and we finished our paperback by candlelight. (It was a Harold Robbins. Mira had read the first half which she tore off and gave to me because I had devoured everything else in the place.)

Next day, with frost riming the ground and the thermometer well below zero Celsius, Mira declared that she had had enough: *I* might be prepared meekly to accept this as my destiny; as for herself, *she* was going to do something about it. 'It's the evil eye,' she said. 'We've been cursed and we've got to exorcise it.' Oh dear, were we in trouble. Had she taken leave of her senses and regressed to her oriental roots? Not quite, as it turned out; somebody had been filling her head with stories about a certain church in Siena where afflicted pilgrims could banish their devils and end a run of ill luck by lighting a candle and saying a little prayer. I had two choices: either to go along with this malarky or risk losing my Destiny on the slippery road to Siena that was covered in ice. I had a mad urge to let her drive but relented in the end and off we slid on an erratic course for the Church of Saint Mary of the Slaves.

Generally speaking, the churches of Siena are not noted for their lavish decoration or ornamentation and I thought it appropriate that the church that had been waiting for us for six centuries should be listed in the guidebook as having not just one work of art depicting the Massacre of the Innocents, but two. It also had various chapels leading off the chancel and aisles, each with its own altar ablaze with candles. I stopped counting after noting 10, none of which bore a sign saying 'EVIL EYE EXORCISED HERE', and the Michelin was no help.

By now I was getting a bit fed up with this little caprice. 'Why don't you ask that old lady over there?' I said more as a dare than anything else, pointing out a hunched figure in black clutching a rosary. 'She looks like a regular who'd know which one to go for.' And Mira duly approached the unsuspecting worshipper, probably interrupting her muttered prayers with her question about the evil eye – *il malocchio*. Never can a member of the congregation of Saint Mary of the Slaves have been so electrified. With a screech she shot out of her pew and fled before the gaze of her fellow parishioners, penitents, tourists and ungodly gawkers such as myself who had come in from the cold just to shelter.

'Come on,' I said, 'give it up now. Let's go.' And she reluctantly followed as I started making my way to the main doors, where we passed a table with a wonderful display of long tapered candles for sale at 500 lire apiece. 'Can you give me a coin?' asked Mira. 'No, I've only got a 5,000 note,' I replied. 'That'll do. Give!'

So I handed her 5,000 lire and she bought 10 candles which she lit and positioned one per altar around the church. Just to be on the safe side.

We awoke to snow the following day. There was that gunmetal light, a vision of blizzarding flakes, and a white-out which we will never forget. It snowed all day, the next night too. Thirty-eight centimetres fell in all, a record, they said on the radio (which was on its last legs, with batteries fading fast). The phone line was down. There was no power. We had only a little firewood and our precious paraffin reserve was reaching danger level. For water, like Arctic survivors, we melted snow. For food we had cans of sardines and tuna and spaghetti. For light we had candles – not that many, just enough to withstand the four days the siege was to last. We played Scrabble and I painted some watercolour shields to hang in each of the apartments which we were going to name after the *contrade*.

So much for banishing the evil eye. We were stuck, truly prisoners. Even if we could have got out, the car wouldn't start: its fuel lines were frozen. We made one attempt on foot in a momentary lull, but found many trees were down, blocking our exit. We also noticed a vast white space where once there had been a lovely tree. We had lost a huge centenarian oak: it just collapsed under the weight of the snow piled up on its winter-brown leaves.

I grew rather introspective at that point.

What had we let ourselves in for? What kind of masochism was this? Could it have been that dear old Great-grandfather had known something when he packed his bags and pushed off to England all those years ago, leaving the colourful warmth of the Italian coast for a future in soot-black Manchester at the height of the Industrial Revolution? What special urge had motivated him to exchange sun-kissed olives, oranges, lemons and bougainvillea for dark oppressive cotton mills and Victorian workhouses, where the only splash of colour came from clumps of willowherb on coal tips? Nobody in the family knew why the old boy had given up *bella* Italia for *brutta* Mancunia. What had made him do it? Had the hardships of rural life such as we were now enduring – conditions even in his day could hardly have been more primitive – proven too much? Had bureacracy driven him mad? *Had the local Montegraspers refused him a loan?*

Just when I was about to ask Mira whether she thought it might be time to pack our bags and walk away from Collelungo for good we heard a noise. The special silence born of a mantle of snow lying on open ground in the middle of the countryside was being broken by syncopated bursts from two-stroke engines revving madly. It sounded curiously like somebody strimming. Surely not Cheeso and a mate? In the *snow*?

It came from buzz saws, wielded by two villagers who had taken it upon themselves to cut their way in through a 1.5 kilometre swathe of fallen trees and broken branches to see if we were all right. Our saviours were two wonderful men we were later to get to know very well: Renato Verdiani and his twin brother, Roberto. They had been born in the neighbouring property called Cereto and knew exactly what deprivations could be expected, they said. Their spontaneous mission of help was typical of the kindness we were going to experience from other Tuscans. What they could not have known was that their warm-hearted act would tip the scales; that this one generous gesture could transport us from darkness into light. Suddenly, we stopped feeling sorry for ourselves.

'That's pretty professional cutting gear you've got there,' I said, perking up at the sight of two giant chainsaws in the hands of these grinning heroes. It was hard to tell them apart. In their mid forties, their only physical difference was Asterix mustachios on one (Renato, aka 'Baffo') and a full beard on the other (Roberto, aka 'Barba'). They had the same mannerisms, the same diffident tricks of speech and the same soft voice.

'This is just gardening equipment,' joked Renato. 'The real

stuff's back at the depot.' And he wasn't pulling our legs: it turned out they were builders with a big base in Castellina, just across the valley. From that moment on we became firm friends. Warming themselves by our paraffin stove and sipping coffee with us they reminisced about past winters when other Castellinese had to be dug out (how flattered we were to be considered worthy of inclusion in the description – another sign of their warmth of spirit).

They seemed in no hurry to leave so we started asking them about Collelungo and the immediate surroundings which were still a mystery to us. Soon the talk turned to the woodland paths and secret bridges and ruined mills that apparently lay on our doorstep, abandoned by man and overrun by nature, making us realise how much we had underestimated the countryside. We vowed we would make it our mission to discover as much as we could about the neighbourhood and its hidden treasures when the better weather came. We were going to see it through, after all.

9

Through the Looking Glass

❧

AND the better weather did come. Finally we found we could open the windows at night, but even then the joys of living in a ruined pile in the middle of nowhere left much to be desired. One single, 40-watt light bulb was like a megawatt magnet to every creature that flew over Chianti. Thousands of brown moths attacked us like a biblical plague, so we shut ourselves in, preferring to face death by suffocation. Even when we switched the light off we were not safe: a bat got into the bedroom one night and half scared me to death with its flapping; another good reason for keeping the windows closed. 'It's only a baby *pipistrello*,' said Mira, who had latched on to another cute Italian word and was quite unperturbed.

In these conditions it was difficult to invite new-found friends to visit us and return the hospitality they had shown us in their comfortable homes. However, when Shelagh and Jonathan Routh agreed to come for dinner ('army style' I warned them), we thought we'd hit upon the ideal solution to the menace of unwanted flying objects. We would douse the light and enjoy their company without any airborne interference by illuminating both their path and our living room with candles. We were so proud of ourselves: just that morning we had been to the Co-op in Castellina and bought three dozen lovely little nightlights, all done up in pretty red plastic holders to protect the flame from the wind. They looked most attractive, lining the way to us, so when the Rouths arrived with worried frowns we were naturally disappointed and took it as a sign of their disapprobation of our living conditions. Not a bit of it. 'What happened?' asked Shelagh. 'Who died?' And she patiently explained that we had gaily decorated their way with votive candles, which all good Catholic families use at the cemetery to honour their dead. Well, I don't know; neither my wife nor I are particularly gifted in the faith department. Jonathan looked as though he'd been caught on *Candid Camera*, the TV show that made him a household name in Britain in the 1960s.

The dinner went very well. For appetisers we had a variety of vegetables – onions, mushrooms, bell peppers, gherkins, carrots and cauliflower – all served *sott'olio* (pickled and preserved in oil). Mira prepared *risotto con i carciofi*, a Tuscan artichoke speciality, and to follow she made a beef and tomato *stracotto*, a stewy cousin of the great French *daube*. Dessert followed local tradition: hard *cantucci* biscuits dunked in *vin santo*, as we'd first enjoyed at Bruno and Gina's.

Our talk with the Verdiani twins had really inspired us to get out and investigate. There seemed so much more to discover about the neighbourhood, which had been as forgotten as Collelungo when the world turned and the flight from the land gathered pace. The problem was that everything was so overgrown it appeared contiguous, unending: one great big green thickly wooded hill and valley leading to the village. It was almost impossible to determine where one property started and another ended. There were no fences, no demarcation posts and only the strangest vestiges of barbed wire divisions within our land which we correctly deduced had been erected by Pepi to corral his horses. These simply confused us further. The mention of Cereto, the twins' birthplace halfway to Castellina, spurred our curiosity.

Like so many city folk raised within urban surroundings we had not been able to see the wood for the trees – literally. We had become so familiar with the picture-postcard scene of Tuscan cypresses and serried ranks of vineyards that filled our foreground that we had overlooked the point that these are man-made adjuncts to nature. The cypresses were planted ornamentally to line roads or shield hilltop dwellings, normally the estate-owner's villa, from the wind and sun. The vines were tamed to grow this regimented way; by nature they are climbers and in olden times were allowed to spread and develop 'promiscuously' as the Tuscans say.

We entered the woods walking down into a fold of hills between ourselves and the village. We crossed through the looking glass to an underworld that was Middle Ages old. There were candelabra oaks covered in lianas of ivy so thick they could have been elephants' trunks. Turkey oaks that in winter still carried their rusty dead leaves like trophies. Lichen-coloured rocks that in coming months were going to be laced with streamers of bryony and honeysuckle. Clumps of juniper and broom on promising paths familiar only to porcupines, foxes, hare and wild boar. Shirt-ripping patches of bramble and blackthorn wherein lay discarded porcupine quills, banded in brown and white, the detritus of battles ancient and new. (We read that they shoot their quills in self-defence when attacked. From the amount we found we must have stumbled on a favourite battleground.)

The whole scene was a perfect match for D.H. Lawrence's description of a Tuscany that 'manages to remain so remote, and secretly smiling to itself'. In *Flowery Tuscany* he wrote: 'There are so many little deep valleys with streams that seem to go their own little way entirely, regardless of river or sea. [They] run and rattle over wild rocks of secret places and murmur through blackthorn thickets where the nightingales sing all together, unruffled and undaunted.' That was in 1927.

We discovered we had our own little stream, the Arbiola. It rose 1.5 kilometres from our home and followed the valley eastward to mark our southern boundary. The undergrowth was even thicker down there where we made our first find: the Verdianis' ruined watermills, places where they probably played as boys and which had remained a secret known only to themselves and other true Castellinese. We came across a lovely waterfall tipping a fast cascade into a bathing pool where we could imagine the village children swimming in summer. But best of all was a hidden stone bridge we literally stumbled upon. Totally covered in ivy and the kind of creeper you could swing from, it had a tiny narrow path made by wild boar leading across it through knee-high vegetation. Crawling underneath, we found that its perfect stone arch was pristine. We disturbed a roe deer as we slipped down to examine at close quarters the hand-hewn limestone, scooped out in two matching places either side of the arch to accommodate what we guessed must have been a wooden beam. Renato and Roberto explained that there had been a complex water management system in the valley within living memory. This had to have been a sluice gate, controlling the flow of water to the mills.

Down there, under the mantle formed by the oaks and evergreens high above our heads, the sensation of being in a timeless place was enhanced by a profound silence broken only by birdsong. Ever since that first magical experience, whenever we can we return to delight in its sense of solitude and peace, enjoying the differences in vegetation at various times of year, with ragwort, violets, coltsfoot and wild fennel on the ground and all around us yellow broom, red berries, purple berries and black sloes growing in profusion. (Mira got a particular gleam in her eye when she first saw those; my mother had given her a recipe for sloe gin and I am still enjoying the result.) In the cool of the shady creek even on a hot summer's day the stream, now a brook, gurgles its way to the sea. Butterflies dance in sunbeams glancing off the water. There are glimpses of bright blue sky and delicate fleecy clouds flying overhead, the type Tuscans call *pecorelle*, or little sheep.

Every time we go there and we edge further towards the village I know its castle tower will start to loom above us through holes in the tree cover. The castle-keep was built in the 13th century to defend the country people from raids by the enemy in that constant state of warfare, often not declared, that characterised relations between Florence and Siena for four centuries. The village's defensive walls enabled it to withstand classic sieges lasting up to 40 days, resisting primitive rocket attack and (as local history records) even poison gas grenades launched from that very spot. The ancestors of these same woodland trees probably surrendered to the warrior's axe to be turned into siege towers for the Duke of Calabria's attacking Aragonese forces.

The two Verdianis were big fellows but gentle in their ways. They were always ready to find good in people when talking about the village, the villagers and village life. We never heard them say anything specifically negative about anyone, so when we told them how frustrated we were with the slowness of our project it seemed out of character for them to say the problem could possibly be our choice of *geometra*. Something must be seriously wrong.

Indeed it should have been evident to us much earlier that engaging Signor Faraoni had been one big mistake. He had been assuring us that delays would be minor and that planning permission would be forthcoming within weeks, but nothing happened. The weeks turned to months. With the overdraft no longer available we could no longer afford to pay him. We were tiring of his forced optimism, his smelly cheroots and his naff mannerisms. Nor were his tortured quirks of speech helping us much. The Verdianis' suspicions magnified our own doubts and we determined that showdown time was coming for the little dandy. The chance to put him to the test soon came, and was to prove a defining moment.

Of all the people you do not want to antagonise when starting a building project in Italy, the village mayor must come top of your list. He can make you or break you, his position is so important. We knew it was vital to have him on our side and we had already had a private chat, with Benito translating, right at the start to see if our plans met his overall approval. They did: his mother had been born at Collelungo, he said, and he was happy to take a personal interest in its redevelopment. It quickly became clear which side of the political spectrum we were dealing with when he then went on to warn us against acting 'like Milanese industrialists' by putting up gates and fences to prevent the local people from taking their pleasures wherever they willed. By which he meant their constitutional walks and hunting rights. It was their heritage, after all. Didn't we agree? 'Most definitely,' we said.

We had sought another interview, officially this time, for Faraoni to plead our case for urgency in the matter of building permits and for help in cutting through the red tape we now discovered mummifying not just ours but all building projects in Chianti. We did not want to seek special favours; we weren't arguing with the health authorities' demands for minimum room dimensions (14 square metres for a double bedroom, 9 for a single) and headroom (no lower than 2.7 metres anywhere). Faraoni started with what we thought was an innocuous matter: our desire to put louvred wooden shutters on the outside of our windows. Our request had been rejected by the borough surveyor's office and the mayor was our only chance of having that decision reversed.

For the occasion our spiffy surveyor chose a little number that could not have been better calculated to put our mayor's back up. He dressed in a white suit with white Gucci loafers. For accoutrements there were a gold necklace, a signet ring with a gold caterpillar crawling over it and a gold-tipped cigarette holder even longer than usual. The mayor, a non-smoker like us, wore trainers and jeans.

'Why do you want shutters?' he coughed as Faraoni fired a fast jet of smoke in his direction.

'Because they keep out the light and heat. They're fine for ventilation too,' said Faraoni.

'They are not traditional.'

'But you see them all over Italy, all over the Mediterranean,' we protested.

'Not on a *casa colonica* you don't.'

And the mayor, a dry cleaner by profession, explained that as the *casa colonica*, or peasants' house, had been occupied by *contadini* who were up at the crack of dawn to work the fields and then remained outside all day, they had no need for ventilation. The opposite, in fact. On leaving for work they would close the windows, and behind these shut the internal wooden panels called *scurezze* that filled the room with darkness, keeping the sunlight out. That way, he said, when they returned home in the evening they would find the room beautifully cool, helped by the thickness of the stone walls. Louvred shutters were strictly for the owner's villa. The *padrone,* being a rich, lazy soul, could lie in bed like a pasha and have servants bring him breakfast. He would need to have his window open, and to protect him with shade this would have to be equipped with shutters.

'Eh?' said Faraoni.

'Bo!' said the mayor.

So much for the harmless stuff.

Then Faraoni brought up the real subject of the meeting: the need to speed through at least one of the permits so that our work would not stall. Our mayor called in the borough surveyor, and it was then that we discovered the full extent of the catastrophe. It seemed our man was presenting plans backwards, upside down, hopelessly wrongly drawn. Not another word was needed. He was evidently a busker and an incompetent, not only insufficiently qualified for this kind of sensitive reconstruction project but also out of his depth with a set-square.

Faced with such a dramatic unmasking, our man might reasonably have been expected to fall on his sword. But not Faraoni. Instead, he went onto the attack. 'I shall accuse you of an abuse of power if you do not approve these plans,' he said, waving his cigarette holder imperiously in the mayor's face. 'I will take it personally to my friend, the *direttore* of the *provincia!*'

We were speechless with embarrassment. The meeting broke up in disarray with Faraoni calling the mayor a '*cretino*' and the mayor spinning on his Nikes and slamming the door.

10

Distractions

WE limped along through 1991, a miserable year all round. We ignored the advice normally given to people who find themselves in a hole and instead kept digging, literally and metaphorically. Massimo and his team were dispirited but went on with the work at a depressingly slow pace. In order to pay them and the very large bills we were getting for building material we decided there was nothing for it but to take out a second mortgage on Mira's mother's flat in Hammersmith, which my Ma-in-law (a widow in her eighties who had survived many personal crises in her own life) kindly agreed to. But as the days passed we grew increasingly alarmed at the possibility that the bank would force us into bankruptcy by foreclosing on our company and thereafter put Collelungo up for public auction. We were in grave danger of losing everything.

Just about then a more immediate problem presented itself. One of the builders had been trying to light a fire in the big fireplace that had been the bread oven back in Migliorini days and for some reason put his hand up the chimney breast. His fingers touched several objects, smooth and cylindrical, and he called his friends over to witness his find. When he pulled them out, everyone recoiled in shock: '*Micci!*' they shouted.

'*Micci?*'

Mira and I looked at each other, racing for the dictionary. 'Oh my God,' we said. 'Detonators!'

The Carabinieri were informed. Statements were taken. Documents were demanded. Panic swept the village. Rumours of Red Brigade activity became rife. The story hit the local press, with the sinister foreign ownership of the farm heavily emphasised and our backgrounds richly embroidered.

We were as mystified as Massimo about their provenance. Red Brigade my eye, I thought. Had they been left over from *contadino* days? If so, what purpose would explosives have served? And why store them in a chimney, of all stupid places? And then Benito, ever the Machiavellian, sowed a seed of doubt in our minds. Had we made any enemies in the village? he asked. Did we know of any rivals who might be jealous; who might fear our venture could take away their business; who might, in short, try to damage our chances by indulging in a spot of sabotage?

We had been staying at a weird kind of restaurant-hotel called the Villa Mafalda, run by a villainous old woman who favoured a turban and sprouted black whiskers from moles on her cheek and chin. It was pretty crummy really, hardly the village Hilton. Mafalda also cheated her diners by pouring slop wine into used bottles and presenting it at an exorbitant price to gullible tourists ready to swallow both it and the story she concocted about the grapes having come from her family's private vineyard. We gave the restaurant a wide berth after falling victim ourselves our first night in residence. But Mafalda ran the one place in town where we could afford to stay for any length of time on our diminishing resources.

She talked a lot, Mafalda. 'Oh, Signor Tony, Signora Mira! Just tell me everything and I will help you wherever I can,' she said immediately she heard that we were the ones who had bought Collelungo. 'I knew the farm had been bought by foreigners but you poor things – *poverini* – you must be very *bravi* to be going ahead with this big project all alone.'

Mira had been cautious, all the same. 'We don't want to tell her too much about our plans,' she warned me. 'You never know where it will go, and nobody says anything good about her. And after all we are going to be in competition once we get going.'

Mafalda? Sabotage?

Further discreet enquiries revealed that Mafalda was also quite a businesswoman. As well as the hotel she owned several apartments that were let out lucratively, a grocery store and a majority holding in one of the village's two petrol station freeholds. Thanks to her propensity for gossip and chat she was also known as 'Radio Chianti' to everyone for miles around. We had been warned.

If anyone had indeed planted the explosives we had a fair idea who it might be but did not dare mention her name to the police. For the next bit of intelligence we picked up in the village came with danger warnings all over it. There was no Mr Mafalda any more – he was rumoured to have done a bunk after a scandal involving a cleaning girl – but the turbanned terror did have a regular and frequent visitor herself in the chunky form of the marshal of the Carabinieri station. She also had influence elsewhere, especially in Siena where she was supposed to have connections in all the right places. Her sister's eldest boy was high-up in the provincial administration, with a fairly open attitude to accepting favours on behalf of the family (which was why, we supposed, the health authorities had never visited the Villa Mafalda to discover its secret wealth of dirt).

How prudent to have kept away from her telephone.

We did have one asset which had been staring us in the face, and it was symptomatic of our city nature that we had not seen it straight away. We had olive trees on the estate. In common with all the others in our area, they had suffered tremendous frost damage in 1985 and were only now bearing fruit again. Being so short of cash, any income was a blessing and even though we knew we would not reap a huge harvest from our little grove it struck us we should at least be trying to benefit from it rather than let the fruit go to waste. We were in a fairly despondent mood, but a few words of encouragement from a local couple we had become friendly with tipped the balance. After all, we had nothing else to do.

Delia and Giuliano Baldini ran a hotel in Castellina that we wished we'd discovered first instead of Mafalda's. They too had run foul of the lady in question when they started their business only a few years earlier, so we had much in common. When we mentioned our experiences to them and told them of the dirt we had seen and her attitude to customers in the restaurant they both smiled knowingly. Then Delia bent forward, looked left and right for theatrical effect – we were miles from anyone – and confided conspiratorially: 'Signor Tony, Signora Mira, if guests ever saw into her kitchen they wouldn't stay a minute!' But how could that be, we asked, when hygiene laws were so strict in what we were hoping to be able to soon call 'our' industry? 'Ha!' she said. 'She has covered all the big shots in flour!' Bribes, that is.

The Baldinis' visits to Collelungo proved a welcome distraction from our problems and the daily grind of worrying about money. The difference between them and us was that they were lifetime olive pickers and knew exactly what needed to be done and where to take the crop to be milled for oil. We agreed to share the labour with them, share the costs of pressing, and share the oil on a 50-50 basis.

Gathering olives is a finger-numbing business at the best of times. As far as I'm aware, however, there is no such thing as the best of times. It seems to me the operation is always conducted in a period of high wind, intense cold and drumming rain, late in November or early December when the days are short and you would rather be tucked up by a log fire with a cup of coffee, sticking pins in effigies of bank managers or surveyors. Instead of which, half-hidden among a million face-slapping wet leaves, you balance nervously on the top rung of a home-made wooden ladder propped against your olive tree and try to ignore the frailty of the young boughs you have chosen to rely on for life-support. It is always a home-made wooden ladder, note: there may be millions of safe, lightweight, modern ones tucked away in Tuscans' homes that are used for internal decorating jobs, but here in the fields Real Pickers Use Wood just like olden times. You cannot risk having a Japanese tourist heave into view, training his Nikon zoom on you, and see you runged in namby-pamby aluminium. Think how that would go down in Okinawa.

The wooden ladders were considered best because they tapered at the top almost to a point and therefore lent them-selves to being inserted into the branches – that is, after you'd spread your net beneath your first tree, struggling with the billowing nylon like a paratrooper and weighting its corners with rocks. Then you had to shake the tree to drop the ripest olives into the net. About half missed on account of their erratic trajectory and the perverse effect of wind velocity upon gravity.

While Delia and Giuliano were swinging along with a rhythm that came as second nature, Mira and I were swaying like koala bears in the silver-green foliage, hanging on for dear life and dropping the olives into baskets tied around our waists. The basket was apron-shaped, flat on the side that strapped marsupially to the stomach, curved in a semicircle on the other. As you leaned forward to fill it you were likely to hear a snapping sound as the elasticity of your particular olive bough reached tolerance limit. Most probably you would drop abruptly a foot or two in your angle of inclination but almost always there was another branch to catch you underneath so there was little reason to worry. Your scratches would heal. The bleeding would stop. The sleeve you just tore could be mended. The alternative to this torture was to take a little hand rake and comb each branch, grooming the tree like a horse, and let the olives that missed the basket fall to the soggy ground. Those that missed the net too would then have to be extracted from the scrub along with the rest before you could move on up the grove to the next tree. There were only 246 on our estate.

After picking, we put the olives in plastic crates and loaded up the Renault to haul them off to the *frantoio*, the olive mill at Panzano, where they were washed, crushed, stirred and pressed. Giant granite stones standing on edge like cartwheels rolled relentlessly over them as they trundled mesmerisingly around a circular trough, but that was the only old technology about the place. For reasons of modern hygiene the rest of the equipment was sterile stainless steel, with electronic lights flashing, centrifugal separators whirring, and state-of-the-art panels monitoring the passage of our precious fruit.

Despite all that, there was no doubting the old-fashioned, genuine nature of the product that emerged in a thin stream of iridescent green at the end of the process. We spent the time with the other producers, each waiting for his own elixir to arrive, in the green aroma of new oil that hung in the warm air. We were in a back room before a log fire in a vast fireplace, pouring the new oil on slices of toasted bread. These we rubbed with garlic and sprinkled with salt – the *bruschetta* that no Tuscan meal would be complete without. It was the food of the gods and we were in heaven, with banks, mortgages, saboteurs, vipers and snakes in the grass all momentarily forgotten.

11

Tangentopoli

❧

WE survived another winter and the calendar turned. That year, 1992, was remarkable for two reasons: how we kept going on a shoestring when Luca finally pulled out, as we suspected he would; and the momentous events about to unfurl nationwide, which became a saga as suspenseful as anything any Hollywood scriptwriter could have invented.

It was the year a Milanese magistrate, Antonio di Pietro, nabbed the manager of an old folks' home who was a bit tardy in flushing down the toilet a stash of banknotes he had just received as a bribe. From this banal beginning sprang something momentous called *Tangentopoli* (Bribesville), an earthquake whose after-shocks are still being felt at the core of Italian society over a decade later. More than 2,500 people were investigated, about 450 were found guilty, a few were put in prison and a score took their own lives. The guilty included a clutch of former prime ministers, most notably Bettino Craxi, convicted of a host of corruption offences involving up to $160 million.

'Supergrass' claims that both he and twice-Premier Silvio Berlusconi were involved in the Mafia's bombing campaign were also investigated by my pals, the country's anti-Mafia force. The degree to which organised crime had been co-opted by the establishment, or had infiltrated it, shocked the nation and remains the most delicate issue in Italy even today. Mr Berlusconi is still not out of the woods, but for other reasons.

The rip-tide of *Tangentopoli* hit Siena in 1993 when the grey vans of the Guardia di Finanza flanked by Ducati motorbike outriders pushed through the thronged streets, forcing tourists and locals aside with their sirens blaring and blue lights flashing, heading for the city centre. Everywhere in Italy, corruption investigations were causing sleepless nights among politicians, businessmen and bankers. The purge was big news.

When the convoy turned and pulled up sharply in front of the Rocca Salimbeni, the fortress and fount of the city's wealth, a force of men in light grey uniforms with yellow flaming-torch cap badges descended while Siena held its breath. Soon everyone knew: not one but two members of the Monte dei Paschi board had been arrested for allegedly receiving kickbacks for granting loans. The bank's managing director, Carlo Zini, also stepped down after being told by magistrates he was under investigation on similar allegations.

The Press reported it as a showdown at the *palazzo*, with the whiff of scandal penetrating its thick stone walls. Never before in five centuries of lending, through the bloody wars between Florence and Siena and Italian reunification, had its reputation faced such an attack, said the *Financial Times*.

Shock, horror? Maybe. According to an article I read in the *Economist*, in the five years following 1992 the Yellow Flame boys, as they were known, set fire to the feathered nests of no fewer than 17 per cent of all those who held top jobs. As many as 57 per cent who held top jobs in politics and 40 per cent of Italy's top businessmen had had run-ins with the law. Corruption fatigue settled on the country.

As it happens, all this proved pretty academic in our case. The bank's lawyers had decided to sue us for the return of the overdraft – and we were suing them back for broken promises.

We felt as though we were suing the Vatican. For added spice, we also sued for damages, on the grounds that our entire business plan had been torpedoed by the withdrawal of our promised loan. Everyone said we couldn't win against the bank but Benito made the point that at least we would gain time: court cases routinely took 10 years to settle. And he did know a very good lawyer in Florence. Florence was the key: a Sienese lawyer was sure to be in the Montegraspers' thrall.

He was a card, Benito. Wasn't there some consumer group, some banking ombudsman, we could appeal to? 'Forget your *Anglo-Sassone* assumptions,' he said. 'This is Italy. Nobody here believe that the law or police or administration exist to serve them. At same time, these organisation do not believe they exist to serve nobody.'

For a man of his experience and talent-span he had a peculiar personal motto, *Nulla Tenente*, which he explained meant 'Owner of Nothing'. We were to discover he had spent much of his life in Kenya (hence his disparaging reference to Siena as 'the bush') where he had been a hotelier, deep-sea diver, scuba diver, spear fisherman and wildlife photographer. Rally-driving and fashion photography were also on his curriculum vitae as well as – I swear this is true – Wall of Death stunt riding. He was also a businessman with fingers in some quite remarkable pies, including consultancy interests in wine and spirit firms in Sicily and Scotland, wholesale garment industry outlets and leather goods factories running Gucci and Valentino lines. *Nulla Tenente?*

The problem was that the preliminary contract we had signed for the mortgage granted the bank a security of three times the value of the loan, not simply loan value as in other countries. Also the bank had immediately registered this three billion lire at the Land Registry even though the deal itself had not been consummated. Worse was coming: we discovered that if we wanted to have this lien lifted – which of course was a prerequisite if we were going to attract funds from an alternative bank – it was down to us to pay the cancellation fees. On a security of three billion lire they came to a hair-raising £10,000. And so we cashed in our last Premium Bond and set about trying to raise new financing.

As far as Faraoni was concerned, there was no reason for us to carry on. He had been a failure with the permits and a failure with his special contacts. Against his violent protestations we sacked him and sent Massimo's team home.

The next three years were passed in limbo. Despairing of the Italian system, we approached various banks with household British or Continental names but every time we kept getting referred back to their co-respondent bank in our area – no prizes, the Monte dei Paschi di Siena. Curiously enough, the Abbey National had just opened shop in Florence and as it had already made a packet out of us in London we thought we might receive preferential treatment here; alas, as in England, it could only make mortgages on a multiplication factor of our annual income, which was now a well-rounded zero.

Only the passing of the seasons marked our progress. We were chasing our tails, making the rounds of the banks and financial institutions, pursuing all sorts of permits, worrying about the court case and looking for possible new investors, but venture capital seemed an alien concept wherever we turned. There was one interlude when I appeared in court on behalf of Pepi at his bankruptcy hearing to testify that we had bought the property from him at a fair price. There were other high-lights, such as the moment Massimo the builder sought and got an injunction against us that could have led to a sequestration order – a nasty little trick Faraoni had put him up to, he confessed. We offered him what little money we could and he withdrew.

We harvested our olives with the Baldinis again and sold our oil to buy groceries for the third year running. Reluctantly, I made contact with London and managed to interest some news-papers and magazines in freelance ideas I thought up – assign-ments that helped to fill our time and pay for most of our household costs, which were now kept very low. This former pair of Dinkies (double income, no kids) had now become Ninkies. Discreetly, we approached a local estate agent and asked if there were any likely buyers on the horizon (poor old Barbara, a diabetic, was now totally incapacitated having had her foot amputated and been forced into retirement). The answer was negative: Collelungo was unsellable in its present halfway condition given the state of the market.

Throughout this purgatory, Benito kept thinking up new wheezes but even his bustling presence could not convince the money men that we had a project worth backing in a Europe still in recession. Then one day we learned to our great surprise that something had come up which might prove our salvation. At last he had found the right man in the right place: the manager of an obscure Florentine bank untouched by *Tangentopoli* and the Clean Hands anti-corruption crusade, a traditionalist unafraid to travel the old '*regalo*' route in pursuit of business in time-

honoured fashion. Considering what was going on all around
him this was a sensational development for us. What was interesting was that this well-placed and most important person
appeared to need something which we could supply (according
to Benito) almost as desperately as we needed his bank's dosh.
The most relevant thing for him, the one item he wanted more
than anything else in all the world, was a wetsuit.

'A *wetsuit*?' we asked Benito incredulously.

'*Si*, a wetsuit. A rubb-air dress.'

'But why doesn't he go out and buy one?'

'Because he no find one to fit. He wider than he tall.'

And so we got our mortgage – due to the fact that bespoke
tailoring for scuba divers is an unestablished art, with every
practitioner of the sport assumed to be of Jacques Cousteau's
stature rather than Michelin Man's. Our contact was massively
girth-challenged and desperately unhappy because he could not
indulge in his great passion to dive. Suddenly he had come face
to face with the one person who could help him achieve this
lifelong dream. Our own Benito, fellow Florentine, a man whom
we had met practically by accident, had amazed us with the span
of the talents we already knew about. Now we discovered he
had a link with a factory in Naples specialising in underwater
sports gear and swimming costumes.

The bank manager got his custom-built wetsuit, its proportions triple-checked by the disbelieving tailors who thought they
were dressing a seal. And he became a changed man, according
to Benito: happy, cheerful and smiling instead of the miserable,
dreary soul everyone in his immediate circle had known him to
be. We never got to witness this occurrence, having wisely kept
a very long distance from all this Medici-style intrigue. Happy,
too, not to have been caught by the diving bug ourselves (or to
have had any free time to indulge in the sport on the shoreline

of Elba where our saviour apparently still likes to frolic and make a big splash).

Diving had had its downside for Benito, leaving him a little deaf, which at first made for difficulties in our dialogue – us with our rudimentary knowledge of Italian, he with his not-always-perfect understanding of the language of Shakespeare. 'What means this. . . ?' or 'What it is, this . . . ?' he would say. Certain words of his were pure Benitoisms (as surely some of ours were Italglish). 'Gluk' kept coming up a lot in the early days for some inexplicable reason, by which he meant 'glue'. It's good to be able to understand your accountant.

A Florentine to the core, he hated having to go to Siena for us when bureaucratic needs called. For him it was like *'il terzo mondo*, the third world.' In no-less-traffic-strangled Florence he managed to avoid the problem by riding a scooter, wriggling through the jams like a fish through a reef. 'Ah, but what happens when it rains?' we asked him.

*'Enny*thing,' he said with a smile as big as a million-dollar mortgage. 'I also wear a rubb-air dress.'

12

Tea and Sympathy

❦

BY the time 1995 dawned we had relaunched our project. We were refreshed, reinvigorated and rediscovering all the good things about Tuscan life, although we were not out of the woods with the Montegraspers.

There was more good news. One day early in the year, on hearing a throaty engine noise from the lane leading to Collelungo, we looked out and saw a chocolate-coloured Jaguar approaching in a stately fashion. As it came nearer we could tell why it was going so slowly: it was so old it was in danger of becoming of historical interest. Closer inspection revealed that it had ancient black and white English licence plates, the steering wheel on the right, and two white-haired occupants.

'Hel-*lo!*' said the driver, clambering out with some difficulty and placing a panama hat on his head, then doffing it in gentlemanly fashion the moment he saw Mira. He wore a crumpled linen suit and white beard, and his half-moon glasses gave him an academic air. From the passenger's side emerged a lady of similar vintage in a printed sunfrock covered in marigolds. 'Hel-*lo!*' she echoed.

Barney and Bunty Whittaker introduced themselves. They were tour operators, working a very small programme for discerning travellers in upmarket places. Barney proferred us their card: 'CROQUET HOLIDAYS', we read. 'We go through the hoop to make you happy.'

The pained look on my face brought an immediate (and clearly well-rehearsed) response: No, said Barney, none of their clients actually wanted to play croquet, though the idea wasn't a bad one, what? They had founded the club in the 1960s in answer to a demand from dilettante friends in the Home Counties who wanted to visit cultural destinations with themselves as guides. He was a retired history professor and Bunty had taught art, having studied in many of the delightful places they now visited on their peregrinations. The programme had begun in India and then spread to other parts of the old empire where the tiffin set once held sway. Since then they had developed a select client base nationwide within the UK, they explained as Mira offered them tea. ('Yes, thanks. Jolly dee!') They needed a new destination to fit their profile and were desperate to have some form of presence in Italy.

Could this be happening to us? we thought as the delightful duo tucked into their biscuits and Earl Grey. Where on earth had these characters come from? We warmed to them all the more as the full extent of their Italian experiences unfolded over the teacups.

It seemed they had been through quite a hoop indeed; they had barely survived a chain of disasters that had left them disbelieving that their Italian dream might ever be attainable.

First, they had been on the verge of signing a contract with a hotelier in a Calabrian fishing village when a representative of what they took to be the local Mafia stepped in. 'He had a black moustache and dark glasses and quite a threatening look. He said he wanted precisely the same sum of money as we were paying the hotel for each guest,' said Bunty, a charming lady of the Joyce Grenfell school. 'I told him: "I'm afraid we don't work like that in England," but the hotel-owner said we'd better pay or his hotel would be burned down.'

Oh dear. They moved on, seeking safer waters. They arrived in the north and were poised to shake hands on a deal with an Italian count in Verona (self-catering units in his castle) when the Guardia di Finanza arrived in a tornado of noise and flashing lights and led him off in handcuffs. Mira gave me a look and smiled. Finally, said the Whittakers, they were about to commit themselves to a contract with a respectable businessman when they woke up one day and found he had gone bankrupt. We exchanged glances again, but no, this was in Rapallo, not Siena.

And so this nice amiable couple found themselves fleeing from organised crime with what they said was a pent-up demand from clients still clamouring for a slice of *la dolce vita*, not knowing which way to turn next. They were on their way home in the Jag and just happened to be passing by Castellina when they stopped for lunch – fortunately not at Mafalda's but at our favourite restaurant, Il Pestello. They casually asked the owner if there was any property nearby with apartments for rent, and he had mentioned us and Collelungo.

'But oh dear,' said Barney, looking around at the damage inflicted on the medieval scene by the Neapolitans, 'I see we have come at an awkward moment.'

'Well, the apartments are not quite ready yet,' said Mira quickly before I could say anything. 'Would you like to have a look around anyway?'

We came to a deal, there and then, that they would revisit Collelungo in six months' time. If they found our project sufficiently well developed they would sign a contract with us for an allocation of apartments and put us in their 1996 brochure. They might even be able to help us with a small advance if required, they said. It was a matter of trust, English style, and we shook hands on the deal.

For us it was a turning point. We now had three essential components in place: the building permits complete with *Belle Arte* consent had finally come through for all 12 units, with some modifications, but everyone – even the mayor – was happy. We had potential income from a tour operator who would support us and market them, though the time pressure was enormous. And we had assured financing. There was just the fourth ingredient missing: the property itself. Time to get a move on, we said. With a new wind blowing and having sorted out Massimo's tiresome legal action, we were delighted when the Verdiani twins mentioned a local surveyor who they assured us was capable of sensitive restoration work in place of Faraoni. He was happy to come on board.

Renato and Roberto turned out to be indefatigable workers, which came as no surprise as we were already well aware of their skills with the power saw. They had told us they were builders; in fact they were working directors of a big local construction outfit called Big Blu which specialised in swimming pools, tennis courts and public housing, but had also sensitively restored a local hotel that was similar in character to our property. Now that we had a new bank's backing we could take on their services knowing we would be in good hands. They even agreed to a schedule of delayed payments which eased the money situation considerably.

The old scaffolding and crane came down, mission accomplished (roof renewed, walls repointed). Miraculously, our pool permit arrived the day the Whittakers departed, and Renato turned up at the controls of a huge bulldozer, ready to start digging immediately. A computer and photocopier joined the fax and phone in the former chicken coop we had fixed up for ourselves as an office. And at last we felt confident that things were going well. We were on our way.

We were now dealing with a serious team of professionals. Nothing seemed to faze them. Big Blu's foreman was Ivo, a strong Tuscan in his sixties with a kindly smile and gentle manner (his name was pronounced 'Eevo' to rhyme with 'Heave-ho'). Under him came a team of three builders, Cosimo, Claudio and Pietro, plus two labourers, Beppe and Alberto. All five came from Italy's deep south and brought with them an eagerness to work that was surprising and a way of talking that was impossible for us to understand. Only Cosimo's accent was penetrable: he hailed from Taranto but had spent much time as a guest-worker in Germany, so his vocabulary was peppered with useful Teutonic expletives which he had clearly learned on the job. Often we had to resort to two dictionaries when trying to communicate with him; more often than not, the words weren't there – unprintable, we assumed.

But we got along fine. Living on top of them, we were able to supervise every move, always present to answer any question. Our new surveyor took the back seat, content to get his fees the easy way and let us deal personally with day-to-day problems. Which in a way suited us well.

But Mafalda was a surprise. She actually had the gall to turn up one day, and continued to drop by on the slightest pretext, arriving at all hours and trying to be chatty when we had plenty of better things to do. Ostensibly the purpose of her visits was to give us friendly encouragement, but she took exceptional proprietorial interest in the building work, asking how much we were paying the men, where we were getting our supplies from, how the programme was developing, how much we planned to charge our guests, and so on. All kinds of irritating busybody questions that in normal circumstances would have merited a very brief answer indeed. I was all for throwing her out unceremoniously. It was impossible to keep her away, short of getting a court injunction, but Mira parried her questions as politely and diplomatically as possible for fear of antagonising her. All the same, Renato and Roberto confirmed our suspicions that the health people did seem to be taking extraordinarily peculiar interest in our project, and it was difficult to avoid the conclusion that her visits were not entirely unconnected.

It was the bathrooms that caused us the most sleepless nights. First, bathrooms and bedrooms could not be en suite, for that would be in breach of the *agriturismo* rules (which had clearly been drafted by the one prude that the government of the day could find). In a hotel or private house en suite bathrooms were the accepted norm, as they were everywhere else in the world. But because our property was classified as rural rather than urban we had to have a proper division between the two to prevent the WC from polluting the bedroom, and this meant an antechamber, not just a door. It was a requirement that defied all logic and called for some creative architecture.

Secondly, each bathroom had to be what the health tyrants described as 'complete' – that is to say with loo, bath or shower, handbasin *and* bidet. 'The rules have changed: you must have one complete bathroom for every six people now, whereas it was one for eight before,' we were told when a health inspector descended on one of her frequent site visits.

'Aha!' we replied, 'we are going to do better than that. We are going to have one bathroom for every two people.' Which was true, though in some cases these were incomplete as there was no room to put a bidet. We talked nothing but bidets to everyone we met. Bidets became an obsession. Bidet catalogues and brochures piled up in our own bathroom, to the extent we could hardly get in to use our own bidet. We covered the waterfront, as it were, and still we had a problem. Nobody made a small bidet.

'The French make a portable one,' said Mira. 'Remember that fleapit in Paris where the bedroom had a sink in it and beneath it we found a bidet, hidden by a little curtain?' I certainly did. It was fixed to a kind of skateboard like Brigadier's and could be trundled out from its hideyhole trailing connecting hoses and waste pipe on an articulated, extendable, chromium arm that was spring-loaded to make it retract automatically. I still bore the scars.

But it was one solution to consider. Our plumber, Attilio ('Attila'), came up with another: the combo-loo that doubled as a bidet. Depending on which function you desired you simply turned a handle and instead of flushing down like a waterfall it flushed up, like a fountain. Accidentally left in reverse-thrust mode it could therefore surprise the following customer with a flushed fundament. Ingenious, but not such a great idea.

Faced with a difficult choice, we let Benito, master of all things mechanical and aquatic, be the judge. 'Are you crazy?' he said. 'This is Italy. You don't unnerstan. These stupid people. They say one complete bathroom enough for six people? Right! Six people it is. Every place you have a bathroom where there is no enough space for a bidet happen to be in big apartment where main bathroom has one, right? So, no problem. If people with small bathroom, no bidet, want use bidet they go through next bedroom and use next bathroom. OK?'

OK, Benito. The health authorities said OK too. We were in Italy.

We settled into a working pattern that was to last for more than a year, a daily routine that had our squad of builders – the *squadra* – working flat out for four hours in the morning and four in the afternoon, with us flat out from 7 a.m. to 9 p.m. most times, with just the occasional visit from the surveyor to make sure all was going well.

Our first house in Ealing had been a modest two-storey affair built by Wates and held together by plasterboard internal walls pinned to stud partitioning, by nature of which interesting results could be achieved with a blow of the hammer and a good shove. From there we moved to a flat overlooking the Thames at Blackfriars Bridge with tired geraniums in window boxes and hardly any view until we put in a raised floor and sliding balcony doors. (We missed seeing Banco Ambrosiano executive Roberto Calvi hang from it in front of us, however. You may remember the bank hung too, with losses of $1,400 million.) Our next property was a derelict mews house requiring a serious makeover which we worked on for four months, nearly Cuprinol-ing ourselves to oblivion when we discovered worm-eaten floor timbers in the dining room we were sleeping in. We sold that and found a bargain of a flat in Chelsea. It must have belonged to someone with more money than taste, for although it was small it contained decorative elements of size and style more befitting Versailles than SW3. So we rebuilt it.

But nothing had prepared us for the task of turning a medieval ruin into a complex consisting of a dozen individual apartments, workrooms, laundry, bar and public lounge.

Astonishingly, the Big Blu team often arrived before the official start time of 8 a.m. They never once played a transistor radio or asked for 'a cuppa' as we would have expected in England. They worked away until noon, then broke for a one-hour lunch they had brought with them – Ivo and Cosimo each with a small gas stove on which to heat up their lunch, the others with tins of tuna and fruit which they attacked with a cutter, never a knife or – heaven forbid – a poncey tin-opener. They would stretch out for 40 winks, then it was work time again from 1 p.m. to 5 p.m., and finally a cheery '*Arrivederci!*' as they vanished with a wave. Only the way they said it, it came out as 'Reevdurch!'

It was just the same in all weathers, Monday to Friday and even Saturday and Sunday on some urgent occasions. The secret lay in the fact that they were all, in effect, guest-workers in their own country: they had had to come north to find work, leaving their wives and families in the south, that other Italy of sun-ripened poverty and crippling unemployment. Apart from Cosimo, who was a widower, they saved up their days off in order to take extended holidays in August and at Christmas. Once in a while Pietro would take off early on a Friday afternoon in his battered old Ford and not be seen again until Monday morning, having driven 1,600 kilometres in between to spend the weekend with his wife and children.

Ivo, Cosimo and the gang had evidently worked together as a team for some time before coming to Collelungo, for they quickly established a rhythm that was magical to watch. Like well-choreographed dancers they dovetailed their responsibilities without the need of conversation – as when, for instance, a bucket of cement needed replacing or a hand was required to shift a heavy load. Everything flowed like a river. To see them putting up heavy oak beams, crossing them with chestnut stringers and then slapping down terracotta coping tiles was to experience poetry in motion, punctuated only by the occasional *Scheisse!* from Cosimo. With Ivo atop a tall ladder a supply line would form below: then, as firefighters might pass along buckets of water, each man in turn would swing along tools, tiles, nails, screws, a cigarette, saws, hammers, a lighter . . . in perfect syncopation without change of pace.

Only once did we ever hear a transistor, and it woke us like an atom bomb at seven o'clock one morning: a noise of disco intensity coming from the concrete pit that was to be the swimming pool. Some specialist tilers had arrived, a group of young men from Venice who were expert in fixing mosaic walls and evidently could not concentrate on the job without the aid of the Italian equivalent of Radio One on their ghetto-blaster. Thankfully, for if we hadn't been alerted by the sounds of heavy metal we would have had a ready-made disaster on our hands. I looked out of the bedroom window and saw sheets of canary yellow going up instead of the delicate duck-egg blue we were expecting. Racing downstairs in my pyjamas I closed with the offending scene in two minutes flat – causing great merriment among the lads.

'Don't worry, *signore*,' they laughed, 'it's only a backing sheet of yellow film! The tiles are exactly the colour you ordered: look!' And with this, one of the boys gripped what I then saw was a piece of yellow plastic film and gave it a big tug. It peeled off, revealing mosaic chequered sky blue and maroon. Someone had misread the order that had been faxed from Big Blu to their subcontractors and a catalogue reference to our chosen colour, ref. 2376, had been taken as 2876. Great, I thought; how many Aston Villa supporters are the Whittakers going to send us?

Home certainly wasn't rebuilt in a day but it wasn't the Big Blu team's fault. They had metre-thick stone walls to deal with, stable floors to be mucked out to a depth of a metre, holes to be drilled for tubing, piping, wiring, cabling, drainage, sewerage. When a pneumatic drill penetrated a hidden space beneath the first building, revealing a magnificently built vault the size of a burial chamber, we all held our breath lest it be an Etruscan tomb, in which case all work would have had to stop and our archaeological discovery reported to the authorities. Like the attempts to dig a metro system for Rome, work would then have been put on hold for years. Fortunately the chamber turned out to be just a cesspit, but a beautiful cesspit at that.

The job was big enough for a team three times the size of ours but we doubted very much if trebling it would have brought proportionate benefits in time-saving. For while we were racing ahead on the construction front, the timetable was truly being dictated by the snail-like pace of Italian bureaucracy, inertia in local government and the dazzling quantity of planning laws we had to plough through. These, indeed, represented the only part of the system that did move quickly: they were subject to rapid change and were often conflicting. The physical task of reconstructing an ancient building was insignificant compared to the hurdles that had to be overcome. Everything had problems attached: water, gas, electricity; septic tank; room height; the depth of the pool. All this in a conservation zone where the authorities drew a very distinct line between restoring a property and rebuilding one.

The laws concerning the pool changed three times while Big Blu's excavator munched into the hillside under Renato's control. First we were told we would have to have a lifeguard on permanent duty while guests disported themselves anywhere near it. OK, I said, that could be me. First change: the lifeguard must, naturally, be the bearer of a certificate of competence that had to be renewed each year following a proficiency test. That ruled me out straight away. Second change: instead of merely a shower in proximity to the pool there must, in addition, be a compulsory shower system obliging anyone entering the pool area to get wet, whether or not he or she was wearing a bathing costume. Third change: such an arrangement must be activated by magic-eye beam rather than physical touch. Finally, on the point of despair, we were told we could avoid all such obligations if the depth of the pool were no greater than 1.4 metres and we described our clients as house guests rather than paying customers. Once again native ingenuity had triumphed over the law, which truly was an *asino*. 'Even then they forgot to pass a law obliging us to fence it to protect stray toddlers from falling in and drowning,' said Mira.

13

Water Rights and Wrongs

WATER quality and supply was something that concerned us greatly. We knew that water in the Chianti hills was almost as precious as wine, and sometimes more so, but a new friend, Giulio Ruspoli, had advised us first to check whether Pepi had registered the water source on Collelungo's land which supplied all our needs. If not, he said, anyone could come along and declare it as his own. He knew because it happened to him at his estate of Lilliano, and Giulio, whose wines were well known, was hardly in our tenderfoot league. He was a prince, of an ancient and respected Roman family, well connected and liked. A pillar of society, you might say.

With 12 apartments, our own office requirements and the need for a public WC we had a total of 17 lavatories emerging from the building site. When we thought of the amount of showers and baths that would be taken daily by up to 31 guests as well as ourselves we knew we would have a sizeable problem should anything go wrong. This was a probability rather than a possibility, given that we were not on the public mains and had an unquantifiable amount of water and an unreliable and often erratic supply of electricity with which to pump it around the apartments. There could be no water without electricity: a difficult concept.

There were three things to be done. First, at considerable cost we put in a generator to provide power when the grid failed (we were discovering we were particularly prone to lightning strikes and power cuts. Several times, ENEL had blacked us out for hours and once for days. Another time, a neighbour digging his vines managed to sever the main cable linking us to the outside world.) Second, we put in a septic tank that came with the description '60-seater' and that seemed to take care of the downside risk. Third, we made an urgent call on the people who control and register all water rights in the province, the Civil Engineers. And there followed a debate about whether we had a well, as we claimed, or a spring – the difference being that in the latter case we owed the *provincia* a lot of money. Collelungo had been stealing water for years from the river that marked our bounds and as everyone knew, river water was State property! An uneasiness descended. This was not what we wanted to hear. The visit cost us around £350 to include all the back years of Pepi's use.

And then the water inspectors dropped in unannounced.

According to Pepi, the spring at Collelungo was so pure and abundant that people from the village used to tramp half an hour through the woods to draw supplies from it. Nevertheless, with modern standards being so high and our business depending on official recognition of its being fit for public consumption, our plumber had insisted we build a small pump room in which he could install some extra purification gadgets to meet today's norms. It was a showpiece of cutting-edge technology, the acme of hydraulics and hygiene. We had spent a fortune installing a drip dispenser for chlorine, charcoal filters and a huge salt vat for softening purposes alongside compression tanks, pumps, valves and a system of piping the like of which I had once seen on a nuclear submarine. Together, we also decided it would be advisable to change the circuit of old white plastic tubing that carried the water supply underground and was so brittle it broke, usually at the most awkward moment, whenever a heavy vehicle passed or someone swung a pickaxe in the wrong place. The new black polyurethane replacement was laid over 1.5 kilometres, where possible out of harm's way in ditches.

First the water was pumped up from the spring to three old concrete cubes that had once been wine vats. At Attila-the-Plumber's insistence, these had been placed on a ledge of sand at a considerable height above the car park. I had expressed misgivings about this position and was worried about the flimsy footing but he was unconcerned, saying the weight of the tanks would ensure their stability, and I had to bow to his evident experience and knowledge. These were simply holding tanks for the pump room below. And indeed the inspectors declared themselves impressed, as I hoped; I was rather proud of the little grotto with all its bells and whistles. But rather than take their samples in that sanitised centre of operations they preferred to decamp to our kitchen, where to our unpleasant surprise they took out a blowtorch and applied a concentrated jet of flame to the delicate brown paintwork of the Terre-de-France mixer tap unit. 'To eliminate germs,' they said, before running off a few litres into specimen bottles. Then they departed, leaving us with a blistered tap which would never be the same plus nagging doubts about our hygiene certificate and the sufficiency of the bottles of grappa we had given each of the three as an incentive.

We waited three weeks before hearing the result of the analysis. The sample showed iron content 10 times above normal: 1,890 units instead of the maximum 200 permitted by law.

'Impossible!' said Benito.

'A disaster!' I said.

'It's wrong!' said Attilio. 'Those readings can't be true. With that level of iron there'd have to be an iron mine nearby and the water should be looking red and tasting funny.'

'It's got to be Mafalda,' said Mira. 'She must have a mole working in the lab to have come up with results like that. I bet someone's tipped a chemical in there. You can't explain it any other way, short of an accident.'

It was no use phoning the health authority, USL; all their calls were routed through secretaries whose sole purpose in life was to protect their bosses from irate consumers.

I decided action was called for, a bit of old-fashioned leg work. 'Come on, we're off to Siena,' I said to Mira, and we struggled for an hour through the tourist traffic to find their headquarters in a red brick monstrosity in Siena's back streets. While other foreigners were admiring the fabled magnificence of the city, its fountains, surging towers, tunnelled alleys, hidden gardens and romantic wells we flew into the building and accosted the first white-coated lab assistant we saw. 'Which way is the Director's office?' I demanded. Ten minutes later we sat in front of a surprised bureaucrat having barged past his outer defences. Brandishing the test results and emboldened by the outrage of anyone even contemplating to stitch us up in such a brazen manner, I pushed the papers across the Director's desk and demanded an explanation I knew would not be forthcoming. 'You must make a new test,' I said. 'If we do not get immediate and satisfying results we shall denounce the lab for incompetence.'

My Italian had come on, you understand, and I was learning

a few native ways. It was an uncharacteristic outburst but it worked. We were visited again by different health inspectors one week later, and soon afterwards received official notification that our drinking water was perfectly safe for human consumption. This time the result showed only 23 units of iron.

It was another little victory, another step in the right direction. But it was also a lesson that we had better watch our little friend with the turban more closely.

14

Conversions

THE process of converting ourselves into Tuscan landlord and landlady was proving a slow and continuously painful affair but we were edging forward, getting to make friends, getting to know the village and getting to enjoy it. It is one of three 'castle towns' that formed the Lega del Chianti to defend the Florentine borders from Siena: Castellina to the west, Radda in the centre and Gaiole to the east. All have taken the proud suffix 'in Chianti' to underscore their ancestral legitimacy. Yet there really isn't a great deal for the casual visitor to get excited about. With its sharecroppers gone, Castellina in Chianti (population: old and dwindling) quickly lost all trace of the pursuits that once formed the fabric of local life: woodcutting, cabinet-making, shoemaking, silk-farming and lignite mining. By the time we arrived, evidence of the village's Etruscan and Roman origins was dwindling too although its 14th-century ramparts were still standing, complete with arrow slits for archers and larger openings through which pitch-burners once applied boiling tar to the heads of attacking enemy footsoldiers. In the 20th century a tyranny of a different sort has imposed itself. Its chief landmark has become a concrete silo, a structural horror visible for miles that serves as a constant reminder of the desperate post-war years when anyone bringing wealth and jobs to the village was allowed to perpetrate architectural heresy. Now, as if trying in some way to counterbalance this atrocity, tourists are greeted by politically correct signs pointing the way to our Ecological Oasis, as we have learned to call the municipal tip.

Seen from Collelungo's topmost vineyard the village rides the horizon like a great liner with a medieval tower for a funnel. It can seem serenely at anchor when the creamy round moon rises aloft behind its battlements bathed in luminescence. It becomes perilously forbidding on stormy nights, with wildfire flashes of lightning illuminating its glistening wet stone. Or, in the rosy aura of dawn, it is just sleepy and benign. Sometimes it performs a vanishing trick: we look up and it simply isn't there, lost entirely in low cloud (we are at 550 metres, about 1,800 feet). The Etruscan tombs at its northern edge lie hidden, too, in a cruci-form group of tunnels following the cardinal points of the compass under a mound of earth like a prehistoric barrow.

Arriving from the north, a newcomer finds himself in the grandly named Piazza Roma, where five roads meet without benefit of traffic lights: a crossroads endowed with a curiously large rusting edifice at one side. This is an old *Vespasiano*, a much-loved and well-patronised curl of iron with patterned perforations named after the Roman emperor Vespasian who actually built the Colosseum but instead had the bad luck to be immortalised for his street urinals. The sight greeting the visitor from the south is no less edifying: an abandoned building whose cathedral-sized doors grace a slaughterhouse that once witnessed the passage of cattle about to be transformed into *bistecca alla fiorentina*, the famous local T-bone steak. The gates stand open and redundant, most meat being embalmed in plastic at the supermarket in modern times.

Between pissoir and abbatoir lies Italy in microcosm: a place of extreme schizophrenia, incongruity and charm where politicians are ritually discredited and re-elected, the Church is both revered and ignored, and laws are openly flouted and ridiculed. Above all, a place managing to be simultaneously medieval and modern, balanced between the secrets it needs to keep inside the family and the *bella figura* it intuitively feels obliged to present to the world outside. I especially savour the fact that the electric Madonna with twinkling stars in her halo shines brightly over the Shell and Fina petrol pumps in the piazza, with fresh flowers at her feet every Ladies' Day and Mother's Day. Down the road meanwhile the latest trashy sex comic can be selling like hot cakes with a front cover showing a hermaphrodite porn star in her (his?) birthday suit and a scratch pad covering the area of doubt.

Seven years were to elapse from the moment we first set eyes on Collelungo to the day we eventually managed to open for business, and in that time the village became more familiar to us than any place we had lived in previously. The pace and pleasures, the intrigues and intimacies of life in rural Italy were an education for two ex-Londoners. Over the years, also, we had come to witness the arrival of a new breed of tourist, one tired of beaches and cities who was seeking to get in touch with nature, craving a touch of simplicity. It seemed our timing was right.

The fun began in spring. We could tell the tourist season was starting when the first foreign buses arrived, towing trailers full of racing bikes and disgorging dozens of cyclists into the village car park. Their exotic Lycra kit in gaudy colours and helmets the shape of giant teardrops might have raised an eyebrow or two but in general the *contadini* shuffling by took it all in their stride quite nonchalantly. They had seen it all before and learned to recognise the new arrivals as the season's first human swallows, harbingers of an annual migration that got whackier every year. They knew they would be followed by camper-vans in the parking lot, lined up in Teutonic precision with names like BAVARIA, HYMER and WANDERLUST splashed across their backsides. Then in successive waves would come the Germans and Austrians, the French, the Dutch, the British, the Japanese. All except the latter would be cocooned in heavy German metal – Mercedes and BMWs and top-end Golfs – from which to observe the countryside. (The Japanese just arrived and departed mysteriously by whatever mode of transport they could find.) Americans came in increasing numbers and through it all, Italian out-of-towners could be relied on to show off the latest Lancias, Alfas and top-end Fiats. It was an endless pageant of colour, style and fashion.

On a typical day Antonio the village bobby can be seen crawling around the cars parked higgledy-piggledy outside the historic centre, checking the blue and white time-discs drivers have to display if the honour system for an hour's free parking is to work. It doesn't, this being Italy. Many of the foreign cars have owners who are unaware of the need to show their time of arrival in the parking zone, and the long arm of the law consequently suffers writer's cramp on account of the number of tickets it has to issue. It is not poor Antonio's only problem. He is looking fazed by the variety of words he is encountering on bumper-stickers that spill all the complexities, cares and cynicism of the modern world into our quiet backwater in language that is often hard to comprehend. He turns to me for help with a translation, handing over a crumpled piece of his notebook where I see something copied that looks like: I BRAKE FOR MOOSE. To my surprise I find moose in the dictionary, and I know the word for brake, but putting the two together and explaining it to someone who is probably descended from the Etruscans is like describing a combine harvester to an Eskimo. I see another sticker, on the back of a big off-roader with AFI (American forces) plates, proclaiming: IF ASSHOLES COULD FLY, THIS PLACE WOULD BE AN AIRPORT. Again I feel the subtlety might just be lost on our local plod. I give a shrug. *'Stranieri patsi,'* I tell him. Crazy foreigners.

No matter what they drive or where they come from, every visitor will bring a bit of his or her own culture that will trickle down eventually to affect the cycle of local life in some way. We have even heard shopkeepers say 'Bye-bye' to please the foreigners. More often than not, the foreigners have enough gumption to respond with 'Ciao!' Aleandro at the wine shop has brought his daughter Roberta into the business because she speaks English. One day we are passing and see their poster supporting a charity called, peculiarly, 'Hospitals Without Walls'. On investigation we learn that in its original, French, form this is Médecins Sans Frontières.

But Castellina is also the crossroads for a widely diversified resident foreign community whose company we were just discovering. Our aim had not been to seek out the companionship of the colony, but there was a natural gravitational pull; an unstated bond among those who faced the strains and challenges of daily life together in a country not of their birth. It was quite hilarious to read that Germaine Greer decided to abandon Chianti after owning a house here for 20 years, at about the time we found Collelungo. No, there was no connection; she had gone to Tuscany, she said, to live among Italian peasants but instead 'found myself living among German hairdressers'. (It seemed no one had polled the German hairdressers or Italian peasants to hear whether they found the idea of living next to La Greer any more pleasing.)

It was nice to mix with people, not necessarily British, who shared an Italy that was different from the tourist version where the sun always shone, the vine always bore fruit, leisure was infinite and threats to one's well-being such as water shortage (or failure to meet critical drinking water standards of purity), hail strike and power failure were items scarcely imagined. For those who had holiday homes and visited the area only for a few warm months at a time – or took a *Summer's Lease* – the dream may seldom have been broken. The difference for us and many of the new friends we were making was that we were working there year-round and had to earn a living out of our investment.

John Mortimer's novel exploiting the notion of 'Chiantishire' rather bothered us. His idea of a snobbish, hedonistic, expatriate world of rich and fashionable socialites was alien to the discoveries we had been making, though for a period after the BBC serialised the book we did notice a perceptible change in the quality of tourists from Britain. Sir John Gielgud had come to epitomise the quintessential Anglo-Tuscan grandee. He clearly developed into a role model for aspiring gentleman tourists, for very soon Gielgud clones could be sighted, whizzing round our rural lanes in Range Rovers bearing what looked suspiciously like Harrods hampers. We suspected it was only Britain's stringent quarantine laws that spared us grand-touring Labradors as well.

Then Bernardo Bertolucci had his sixpennyworth of fun, demolishing the Mortimer myth in his film *Stealing Beauty*, which we saw one night in the village of Greve in company with an awestruck audience of hard-working Tuscans. We were sure their culture was rather different from that depicted on the screen: a decadent society concerned solely with sex, pot and self-interest.

In truth, both images were a pastiche. The Chianti hills certainly harboured their share of occasionally dotty, sometimes delightful, foreigners and the true Anglo-Tuscans (the artists and the art historians) were always being rude about the new Anglo-Tuscans (the bankers, the accountants, the media moguls, the people with money and most certainly those without, such as ex-journalists and ex-travel agents). *Panorama*, Italy's leading news magazine, was the first to identify the core eccentricity when it cited the case of the ex-Indian Army colonel 'who as soon as he arrived in Chianti asked quite naturally of his compatriots: "Are there any other Europeans around?"' Such excruciating old fossils had thankfully long vanished but we were constantly being reminded how lucky those who got here first had been. We picked up an article in the *Daily Mail* in which Isabel Colegate, another early literary émigrée, remembered sharing the £4,000 cost of a square stone farmhouse at Castellina with a friend. It was surrounded by 57 acres of crumbling terraces and unpruned vines and olives which she said seemed to be thrown in with the house. Their buy had been fairly typical. No one wanted land in the Chianti hills in those days.

By the time the myth of Chiantishire gained currency dreams were not coming cheaply any more. Plus, there was a sea change in the composition of the foreign community. It may well have been the British who led the invasion but subsequent settlers spoke German, Dutch, Japanese and English with an American accent. Ms Greer was not far wrong: German residents soon probably outnumbered the British by about four to one. But by then there were very few Italian peasants left anyway.

Our own immediate neighbours are fairly typical. Down the lane live Betty and Louis, two charming former college professors from the United States whose home may be the size of a doll's house but whose pride of ownership makes it seem like a castle. Within the estate of Collelungo there is another house, Campocerchi, which was chopped out of our deeds long ago and sold first to an Englishman who sold to a Dutchman and now belongs to Antonia from Milan and her husband Willi from Switzerland (as I write, some Germans have made an offer for it). The site is of Roman origin, named 'camp of the circle' from the ring of stones that once protected it. Italians Mimma and Franco Ferrando have a most beautifully restored property on the hill opposite us, having returned to Italy from living abroad for many years and thus, as non-Tuscans, confess to feeling rather like immigrants themselves. Finally, in complete contrast, there is the Pitigliani family, the local nobs, still in occasional residence at the family seat of Sommavilla – originally a baronial home, now converted into a condominium of nine apartments and used as weekend retreats, mostly by other Florentines.

It was here one evening that we encountered another unexpected side to life in the Tuscan backwoods. The village choral society gave a pretty performance in the family's private residence in gratitude for some smart new costumes which these good patrons of the arts kindly presented them. We were to hear the choir sing again – beautifully – soon afterwards, in the private cellars of our aristocratic friend Giulio at the Lilliano winery. Their *pièce de résistance* was a rendering of the Beatles' *Yesterday*, sung in such astonishingly clear English that I was prompted to ask the choirmaster who their language tutor was. 'Why nobody,' he said in surprise. 'They don't speak a word of anything except Italian.' Then with a smile he showed me their lyrics. Everything had been written phonetically, in English with Italian phrasing: *Iessterdai, ol mai trobels siimd so farauei* . . .

As we were learning, old money in Italy has a way of lying low; it is never flaunted. The outsides of houses are left peeling, stucco cracking, shutters flaking. Everything is a matter of studied disintegration and distress, which is the image the country as a whole likes to project to the world. Understatement is the order of the day; pristine plaster and shiny paintwork such as might grace a suburban home in a Dulux ad are definitely not desirable. Good taste is only partly responsible for this phenomenon. Security, or more precisely the fear of burglary, is the root cause. On the outside everything is left to take care of itself; the beauty lies hidden within, in exquisite order as in Roman times when villas were built introspectively around a central courtyard.

That summer before we opened for business we were given a privileged insight into all of this when we were invited again to Lilliano where Giulio was having 'a little get-together' to celebrate his 50th birthday.

Twilight fell as we approached the prince's Palladian edifice, no more than 15 minutes' drive from Collelungo. Flames from wax burners made patterns of gold and amber dance over the wisteria that wound around the colonnaded façade, highlighting the stone putti with their age-spots of lichen who gazed down from the eaves. In the hushed and perfumed garden below, Italy's beautiful people were foregathering amid amphorae and terracotta pots filled with lemon trees in full fruit. Stewards in white jackets circulated artfully with champagne flutes on silver trays. It was a fashion parade of a kind we had seen only in the movies. Mira pointed out an impressive amount of Gucci, up from Rome on the shoulders and feet of politicos and aristos we only vaguely recognised from the TV; and there was Versace down from Milan on the bodies of women being escorted by bankers, fashion designers and industrialists who also regularly made the 8 p.m. news. Everywhere, it seemed there was much kissing of hands, and women pretend-kissing to avoid smudging their make-up. It was an insight into drawing room society, where the real seat of power is shared between aristocratic families, the jet set, and the very seriously rich.

Totally unprepared for the magnificence of the occasion, we felt privileged, underdressed, undeserving intruders in that precious world. Fireflies danced in the gloaming as we drank our Krug, watched the sun set and witnessed the rising of a brand new moon. The sound of tinkling glasses and laughter drifted across the whole magical scene.

15

Discoveries

A place called Poggibonsi had been mentioned to us as a good
source of supplies for the scale of our shopping that was rapidly
becoming apparent. The name, pronounced correctly, sounded
like 'Podgy Bonsi', for which reason English-speaking visitors
seemed to find it especially droll and cuddly; but apart from
being on the road to San Gimignano (which few of English-
speaking stock could pronounce correctly: 'San Jiminyano') it
was of little touristic significance or artistic merit. Its main claim
to fame seemed to be the Sanctuary of Santa Maria a Romituzzo
where a collection of more than 5,000 legs, arms, heads, necks
and whole bodies could be found in the form of tin votive offer-
ings. According to the guidebooks the big excitement at
Poggibonsi came in the 13th century when a Gothic church was
built and the Della Robbia gang installed an altar. Things have
calmed down a bit since then.

It remained out of the history books until the Second World
War when it took everything the Allies could throw at it in their

advance up Italy. It was rebuilt hurriedly after the war, like most of modern Italy, in the frenzy that marked the need for emergency housing. Consequently, apart from its historic centre it was not a pretty sight. Mercifully for those living in the vicinity, prices had not been pushed up by tourism. It was where the bargains could be found.

It was where we came across an amazing three-storey emporium, Tutto Mercato, ruled by a man called Umberto in a string vest with a bar-code moustache and foghorn voice. He was barking his special offer of the week as we walked in: for every £80 spent there was a free gift of 10 kilos of pasta. As our spend was likely to be rather more in the region of £8,000 the thought occurred that we might be better off forgetting *agriturismo* and going into the grocery business. 'It looks as though we'll need more planning permission for storage space,' I said to Mira.

At ground level one could find an assortment of Chinese bric-a-brac, kitchenware, utensils, crockery and cutlery. The first floor was a jumble of washing machines, cookers, old-fashioned parlour stoves, fridges, dishwashers, curtain rails, lavatory seats, TVs, hi-fis, armchairs and sofas, carpets, matting, light bulbs, toasters, vacuum cleaners and bathroom fixtures. And on the second floor we found furniture of exactly the style we wanted and had seen elsewhere at alarming prices: *arte povera*, as it's called. Pauper's art, basic and simple, was just right for a restored Tuscan farmhouse. Umberto, a curious cross between Mohammed Al Fayad, circus ringmaster and truck driver, showed us some lovely items at really knock-down prices.

We came out of Umberto's place feeling greatly relieved and turned left into an avenue of plane trees. Once we had crossed a disused railway track we plunged into the *centro storico* (historic centre) of Poggi-B and made another great find. It was the handwritten sign in the window that caught our attention. 'Do you want to kill your enemy mice once and for all?' it read. 'Apply within.' We did, and became instant friends with a man called Natale, 'Christmas'. It was more a long and narrow Aladdin's Cave than a shop, filled with chimney-sweep brushes and poles, carved olive-wood chopping boards, clamps to hold shanks of ham, bottling machines, barrels, bottles, corks, capsules . . . a real old-fashioned hardware store where nails and screws were sold by weight, kerosene was dispensed by the jerrycan and advice was given freely on subjects from woodworm to winning the Lotto.

Also in Poggibonsi we found a man who would make light fittings to our own design for the total of 15 bathrooms that we needed. For our 12 kitchens we signed a contract with a manufacturer who agreed to put in marble tops for the price of Formica. Any tricky bits of woodwork were entrusted to a carpenter whose workshop we came across unexpectedly in woods adjacent to Collelungo. Wrought-iron railings, hand rails, grilles, doors, window frames and garden lights were the responsibility of the village blacksmith, Graziano, back in Castellina. His was a working smithy, a smoke-blackened forge that had rung to the sound of hammer and anvil for half a millennium but now hissed with jets of oxyacetylene torches.

Castellina lies on the old Chiantigiana highway between Florence and Siena but the modern road skirts the village, leaving it marooned with a medieval main street hewn from stone pretty much as the Medici may have remembered it. Except in very recent times its ancient paving has been dug up piece by piece so that fibre-optic phone lines and a new mains cable might be laid. Each numbered stone has been carefully replaced in precisely the right order, while any that might have been considered dangerously worn has been renewed and an instant patina of antiquity applied with compressed-air chisels carving individual furrows in each block. We both think it a masterful sleight of hand in a country where decay is both cultivated and worshipped.

Through this street in summer hydrangeas sprout from hollowed-out tree stumps strategically placed outside the shops. The only break in the pink and blue line of blossoms might come from an azure rosette with ribbons fluttering from a brass door-knocker. Attached to it will be the joyous announcement: *IO SONO ARRIVATO* (literally, 'I've arrived!'). It's a boy! And a precocious one at that, in the manner of all Italian males.

Mario, who runs the village antiques store, might be rearranging the display of 'medieval tapestries' he sells successfully to tourists who wish to have the skyline of San Gimignano or bell towers of Arezzo hanging on their living room walls at home.

Sabrina might be setting out her supply of eggplants, mushrooms, fennel, tomatoes and outrageously big red bell peppers on the rack outside her greengrocery, a kaleidoscopic display tourists find hard to resist photographing. We watch the seasons change just by monitoring her stock: asparagus in early spring, cherries a little later, peaches and watermelon in summer, pumpkins in autumn, chestnuts in winter. When we ask Sabrina if her tangerines have pips, however, she confesses she has no idea. She doesn't like the fruit and never eats it.

Facing her is the reconstituted Roman-Venetian church, completely fake, built in a rush in 1948 to cover the hole in the ground the Germans left when they blew up its predecessor four years earlier. I am not alone in thinking it a pity they had not also destroyed the sacred relic that lies within it: the embalmed and blackened remains of the Patron Saint Fausto, which are paraded through the village streets once a year to bring terror to little boys and girls who forget to say their prayers. As we had been warned, the village votes Communist, always, and its diminutive priest, Don Gino, has long ago reconciled himself to the losing battle. His antagonist, our friend the mayor, is a very large and rotund Refounded (but not Reformed) Communist who, despite his disdain for Faraoni's foppishness, is not beyond a bit of vanity himself. His love of pomposity is well served when occasion calls for him to wear his one and only suit and don his red, white and green polyester sash of office. The priest consoles himself with the knowledge that instead of enhancing his standing and authority as first citizen many parishioners think it has quite the opposite effect: His Worship the dry cleaner turns into a giant Easter egg.

Along the road there is an ancient and austere family *palazzo* bearing the crest of the Medici dynasty on its crumbling façade, behind which a luxury hotel has been developed; vaulted storage space that has metamorphosed into a cocktail bar; some stables that only a while earlier had housed horse and farrier and have become a smart pizzeria. We also have a barber's that has changed little in half a century, where customers take their chances in a cracking plastic chair surrounded by magazines that look as though they have survived since the 1950s.

A similar retro look graces one of the three village restaurants. As the 21st century loomed it still had a retouched photo of its owner, a once-handsome racing driver in the Fangio mould, on the receiving end of a kiss from none other than Claudia Cardinale, clearly his one moment of fame in his glory days. *La bella Claudia* had hung on the wall for well over three decades, her fading hues having to be re-tinted so often that she had assumed the electric qualities of those magic paint colours we kids who grew up after the Second World War achieved by wetting the page with a brush dipped in water.

For Mira and many of our guests village life revolves around a shoe boutique, owned by the former mayor who after a record spell in office also owns a second home in Cuba. To the uninitiated, he is a die-hard Communist with impeccable left-wing credentials, but life has taught him that market forces and the philosophy of Fidel are not mutually exclusive. (Another place central to our well-being is the chemist's, where we buy remedies for the usual ailments plus, in my case, a special home-made brew Alessandro the pharmacist describes as a baldness cure. I have to tell you, it doesn't work.)

However, it is the bar that is the nodal point in everyone's daily existence. It is a clearing house of information where, for the minimum investment of a thimble of espresso tossed back standing up, the return can be most rewarding. The premises also function as a free mailbox, where letters can be left for fellow villagers: a more-than-handy facility in a place where the concept of customer service has totally escaped the bureaucrats who run the real post office. It also serves as headquarters for a volunteer forest fire brigade which boldly goes where others fear to tread in its one antique Fiat 500 with a whiplash aerial stuck on with a suction cap.

Apart from our tombs and medieval fortifications, tourist attractions per se are few, and the best of these is unintentional. It is at the bank, where the Italian love of technology can be seen in a fiercely intimidating glass security chamber that customers are forced to pass through on entering. A vertical drum, its sides bear pictograms helpfully illustrating the types of object we will not be allowed to carry with us. These include an umbrella, a camera and even, strange to relate, an automatic pistol. Loudspeakers are installed in the front of the open drum and every so often when a prohibited object is detected a recorded message might blast out in Italian, English and German, causing the whole village to jump up and run to its window. Usually, to the disappointment of all, it merely signifies that a luckless tourist has been trapped in its cylindrical clutches.

And that is it, apart from a doctor's surgery, a Co-op, a butcher's, a nursery school and playground, the Carabinieri station, the Consorzio Agrario and the abattoir. An official bus park large enough for only one single-decker marks the end of the village. As many as six bus services a day connect Castellina to Siena, but there is only one to Florence, the more important regional capital. Curiously, that leaves very early in the morning and returns quite late in the evening, void of passengers in both directions. Cesare, the young man who drives it, lives in our village and has the bus company's permission to use the vehicle to commute to Florence where he spends his working day on suburban routes before bringing it home at dinner-time.

Six centuries have passed since the Florentines and Sienese settled their squabbles about where the boundary line between their two territories should be drawn. Yet the fact remains, the only reason we have a public transport link to the capital of Tuscany is because poor Cesare lives in the village and wants his pasta cooked the way only Mamma can make it.

Nothing much happens in Castellina, the highlight of the week being the Saturday morning market with its fish stalls and counters selling slices of roast suckling pig. So when we awoke one morning to hear there had been a murder in the village we were electrified. A lone woman, out walking her dog one night past the Etruscan tombs, had been led by the animal's frenzied barking to a grisly discovery: the body of a young female lying in the tunnels beneath the ancient burial mound.

Police eventually identified the victim as a 28-year-old taxi driver from Siena but the murderer and motive remained a mystery. At the bar we heard idle talk of black magic rituals and drug dealing and, though the girl was unknown in Castellina, her name became linked with a villager the locals were convinced was somehow involved. Soon, half the village was expecting the resident rag-and-bone man – known to all as The Pilferer – to be brought in for questioning: after all, his son-in-law was doing time for the murder of a local girl a few years earlier, wasn't he? The logic was lost on us.

One morning a few days later when we dropped in for our habitual morning coffee the bar was full of busybody gossip as usual. But unlike previous occasions when our fellow villagers had been only too keen to buttonhole us for a chat, we detected an unexpected coolness instead. 'They're closing ranks, I suppose,' I said. 'They probably don't want to talk to outsiders right now because of the Press and the bad publicity all this has brought the village.'

Mira didn't reply. She thought it was very strange. We were getting some really odd looks and she could have sworn the usually talkative barman, Fabrizio, was trying to give us the cold shoulder.

'Come on, Fabrizio,' she said challengingly. 'What's going on?' I followed Mira's gaze and began to entertain a suspicion.

'I bet you Mafalda's been here poisoning the atmosphere somehow,' I said loudly in Italian, and Fabrizio almost choked.

'Meestair Tony, yes the Signora has been saying things about you,' he admitted. 'But it is not anything to do with this girl. Oh no! It is about your blue movies.'

'What?' we asked in unison, shocked. 'What do you mean, *blue movies*?'

Pain passed through Fabrizio's eyes.

'Please! Do not think badly of us but we all hear what she

say, how you want make sexy films of the guests at Collelungo and place video cameras in all the bedrooms.'

We looked at each other, aghast. Mira giggled. Then we burst out laughing. Blushing, Fabrizio scurried away with a tea towel and busied himself wiping coffee cups from a safe distance.

The idea of making blue movies was preposterous. We had told the village electrician, Leandro, to cable each apartment with the aim of putting TVs in their lounges and bedrooms and *play*ing videos for guests to watch if they wanted some evening entertainment. Mafalda had evidently got wind of this from the lad himself and did not like what she heard: the facilities at Collelungo were going to be more luxurious than hers. Also it provided her with a wonderful opportunity for mischief.

'Oh Mafalda!' we cried, and the entire bar turned in our direction. She had to be stopped, one way or another.

16

Countdown to D-Day

IT was 1996. Year Zero. It was still January, and panic was setting in. Barney Whittaker had paid a second visit as promised and pronounced everything to his satisfaction ('Tickety-boo!'), for the pool was finished and the apartments were well on their way. But now the pressure was on. The property looked awfully raw and immature despite its medieval provenance. Big Blu's scaffolding had gone and all remaining building materials had been tucked out of sight, exposing a scene starkly in contrast to the picture-book image of the Tuscan idyll. The garden lay bare. The pool bore a lake of rainwater on top of the green tarpaulin stretched over its surface. But the apartments were far from ready, lacking furniture, kitchens and tiling let alone decoration work. The old stone walls had menacing dark patches as if rising damp were going to be a permanent design feature. The parking area was ankle deep in a rich mush of mud and fallen acorns. It was a bleak time of year.

But the central heating worked. Attilio's plumbing was efficient.

The holding tanks above the car park contained enough water to keep us going through the worst drought summer might bring. This system had been an ingenious solution to an age-old problem that could turn into a crisis with paying guests in residence. Cheap, too, considering it did not need deep foundations. The old tanks were surplus to requirements anyway and could not be sold, as modern winemaking employed stainless steel vats instead of concrete and we still had no intention of getting involved in that. The electrical set-up also appeared to function as intended, apart from a faulty circuit in the pump room which young Leandro was busy sorting out. Even Mafalda was keeping her distance. It seemed safe to start our preparations for D-Day.

As far as the grounds were concerned we really were having to start from scratch. It was evident that luxuries like flowers and shrubs were elements conspicuously absent in the age of the *contadini*, when anything grown had to have practical purpose, so their farmhouses simply started where the countryside ended. This made Cheeso's gift of roses even more touching and unexpected.

We'd never intended making English-type gardens around Collelungo: they were neither desirable nor practical, given their need of constant care and watering. Nor was it our aim to suburbanise the countryside. Such landscaping as we had done had been with the cooperation of Renato and his bulldozer. We made terraces to the west of the houses and argued passionately about how they should be retained, with low walls in stone or wood. The master mason in Renato wanted nothing to do with wood, even though we had recuperated several collapsed beams and put them aside for the purpose.

'Listen, they're full of woodworm,' he'd keep saying, twirling his Asterix mustachios faster and faster the more agitated he became. 'How long do you think they're going to last when you put them against soil, eh? Ten years? Five? Ha! It would be far better to use stones. They'll last 500!' He positively glowed at the prospect, until we pointed out politely that it was us who were living at Collelungo, not him, and even 50 years' life expectancy for the rotting oak would be more than enough to see us out. 'OK, feefty-feefty,' he said. The terraces stood there that January day, a triumph of compromise in alternating stone and wood, bereft of botanical life.

Both Mira and I appreciate the value of flowers, and as geraniums had been the only variety we'd had experience with they seemed a logical choice to give a good show for opening day. Roberto said he knew of a nursery some distance away where prices were half those charged by local growers and we piled into the Renault and set off, heading east across the Chianti hills and into the Arno valley, fired with enthusiasm. He was right: the market garden he talked about had a great variety on offer at a fraction of what we feared we would have to pay – and better still, delivery was included. It was still too early for the babies to be planted out, so we left a small deposit and ordered an entire truckload for delivery in April, together with some lavender and other shrubs. This would be in plenty of time for the big opening we had planned for Easter.

Months passed. The daily routine became automatic. The furniture we'd ordered arrived, the kitchens were fitted one per apartment, the floors were tiled, the walls were painted, white curtains were hung at the windows, and a cleaning lady we had hired from the village, Franca, set to work, preparing everything with gusto as we edged towards the big day.

Franca turned out to be a treasure. She was no spring chicken but what she lacked in youth she more than made up for in enthusiasm. Everything she tackled she did with such force, quite a lot of muttering and the occasional burst of song. She was always huffing and puffing, being vigorous to the point of destruction – such as the time we saw her swatting a cloud of hornets with a broom, which broke after being arrested in mid-swat by a large piece of 14th-century masonry that got in the way. (The hornets had nested inside the first building and were reluctant to buzz off after being unmolested for generations. In the end we had to blast them out with insecticide and fill in their front doors with cement.) A new broom was procured and Franca went off like a Whirling Dervish in a spiralling plume of dust, singing her heart out.

Oh, Franca sang. She sang in the village choir and once went to Rome by coach to cheer up the Pope when he was unwell: a major highlight in her life, though history does not record what effect it had on Il Papa. Her secular repertoire ran from '*Arrivederci, Roma!*' through all the old numbers from the 1950s, her favourite reprise being 'I Found My Love in Portofino'. For special occasions she resorted to something much more ambitious such as the Hebrew Slaves' chorus from *Nabucco*.

The downside to Franca was that she had an insatiable appetite: when her mouth wasn't open for singing it was open for eating, both on and off the job. This caused crumbs. But Franca, being short-sighted, missed them. Consequently we had to follow in her wake to make sure the apartments really were clean. (When we did eventually get up and running there was more about Franca that amused us. Guests were by then referring to her as Portofino and as they vacated their apartment on their last day, Franca would rush in, puffing and emitting little shrieks of 'Heh!', to see what might have been left by way of a tip. Sometimes she was lucky, but more often than not she had to make do with whatever goodies might have been left in the kitchen. Her daily swag often contained riches like eggs, butter, milk, pasta and sugar. We got Franca's rejects, things she didn't understand like balsamic vinegar, Nescafé and cornflakes.)

Finally we awoke one morning and the transformation was complete. The avenue of cypresses leading to the farm had been trimmed back and the approach fanned out into a parking area that Renato had bulldozed and covered with gravel. The two massive oaks guarding the entrance to the property had been clipped of their girdle of ivy whose cords were as thick as hawsers, throttling every branch; they were in perfect shape and even had spotlights at their base. The small CO LE NGO sign of old that had been nailed to a tree had been replaced by the name I painted by hand on a very large rock.

Directly in front of it, our two stone buildings smiled at each other in harmonious tones of oatmeal, grey and terracotta. A long fence of criss-crossed chestnut palings guarded the steep descent between the two houses, filled with Cosimo's showpiece steps descending invitingly over what had been overgrown land. The first building with its Tuscan loggia was back as the original designer intended, reroofed, reglazed, repointed, restored. The only difference was something that could not be seen: its ancient walls were now pierced by hot and cold water pipes, waste pipes, sewage pipes, central heating pipes, gas pipes, electrical cable, telephone cable, closed-circuit cable and another coaxial cable for satellite TV. Two of its original oak beams were intact but the rest were brand new (and distressed by the sandblaster) as were the ceilings with exposed terracotta brick and chestnut rafters. Copper guttering glinted in the sunshine.

The second house was equally transformed, with louvred shutters hanging at every window (I decided to ignore Mister Mayor). There was not a trace of the ugly almond tree whose roots had invaded the front of the house; instead, land had been scooped out to make a clearing and on the wall of the former chicken coop a pretty piece of gnarled wood hung, bearing the legend: RECEPTION.

We were ready – but there was still no sign of the geraniums.

Where were the plants? All day long Mira and I took turns to phone the nursery, which went by the incongruous name of La Ballerina. By evening we were still none the wiser, and then at 8 p.m. came the call we were waiting for. A woman sounding a long way off and far from happy said her husband had loaded up his lorry and was setting out for Collelungo at that very moment; would there be someone to receive the plants even though it was dark? Certainly, we said, and gave her precise directions from the Arno valley. Counting on a slow drive we estimated he should be with us around 10 p.m.

At 9.30, leaving nothing to chance, I went to the office. By then the light drizzle that had started soon after we'd put the phone down had become a steady downpour and by 10 o'clock the wind had backed, driving the rain sideways. When 10.15 came there was still no sign of the man, but the wind had risen to gale force and the farm was being buffeted like a Hull trawler on the North Sea. I switched on all the outside lights and peered into the blackness from my bridge-like position. Nothing. I sank back, nursing a whisky and wondering what to do with 150 geraniums in a monsoon.

It was close to 11 p.m. when the van arrived and by then the tempest had developed nicely. Collelungo was under attack from thunder and lightning, with vivid flashes illuminating wave after wave of slanting rain that splattered sideways onto the window pane. I was on my third Scotch and was lost in a John Grisham novel, which probably accounts for the fact that when I suddenly saw lights moving like a comet across the streaming glass I did not immediately connect with the business at hand. These were the headlights I'd been waiting for but they were too fast: they'd vanished in a downwards arc, well past the unloading point, before I could grab my waterproofs and dash outside to stop the driver.

Struggling to keep upright in the wind and rain, I fought my way into the storm but could see no sign of the van. Then I realised: visibility was so bad the driver had probably mistaken the vineyard for our road. He must have taken the perilous descent between Renato's terraces and the west-side vines – a 60-degree tractor slope for four-wheel drive vehicles, only in the dry. Just then a blinding vein of lightning lit the scene with massive candle power. Ahead of me in that frozen time-frame I saw a big white van embedded in the vines, furiously spinning its wheels and spraying a fountain of mud into the air. My torch beam picked out what appeared to be a giant purple flower, a fuchsia that must have been a couple of metres tall, painted on its side. Lightning zinged again as I approached the stricken vehicle, carefully avoiding the geyser of mud. The noise of the revving engine and whizzing wheels was lost in another crack of thunder and an instant electric flash, revealing the flower as merely a platform for a tutu-clad dancer standing on points on its uppermost petal. Beneath it were inscribed the words LA BALLERINA.

'Hey!' I shouted as the ensemble sank another foot deeper into the mud due to the driver's misguided efforts of acceleration. A face as crumpled as Popeye's looked out of the window, his glare caught in the flashlight, and then he started revving again, the wheels spinning even faster, more frantic, producing blue smoke to blend with the eruption of mud now spraying me too as the machine started to slither and slide. Only when the big Mercedes began to tilt dangerously to the left and look like tipping over did the driver appear to see reason and stop. He jumped out of his cab and into the quagmire he had created. 'Come on! Give us a hand here!' he shouted at me over the lashing gale. Then he raced around frantically and began to throw gravel under the wheels along with whatever else he could find in the way of planks, rocks and woodwormy beams on which his tyres might grip.

When he tried again the futility of it all was obvious: bits of wood, stones and rocks flew in every direction and still the Ballerina was trapped in the vineyard's clutches. Popeye was 20 metres down a 60-degree slope with a cargo of 150 geraniums. '*Basta!*' I shouted. And above the howl of the wind I thought I heard the reply: 'OK!'

Just then an enormous sound eclipsed even the violence of the storm, the kind of monster crash a tidal wave might make when hitting a beach.

'Oh my God,' I yelled. 'The tanks!' Instinctively I turned around, flashing the powerful torch beam uphill to where the water cisterns were. Only where I should have picked out concrete there was darkness. I felt something tugging at my feet. Fast-flowing water was flooding over my ankles and up my legs, rushing on past the mired Mercedes and into the blackness of night.

Standing there in the vineyard, wet through and covered in the mud of Collelungo, I had another one of those moments of self-doubt. But there was no time to waste: together Popeye and I started back towards the house like shipwrecked mariners. Exhausted and emotionally spent, intuition told me precisely what had happened and I saw no point in further investigation until the storm had passed, by which time it could be dawn.

It was now past midnight and we retreated to the apartment where Mira poured each of us a large Scotch. She was horrified to hear what had happened. However, the water tanks were not the immediate worry although the extent of the damage remained to be seen and repairs were going to be costly. It was Popeye who seemed to have the greater problem. It wasn't simply that he was upset at having bogged down his nice white Mercedes; he had to have the vehicle on the road for 10 other deliveries at breakfast-time, he said. We gave him another Famous Grouse painkiller and the spare bed and told him to get a good night's sleep; Renato and his boys would be there in the morning to haul him out early enough with their tractor.

But all the same we were awakened at 6.30 a.m. by the sound of his heavy diesel engine screaming, tyres churning and Popeye cursing. The sun was out, and we left him to it to investigate our own disaster. What we found was not encouraging: all three tanks lay on their sides, cracked open by the impact caused when they tumbled into the car park from their lofty perch. Under assault from the driving rain and rising water levels, one of the tanks must have first dislodged itself from its sandy footing, breaking away and pulling the others with it by the connecting piping. The whole system had collapsed.

17

Rising Above It

❦

APART from totally rethinking our water supply system only a couple of important things remained to be done. One was to hold an end-of-work party for the boys from Big Blu and ancillary workers; the second was to find the last occupants of Collelungo, the Migliorini family, to give them a party. (In the meantime our road signs pointing the way to Collelungo had mysteriously disappeared – another wrecking attempt by Mafalda, we presumed. We decided we would rise above it for the moment.) The party was Mira's idea: to invite the former occupants to return to Collelungo as our guests for lunch, not so much to show off as to try to learn about how life had been in the old days and better understand the history of the place. It turned out to be great timing: we discovered it was Dina Migliorini's 74th birthday.

So it was that one Sunday around noon a small convoy of locally registered cars came bouncing down our lane slowly, stopped in our newly created car park, and when their doors flew open out stepped 14 Migliorinis in three generations. Wonderment filled their faces. The amazement at the scene before them briefly swept away their power of speech. It was minutes before the surprise of seeing her old home again prompted one of the younger ones to break the silence. '*Ma guarda!*' she said. 'Just look!'

Apart from the gossip about the transformation of Collelungo which had washed through the village on the waves of Radio Chianti there had been other tantalising bits of information recently to whet inquisitive appetites. The local monthly tourist sheet, *Chianti News*, had done a really amazing publicity job under the immodest banner MIRACLES IN CHIANTI CONTINUE, telling (in four languages) the story of our reconstruction efforts and simultaneously managing to print all the photos I had given them back to front. It must have been to the Migliorinis' great relief that they discovered the buildings they remembered so well had not in fact been reoriented 180 degrees. But that was about all that remained familiar.

'*Ma guarda!*' became the leitmotiv for the day as our guided tour took them past the room where the shepherd had slept, the store where fodder had been kept, the former chicken shed, pigsties, wine vaults, cow byre, the well (where a pig had once fallen in, we were to hear), and the terrace where Migliorini children skinned rabbits – '*Ma guarda!* There's still some skin left on the stick!' said one of the youngsters delightedly, pointing to some feeble membrane attached to a vine shoot bent into a V shape. But the old place was under new management and these locations were better known now as Luxury Apartment Type A, the Honour Bar, the Office (Reception), the Loggia, the Honeymoon Suite, the Lounge with its satellite TV system and library (the manger full of books), the Water Purification Plant and the Patio Rose-Garden whose main attraction was panoramic views rather than a dead bunny.

Sitting down to eat in the old winery beneath the second building was a poignant moment. When we first saw that space it had been like a cave, lacking light and ventilation, with a floor of living rock on which it was impossible to walk without twisting your ankle or encountering cobwebs and skeletal remains of rats. Giant barrels and vats and stacks of demijohns loomed out of the blackness like boats in a fog. Now its entrance was graced with ceiling-to-floor glazed doors with ornamental wrought-ironwork. What the visitors saw next was a 16-seater refectory table covered with a chequered tablecloth with candles stuck in Chianti flasks, barrel ends sunk into repointed stone walls, pieces of old farm equipment suspended from hooks in strategic places, halogen lighting and terracotta flooring. It may have owed more to Disney than Dante but we thought we had created a reasonable dining room and an ambience the Italians like to call *suggestivo* (meaning 'evocative' rather than the more obvious English translation favoured by *Chianti News*). The Migliorinis were suitably impressed and sank to the table gratefully, there to set about Mira's banquet and some wonderful reminiscences as the wine flowed, a steaming mountain of pasta appeared and we all let Dina have the floor. Amazingly, we found we could follow almost every thread.

It transpired that the old cellar had been their shelter in wartime. Italy broke with the Axis powers in July 1943, and thereafter this was where they had spent much of their time in hiding – first from the Germans and then from the Allies. Collelungo's problem was that it was in a prominent position, close to the road that followed a high ridge between Castellina and Radda. Along this the Germans had set up the Irmgard Line, one of their key fortifications for the defence of Florence, and fought desperately to maintain it in face of the Allied advance. So well dug in were they that it took three weeks to dislodge them, during which time the village changed hands three times before being taken finally by New Zealanders. Collelungo was caught in the midst of an artillery duel focused on the neighbouring farm where the Wehrmacht had established a major gun emplacement. For the *contadini*, it didn't matter who was doing the shooting; they just remember getting shot at, the incoming mortar rounds remaining forever in their minds as 'American bombing'. Collelungo's walls registered several direct hits. (I had already found a souvenir of this period, in the form of a rusty jerrycan with USA stamped on its side.)

At the time of what history records as the Capitulation, I was four days old. One year later, from my bunker in the air-raid shelter in my family's back garden in the Manchester suburb of Gatley, I was not quite able to appreciate the significance of the Allies' arrival in Chianti or indeed my father's part in Mussolini's downfall (he was on active service in Italy with the Royal Navy, unable to speak a word of Italian as by his generation our family had become totally English. In later life he tried a Linguaphone course without any luck.) So it drew me up short to hear that a Migliorini had actually been born in the cellar during this difficult period, and not only that: there he was in front of me now, tucking into his pasta with relish. Luigi (known to all as Gigi) was a ruddy-faced tractor driver who had spent his working life on farms in the neighbourhood. Amazingly, he was already retired.

To steer the conversation away from the war I asked about sharecropping. For in truth in heavily rationed Britain the populace had been much worse off, having to eat Spam and turn saucepans into Spitfires, than in rural Italy where the peasants just went on with the old rhythm of ploughing, planting and harvesting, milling, making cheese, pressing the grapes and olives. By far the best person to tell us about it was Dina, the matriarch of the Migliorinis who had held the coveted position of housekeeper, the most important woman of the house. Widowed now, she was still bright and cheerful, living alone on a new public housing estate in her own home and enjoying its central heating, hot and cold running water, decent plumbing, wiring, telephone and TV – in fact, all the luxuries we had given up in favour of our dream of rustic bliss.

Soon, though, it was evident that she felt wistful about her time on the farm where she had lived for 47 years after arriving as a young bride. Dina gave a sigh and launched into a long reminiscence, much of which was lost on me due to her use of dialect and my use of rather too much Chianti. Luckily Mira's Italian was streets ahead of mine; she took notes and even had a tape recorder handy (role reversal for the ex-journalist). What follows is Dina's story as best we can remember it, told in her way.

18

Dina's Story

❧

LIFE had been simple and co-operative most of the time, said Dina. This was just as well as there were up to 20 of them in different families living under one roof – always Mamma and Babbo (Mother and Father), the *bambini*, Nonna and Nonno (Grandma and Grandpa) and perhaps an old Zia and Zio (Aunt and Uncle) or two as well. In this extended household of three or more generations the '*bambini*' were happy to remain long after their own wedding and the birth of their own *bambini*. Nothing could have been more natural, for they simply added extra rooms to the house or divided existing large ones with partition walls. You could hang your hams on this side of the storeroom, slung beneath the chestnut beams, safe in the knowledge that Zio Maurizio would be hanging his *prosciutto* quite separately on the other side and there would be no confusion.

Life revolved around the hearth, the live-in fireplace that was to a Tuscan peasant house what the altar is to a church. Here it was possible to rest one's weary bones on benches under an outsize canopy after a hard day's work, for it was spacious enough to walk into. Not one but two benches could be placed beneath the huge hood, one on each side of the fire itself and here too the family elders would gather to gossip, discuss important matters or roast chestnuts on winter nights and feast days. Sometimes the hearth became a theatre where the family would assemble, often with friends and neighbours, to chat, exchange views, give and take advice or, if someone was good at story-telling, to listen anew to age-old fables that appealed to young and old alike.

We were rapt as Dina's own story developed. We could readily see how important those gatherings must have been at a time when communications were difficult and hardly any other form of amusement was available. Yes, said Dina; people would reunite around the blazing fire, or outside in summer when the threshing floor made an equally splendid focal point. Fairy tales made a particularly pleasing form of entertainment. Without any form of lighting effect or music the narrator had to use mime, timing and mimicry to hold the audience's attention. Then he or she would start with: 'Once upon a time . . .' and once again the old stories would be trundled out to everyone's delight. The youngsters always asked for the old ones first, the stories of Pinocchio, Petuzzo and Menico, and welcomed them like old friends. And woe betide any narrator who made a mistake in the telling of them! The fireside fables represented everything for those who had no television, no radio, no books – and who would not have known how to read anyway.

Dina was now in full flow, and happily not even the arrival of the main course that Mira had prepared could stop her. All the others around the table were attentive, like their hosts.

Not surprisingly, the hearth would occupy a fair proportion of the kitchen. Built into the corner next to it was the bread oven, a feature of every home. It was traditionally at waist level. Like a pizza oven, the inside was domed and you either lit a fire in the oven to bring it up to temperature or you took embers from the fire and shovelled them in. Monday was the day for baking. Several large 2-kilo loaves were made and usually some pizza as a treat. The flour was home-ground. The water was hauled up on the women's backs from the spring, 500 metres below the house down in the bottom of the valley next to the river. 'Only there was no pump then!' said Dina, spotting me and giving a great cackle as if the mere thought were funny. Once, she said, she had been heavily pregnant with her second child and had had to carry a tankful of water as well as a stack of animal fodder up that long hill. To make matters worse, her elder daughter Vittoria wanted to be carried, too. That night, Vittoria was sent to sleep with her Zia and by morning her sister Mirella was born. (Listening to this across the table, Vittoria and Mirella – now in their forties – just nodded and smiled.)

How those women used to work! Dina explained that drawing water was traditionally their job and in Chianti its source was rarely close to the farmhouse. Zinc buckets and copper containers were their sole means of carriage, and they hefted them by a pole shoved under the handles. The pole was then carried across their shoulders like a yoke. It was women's work, too, to look after the rabbits and pigs, the chickens, capons, geese and turkeys, and collect eggs or put them under the brooding hen. They were also busy bringing up their children (who themselves were sent out to work in the fields as young as five); helping their menfolk with whatever needed to be done in the fields; collecting acorns to feed the pigs; and dealing with passing hawkers who used to arrive by horse and cart to sell aprons and hairpins and cotton and wool for sewing, darning and knitting. They even had to walk to Poggibonsi, 20 kilometres away down in the valley, in order to sell their animals from time to time – and then climb all the way back up again.

But most importantly they had to prepare the midday meal and supper, typically a single dish based on green-leafed vegetables such as chicory and chard. Peasant cuisine was poor, with simple ingredients that were generally the product of the kitchen garden. Beans were an everyday staple (which is why other Italians still called Tuscans the bean-eaters, *mangiafagioli*, we realised) though something fishy like salt cod, herring or anchovy would sometimes be added to lend flavour. On Sundays the women would be expected to prepare two courses: first of all their own home-made pasta (most probably pencil-thick spaghetti known as *pici*) followed by chicken, pork or rabbit, naturally all home-raised and home-slaughtered. The only item ever bought from the village butcher would be boiled beef, and then exclusively on grand occasions. Everyday fare would be accompanied by watered-down wine known as *acquarello* (literally, watercolour) while their real Chianti was reserved for sale, or weddings or harvest time. (Just how preoccupied they were with the value of food we understood from the fairy tale of Menico, a Tuscan Ali Baba. In the story he gains access to an enchanted cave and his eyes bulge when he sees the cornucopia of riches facing him. He fills his two donkey baskets with piles of coins as well as hams, sausages and chickpeas – all itemised, note – before making his exit. As far as I remember, 'our' Ali Baba simply took gold.)

Even after the invention of bottled gas, cooking was done on the open hearth. Beans were cooked in a big terracotta jug placed at the side of the hearth and left overnight, as was *ribollita*, the thick Tuscan vegetable soup made from leftovers, bread and olive oil, 'reboiled'. Very little other food was bought and hardly anything was wasted or thrown away, for these were frugal people. There was no greengrocery in the village until well after the war and every available scrap of land was pressed into use as an allotment for vegetable production. Trees were planted for fruit (figs, cherries, pears, apples) or nuts (walnuts, almonds). Bee-keeping was popular for the honey it produced. There was no room for anything non-productive, and to keep a dog as a pet was considered madness, said Dina; a dog would eat as much as three hens and lay no eggs (she paused for a huge cackle; it was clearly a favourite joke). There were no flower gardens, just the occasional geranium in a pot for beauty. In short, food was hard fought for, but considered a just reward. And until sharecropping fell into disrepute there was rarely a bad word between *contadino* and *padrone*.

The sharecropping system worked well because there was no need for money. The *contadino* signed his contract with the landowner who in exchange for 50 per cent of whatever the farm produced allowed him full use of his land, buildings, cart, working animals and implements. The crafty squire would usually add some rider to the effect that you should also supply him with 10 or 12 dozen eggs during the year, four of your fat capons at Christmas, two chickens at harvest and two more during the grape harvest. Everything would be written down in your peasant's book with anything missing going straight into the debit column. Unsurprisingly therefore, despite the happy-go-lucky philosophy of most *contadini*, the landowner remained a person to be feared. There was no security; just an assumption that because life had always followed this course it always would. But after the war there were many stories about *contadini* having their contracts terminated without warning. No matter how numerous the families were, they found themselves thrown out without home, work or money . . .

Dina finished off her story by saying: 'Would I like my old

life back? I would not!' Her husband, Terzo (literally, the Third), would have agreed with her if he had survived, she said.

What happened to the Migliorinis was typical of what befell millions of sharecropping families when the system collapsed after many centuries. They went their separate ways: some got jobs and continued to earn their living through hard work, but many found the new world a harsh and alien environment and had to rely on the state for support.

It was clearly the end of Dina's reminiscences, and the younger element took the cue to talk about the world's new realities, saying how it was that many people over 40 were still adjusting to factors like consumerism and wealth, finding it hard to come to terms with the concept of living in the midst of the prosperous community that modern Italy had become – in the north at least. One of Dina's sons-in-law, Urbano, put his finger on it when he said people delighted in spending ostentatiously; there was an abhorrence of anything that recalled the poverty of olden times.

Oh dear, we thought simultaneously, how insensitive we had been. Back at the beginning, before Dina had started her long narrative, we had asked the family to identify the various pieces of farm implements we had casually hung on the walls in that room as decoration. For us city folk from far away they were talking points, a bit of fun, museum pieces; for the Migliorinis they were reminders of back-breaking work in all weather, from the crack of dawn to dusk, what seemed like a thousand years ago. But all this, we kept reminding ourselves, had been only a generation ago. In Britain we would never have had the privilege to meet such an eye-witness to history: the conditions she described could have applied to pre-Victorian times.

The party finished on a happy note, hearing how the children used to enjoy romping on the cut hay the family stored in what we had turned into the wine bar. And how Vittoria's pet pig who followed her everywhere went to the well with her one day when she went to do the washing – and fell in, and what a job they had to get it out. Finally, how the children had to turn to nature for sources of amusement whenever they had the opportunity. Vittoria said catching fireflies had been a favourite game on summer evenings. They'd catch them by hand, then put them under an upturned glass because, the grown-ups said, during the night the industrious little things would work and make money. While the children ran through the fields catching their money-makers they would sing the firefly song, which went:

> *Lucciola, lucciola, vieni da me;*
> *ti darò il pane del re.*
> *Il pan del re e della regina –*
> *lucciola, lucciola, vieni vicina!*

> Firefly, firely, come to me;
> I'll give you the bread of the king.
> The bread of the king and of the queen –
> Firefly, firefly, come close to me!

But nobody had a clue what the bread of the king was, said Mirella with a girlish giggle.

19

Life's Rich Tapestry

WE would have liked to ask Dina more about how they were fixed for medical care in the old days, to see how different it had been from our experience.

One very hot Saturday afternoon in June I was taking a siesta. Mira decided she wanted to wander around the property a little and hadn't gone far before she came across a mulberry tree in full fruit. The last time she had seen a laden mulberry was in her own family garden in Israel when she was 11. And here she was, face to face with a handsome tree covered with fruit so perishable they just had to be eaten there and then, straight off the bough. She couldn't resist; she picked and savoured. As always the biggest and best berries were higher up, and she found a big breeze-block left over by our Neapolitan builders handy for standing on while she stretched upwards – and lost her balance. She toppled over backwards, hitting her head on a rock.

From Mira's diary:

Oh God. Tony's sleeping. There's no one else about. I've hurt myself. The only person who could help would be Tony and I know my voice doesn't carry. He's on the third floor directly above where I've fallen. A groan escapes while I gingerly touch the back of my scalp. I look at my hand and it's covered in blood. Now what? Miraculously, Tony's heard my groan. I guess by now he knows what to listen out for. He's kneeling beside me, and holding me in his arms so tight I can feel his heart thumping. I really have given him a fright. He helps me home, we wash the wound and it is bleeding. What is the emergency number? We don't know. We find it in the book. My Italian is better, so I dial and hear a recorded message. We can't believe it. It's the weekend so this emergency number is temporarily closed. Call Florence for Fire, Siena for Ambulance and Poggibonsi for Police – here are the phone numbers! This was not at all comforting. Nightmare visions of what could happen if this was a real emergency – heart attack? Forest fire? Don't think, not now, be practical. So I phone my friend at the hotel. Unfortunately, we have to go through a lot of small talk first but when she launches into all the things that have happened to her since our last visit, I try to interrupt.

'Delia, I've had an accident.' She carries on with her story regardless.

'Delia,' I say a bit louder, 'I've had an accident!' But still she carries on.

Suddenly she stops. 'What did you say?'' So I repeat myself.

She tears me off a strip. 'Why didn't you say so before? You should have stopped me rabbiting on. What happened?'

'I fell and hit my head, there's blood.'

'*Madonna Santa*, I'll come and get you. Don't move.'

I was relieved that she was taking charge, but we didn't want to wait for her to come. I told her Tony was able to drive, but where should we go? What should we do?

The answer was waiting in our village: with our GP running a strict Monday–Friday roster, a locum was present on Saturday afternoons. We used kitchen roll to dab the blood, and, to avoid shocked looks and questions, I found a cap for her to wear. If she carried a camera she would have passed quite well for a Japanese tourist, I told her just to cheer her up.

The locum said she was not seriously concussed but we agreed it was better go to Siena hospital to get the wound seen to rather than have him dress it. I drove the 20 kilometres on full headlights at ambulance speed, parked outside Casualty without asking (the alternative being a 1.5 kilometre walk) and we were immediately enveloped in that clinical inertia big medical institutions reserve for the walking wounded. Various people sat around with worried expressions – we were unclear whether they were patients or relatives. Nobody registered us, although it was not too busy and nurses made brief appearances from time to time. Finally they got the message that this was a medical emergency. We were escorted through a maze of corridors to the X-ray theatre by a nurse who lost her clipboard along the way, having paused three times to chat with other staff, and it was fully 90 minutes later that Mira's wound was finally seen to, as she sat next to a *contadino* who'd chainsawed through his thumb. They told her to see our own doctor to get the stitches removed and we weren't asked to pay a thing, which was OK with us – but the whole experience had been a lesson in luck. It left our confidence about our capacity to cope with emergencies somewhat shaken.

Our GP's style was more *M*A*S*H* than *Doctor Finlay* but I won't hear a word said against him. When *I* took a chainsaw to *my* finger in an aberrant moment, working alongside the boys from Big Blu, he did a superb job of putting it back together again. He was to come to my rescue again years later when I took a serious tumble and started a deep vein thrombosis. When I put copper sulphate solution in my eyes, mistaking it for eyedrops, he knew the right specialist and bundled me off instantly. It was never a pleasure, visiting him, but we were in a waiting room where everyone knew each other and enjoyed having a friendly chat with our co-villagers about life's little setbacks.

Someone else we could not have done without was Big Blu, or more particularly the Verdiani twins. They rescued us more than once after digging us out of our snow hell that awful winter. When we set fire to a chimney one night and flames were roaring into the sky like an Etna eruption they sent a workman to climb the frozen roof in total blackness, no matter that its tiles were covered in ice, and pour water down to douse it. Only days before we welcomed our first guest the main water pump packed up – the one 500 metres downhill from the houses. To replace it another Big Blu hero had to shift its 10 kilo weight onto his shoulder and struggle all the way back up, only to repeat the trip back down two days later with a new pump. There were countless times when we got into trouble and had them to thank for pulling us out of it. All part of life's rich tapestry, as my old editor friend might have said.

20

A Fine Start

THE road signs pointing our way vanished two weeks before Easter. They were vital to our hopes of attracting customers and we were furious. It had taken us 18 months to get permission from the regional road authority to install them and we'd paid a publicity firm more than £1,000 to make them. We were in such high spirits when their workmen came to erect them on the roads around Castellina that we took photographs of the great occasion. Nobody could therefore deny the signs had been in place; here was crucial evidence of their existence, copies of which we took great pleasure in placing before the Carabinieri when we reported the incident.

'Someone has stolen our signs,' Mira told the duty officer down at the village police station. 'We wish to report a theft.'

Fully aware of the culprit's long-term relationship with the man's boss, I added: 'We don't wish to make trouble but we could take things to a higher authority if they are not reinstated immediately.'

(*Above*) *Collelungo* as it was
when we purchased the property

(*Right*) *Collelungo*
after renovation

(*Above left*) Dina,
matriarch of the Migliorinis

(*Above right*) Cheeso,
our neighbour

(*Left*) Jon, doing his bit
to keep Tuscany green

(*Above left*) Mira (left) and Manuela, our agronomist, checking the grapes' progress
(*Above right*) Alberto, our winemaker
(*Below*) François, who came from Colorado to help with the harvest

(*Above*) Castellina, our view from *Collelungo*

(*Below*) *Collelungo* amongst the vines

(*Left*) The Verdiani twins, Roberto 'Barba' (left) and Renato 'Baffo'

(*Above left*) Our Girl Friday, Fabiola, and (*above right*) her mum, Franca

(*Left*) Anelio, clearing away the grape stalks

(*Right*) Grape harvesting the old Chianti way

(*Below*) Grape skins after pressing, ready for the distillery

(*Bottom*) Toasting our first harvest (Tony second from right)

(*Above*) The Black Rooster, symbol of the Chianti Classico consortium

(*Left*) Castellina countryside in spring

(*Below*) Looking east over our vineyards

The officer said it was 'beyond his competence' but he would report the matter to his superiors. Five days later all six road signs were back in place. No further questions. We were quickly vindicated for when our very first guests arrived, a Scottish couple driving down the lane gingerly in a rented Fiat, they said they had stumbled upon a Collelungo sign by chance and decided to investigate.

Mafalda's spoiling tactics were starting to grate, her childish game now causing considerable annoyance. 'If that woman does one more thing to upset us I'm going to fight back,' I told Mira. 'What,' she replied, 'and report her to the health authorities? A fat lot of good that'll do us. Mind you, I suppose we could write to the guidebooks she's listed in.'

'Or write a story about her.'

'I hadn't thought of that. You still have some good contacts in the Press, don't you?'

'Let me think about it,' I said as the germ of an idea began to form.

The Scottish couple had thought our prices were so appealing they wanted to pay cash for their three nights' stay. Carefully peeling off a series of 10,000-lire notes, they stopped when 16 (about £66) had accumulated and then began to make happy farewell noises, with promises to recommend us to everyone north of the border plus the entire National Trust, for which they worked. Genuinely, it appeared that they reckoned £22 a night for two people was a fair rent for a fully furnished two-room apartment with all cooking facilities, hot water, heating, power, light and gas, fresh linen and VAT. Once it was explained that £66 was the price per night for two people the smiles froze, and they wrote out a Eurocheque as carefully as if their lives depended on it.

A fine beginning. But it was to get worse.

We had a few passers-by dropping in for short periods. We had one or two inquisitive souls and quite a few villagers pop in for a look, drawn by native curiosity – and nobody else. Having to rebuild our water system was demoralising enough, but our spirits bottomed out when an English tourist appeared, asked the price of a night's stay, then declared sniffily: 'Ha! You'll be lucky.'

We contemplated having an Open House for friends and villagers, with a buffet and music and flags and a blessing from the village priest, and maybe even getting the mayor himself in all his regalia to perform a tape-cutting ceremony – and rejected the idea quickly. It would be impossible to control the crowds of well-wishers, who would come as if on a family day out and remain unsatisfied until every door had been opened and every cranny scrutinised. No way would the genteel concept of 'show flat' satisfy their inquisitive lust. They would feel honour-bound to test every bed, flush every toilet, check the gas, the lights, the ventilators, the shutters. There'd be no geraniums left.

I wrote frantic letters to 'all my contacts in the Press', but the immediate results were disappointing (only much later did we have some fabulous publicity, but it would have been more valuable right then). The closest we came to succeeding was when a writer for a British tabloid descended, promising 'to do a piece' on us; instead he 'did a number', for the piece never appeared. It was one whole week wasted, of being polite, pouring drinks, ogling his girlfriend's breast implants as she flounced topless around the pool while Big Blu put in *their* implants – brand new fibreglass water tanks embedded in a base of solid concrete. Mira worried about how we were going to meet the bill for all this extra work while I rattled off scores more press releases to everyone I could remember from Fleet Street and the media, an experience which served only to totally expose my inadequacies as publicist and PR man. Only *The Times* responded positively, allowing me to redeem some pride from my efforts with the promise of an article in a few weeks' time as part of an Italian travel supplement.

Delighted with this flicker of success, Mira and I counted down the days, anticipating a glowing spread. Sure enough, on the appointed day an article did appear. It was not the longest nor the most erudite text ever published in the glorious history of the famous Thunderer, but it was remarkable all the same for an originality we had not expected. It ran five lines long, and told readers our nearest airport was at Pizza.

It was not going well. And that was before we heard the bad news from Croquet Holidays. They had failed to sell even 10 per cent of what they had estimated.

When Barney Whittaker had revisited Collelungo six months after our initial meeting we had signed a contract for our first summer season, which pleased us as it gave us reassurance that if our own marketing flopped, at least there would be an arrival of Croqueters once a week to fall back on. It now transpired that this was not to be, at least in those crucial first few months; they had been over-optimistic. However, as a sign of their continuing good faith the Whittakers advanced us £10,000 against future bookings which they assured us would be forthcoming.

We were back walking the high wire again, and the second couple of guests to book in (Italians) did nothing to lift our spirits when they claimed to have found a nasty insect in their apartment. We heard a scream. They had a little baby and the husband said he was sure it had been attacked in the night by a flea. The man was a doctor, and held out a microscopic piece of evidence for me to scrutinise – something that looked like a

10-point full stop on our computer screen. They left the next morning and in all the years that followed we never once had another complaint like that, although we had our share of awkward surprises. That first spring, the poor swallows that had been so used to swooping through ruined Collelungo's glassless windows found it incomprehensible that their way was now blocked by flyscreens and many a one crashed to its death. The odd snake popped its head out of the terrace walls. One or two scorpions, the small and friendly European variety (you try telling that to Americans) appeared inside the flats. The lizards were a constant source of entertainment.

Thankfully we had other guests. Some were lured by tactics alien to the Italian psyche: I painted VACANCY signs (preferring the American version rather than 'VACANCIES' which has too many letters) and hung them from the wandering Collelungo ones, motel-like. I was more than a little annoyed when I discovered they had been snapped off some days later. So I put them back, only to find them lying in the ditch again after a while. On again, off again? This was getting to be a habit. Mafalda?

Others came, attracted by that 'Miracles' article in *Chianti News* and a very nice cover story which a good friend in France, Mike Meade, spread all over his magazine, the *Riviera Reporter*. We advertised successfully in the *Frankfurter Allgemeine Zeitung* and *The Sunday Times* and far less successfully in Condé Nast's *Traveller*, the *Independent* and the *Guardian*. Generously, our friends the Baldinis sent us clients when their own hotel was full, with Delia herself turning up on one occasion to help make the beds when we were very short-staffed and under pressure. And we received many a customer from the tourist information office in nearby Radda, which was also pulling out all the stops for us. Most notable of these was someone with whom we were to become very close friends: Jon Cousins, an advertising man with an artistic flair who volunteered to design a new logo for us and help me create a guide for our guests.

We mobilised all the help we could. Friends rallied round and came from England as paying guests and sent their friends in addition. The first truly happy and satisfied customers were Germans, Peter and his mother Liliane, who even insisted on planting our garden for us. Then there were couples from Nicaragua, from Hawaii, from South Africa. A Japanese professor came from 'Oxfod Ingrand', a drugs squad detective from Munich, a fire chief from Hamburg, a fireman from Belgium, a used-car salesman from Chicago, a High Court judge, an eminent silk and even a soldier of fortune 'with a bank account in Marseilles and a flat in Amsterdam'.

We were picking up pace nicely when the Duchess of York and Tony Blair entered the frame. Separately, you understand, and not in person. The *Mail on Sunday* had run a breathless piece under the headline: 'Fergie set to buy an Italian ruin'; I got a call from an old Fleet Street friend who tried to tempt me out of journalistic retirement with promises of great riches if I could find her '400-year-old former Medici farmhouse'. I passed, deciding another Tuscan ruin was more than I could face. Concerning Mr Blair, the *Sunday Express* asked me to check out the home of MP Geoffrey Robinson, which I found was disconcertingly close to Collelungo. Tony was months away from his 1997 electoral victory and Robinson's generous offer of the loan of his villa for the Blairs' Tuscan holiday was big news back in England. To show you how low I had stooped, I crawled around the place posing as a French postcard photographer looking for views of the rolling countryside, and when the caretaker's back was turned pointed the lens instead on the house and the fountain he'd had specially imported from England. Coals to Newcastle? Maybe. Everyone there was in awe of 'Lord

Robinson'. (I stopped writing for newspapers after that, resisting the temptation to get involved when Blair's decision to attend the Palio made front page news following criticism from animal rights groups. There was another chance in 1999 which I deliberately avoided, when he stayed at a seaside villa owned by the Tuscan government and there was uproar because the police decided to close a beach to other holidaymakers. By then I was past caring.)

We had Pot Luck dinners with everyone invited to bring a plate, where a Tornado pilot, a dab hand at lasagne, chatted up a diva from the Swedish National Opera in front of her boyfriend, the opera's chief percussionist, who had whisked a memorable tiramisu by hand and given half a chance would have whipped the flying ace as well. We had Happy Hour parties and when it rained turned them into Rain Festivals at which a lot of wine flowed and sausages sizzled in the bread oven fireplace. The first of these didn't go too well because we had a house full of German guests and I had forgotten how literally they take their language (which I don't speak). With the help of a dictionary I penned a few words of invitation on the computer and shoved a little note under each apartment door, inviting guests to the Bread Oven for drinkies. We wondered why they hadn't turned up; then, an hour late, a group of bedraggled guests arrived, tired and fed up, having walked in the wet to the village, where they stood outside the bakery waiting for its doors to open, asking everyone they saw where the action was. After that, other Germans left their special mark on Collelungo by setting fire to their apartment. We'll never forget Jurgen and Carola. He was so pleased to be with us he left common sense behind and draped his wet towel over the lighting sconce in their bathroom. I could still detect the stink years later.

Surprisingly, many people extended their stay. A great Dutch couple, Pierre de Bresser and his wife Elly, even extended their commitment to Collelungo in quasi-perpetuity; they made at least nine repeat visits in subsequent years. Other faithful customers were equally complimentary by returning several times, and it was always a huge pleasure to welcome them back. Peter and Myranda Van de Graveele from Belgium always brought us beer, chocolates or some such thoughtful gift from their homeland.

So we were doing something right, evidently. It's just that in the early days we felt insecure not knowing how the Croquet contract would turn out, and more particularly the Monte dei Paschi threat was still rumbling away in the background. And there was Mafalda to contend with. Somehow we had to kick her into touch.

I put on my worn old journalistic hat, fired up the Macintosh, and flexed my fingers. 'BEWARE THE GYPSY WOMAN'S RUSTIC CHARMS . . .' I began to write.

. . . You won't believe your luck when you turn that bend and come across Mafalda. With her five o'clock shadow, Gypsy Lee headband and curtain-ringed ears she seems an improbable figure in this day and age, though tales of the unexpected are ten a penny in these Chianti hills.

Which driver would not brake at the sight of this typical and seemingly impoverished Tuscan Mamma pegging out the washing between the roadside poplars? They billow like *Cutty Sark*'s sails, defying the winds of time in a country where the 18-programme Zanussi has long lost its novelty.

One look at the cars regularly parked outside her establishment at Castellina in Chianti, north of Siena, gives you an idea of her international clientele. Swiss, German and Austrian BMWs and Mercedes mix with Rovers and Volvos of British provenance, and it is easy to imagine the conversation as she lures them in. 'Quick, the camera, now, over here! Isn't that a trattoria there – there, darling, next to that sweet little deli she's beckoning from? I say, what have we found here?'

To step into Mafalda's parlour is to enter a scene unchanged in more than 300 years. Duck if you don't want to be cudgelled by hams, dried sausages and stalactites of salami, or luscious links of *salsiccia* and tresses of garlic. You should mind those hogsheads of red wine alongside racks of the best Chianti Classico the region has to offer. Cartwheels of hard cheese, aged on walnut leaves, walls lined with deep green bottles of olive oil and *panforte di Siena* complete this Aladdin's Cave. You could lose your mind in a place like this.

Many lose their wallets too.

For a start, Mafalda has turned into an art-form the dodge of coming to your table and verbalising the contents of the kitchen – dishes you have never heard of and certainly cannot look up in your gourmet guide.

She embarks on her recital, fully aware that you might catch only one word in 10 and that you are so beguiled that you will latch upon a half familiar dish like a drowning person reaching for a lifebelt. And *per bere, signori*? Why not a bottle of Castello di Ama, a local Chianti? Its reputation is good: the name is emblazoned all around you. That it comes to your table already uncorked with the vintage year scratched out of a disintegrating label only adds to the rustic charm.

Two of us ate supper of salad, pasta and lamb for a bill at least 50 per cent higher than even the best local establishments and at least twice as much as the prices on her stained and grubby menu. The check did include a second bottle of wine, as the first turned out to be undrinkable – our insistence that it should be served 'closed' only filled Mafalda with amazement.

Purely by chance we discovered more the following day. A titled German lady in the village told us she had seen at first hand the canny *casalinga* pouring old wine slops into recycled bottles.

Worse was to come. The accumulations of disorder and the incrustation of grime we found in our bedroom at the Villa Mafalda, the adjacent prison-like property which she has the cheek to call a 'hotel', made us question whether the health authorities ever cared to visit. The bedsheets were filthy, there was evidence of rodent activity, and an old sanitary pad joined a clothing label and balls of dusty fluff under the chest of drawers in front of my nose as I indulged in press-ups the following morning.

Honest locals feel upset that tourists who generally get good value for money in this part of the world should be fleeced so easily. They realise there is no redress because of the language barrier and are particularly pleased when someone puts Mafalda in her place.

Only the other day, an Italian doctor, an outsider himself, had ordered his meal – a huge *bistecca alla fiorentina* and a bottle of the same Chianti – when a little mouse appeared and ran up the table leg and across the table. Mafalda feigned horror. No, it was not a plague, she insisted; it was one solitary mouse that had troubled her for years. Try as she might she could not find a solution. Did such a famous *medico* as he know a way to keep it at bay? The doctor said he did and would divulge the secret after his meal.

When the check arrived he was genuinely shocked, as

the mark-up was outrageous. But he accepted it meekly, and made as if to leave. 'And the formula, *dottore*? You haven't forgotten what you promised to tell me?' asked Mafalda.

'Just show him a copy of this check,' said the doctor. 'Then he certainly won't come back.'

I recommend readers do likewise. Avoid Mafalda's like the plague!

I posted the article on the Internet, a useful tool that was just in its infancy and was to prove a lifesaver for us in the end. Within a couple of years almost 90 per cent of our business was self-generated from the WorldWideWeb.

21

Official Business

꧁꧂

I don't know whether we were naive, but we had no idea that running a guest house could be so complicated or how regulated and controlled the business would be. I suppose, like other foreigners, we saw Italy as a country with a lackadaisical approach to rules and regulations and a citizenry with a healthy disregard for authority. The image is self-perpetuating: you only have to be here five minutes to notice the difference from other nationalities – in the way Italians park their cars, for instance, sometimes diagonal to the pavement, sometimes even on the pavement. Nobody bothers; there is tacit acceptance that a citizen's right to 'do his own thing' is greater than his duty to observe by-laws. So once we had our *agriturismo* licences and everything was up and running correctly we thought we had seen the back of pettifogging bureaucracy. How wrong we were.

Very early on we had taken to heart a well-meant piece of advice dispensed by our friend the Comandante. 'Don't come here with your foreign ways and expectations,' said Bruno. 'You will find things strange, but learn to adapt. Just accept it as it is.' (I knew what he meant. He drove a Citroën and I had our Renault; anyone who has ever owned a French car with its peculiar knobs and levers will understand.) So from that moment we stopped trying to compare Castellina with other places we knew. Italy was, simply, different. Back in Britain, for instance, we were used to referring to the law-enforcement agency, 'the police', as a single entity no matter what shape it came in from uniformed bobby to plain-clothes detective, from motorway patrol to anti-terrorist unit or bomb squad. Police were simply the police. But here? We had already encountered as many as five official police forces and were adding to the list almost daily. At the last count it came to eight if we included the Forest Rangers, the prison police and the railway police, all of whose vehicles with blue flashing lights we saw regularly on our car journeys.

The first force for which there was no direct British equivalent was of course our bank-raiding heroes, the Guardia di Finanza or fiscal police. The risk of encountering them was very real, for they took their fight against business malpractice, tax evasion and drug smuggling to the extreme of setting up armed roadside checkpoints at the ring of a cash register. But equally we could be stopped by someone else in a designer uniform toting a standard-issue machine gun, waving a baton like a red lollipop stick and wearing the badge of either the Polizia or the Carabinieri – both of whom had parallel but overlapping roles, the former under the Ministry of the Interior, the latter the Ministry of Defence. The Provincial Police was another force to be reckoned with whose responsibilities spanned country matters such as poaching, hunting violations and lost dogs as well as the wider implications of *agriturismo* activities.

But it was to Antonio, the village copper (real title Vigile

Urbano) that we poor farmers had to turn for the administration of the basics of agricultural life. Only a third of his work involved dishing out parking tickets, seeing children safely across the road at the school crossing and disentangling traffic jams and bumper stickers. The rest of the time in the two daily office hours he was open to the public he was to be found weighed down with admin work in the town hall, frenetically stamping documents, poring over ledgers with column after column of figures, dealing with applications for road signs, permissions for directional arrows, permissions for new *agriturismi*, permissions for hotels and prosecutions for anyone abusing the building regulations. It was from this bureaucratic nest that I acquired the tablecloth-sized forms we had to fill in every 15 days, listing the presence of guests and analysing their provenance.

If, as a resident of Italy, you invite strangers to stay under your roof (and by 'strangers' the law means anyone not registered as resident at your address, even your parents) you must report their presence to the Carabinieri within 24 hours. This appeared to us to be a chilling echo of the Mussolini era, an anachronism which would surely vanish with the evolution of the European Union. But no, there we were from Day One, filling in police forms in duplicate, giving our visitors' date of birth, address, signature, passport number and date and place of its issue – plus, of course, our own business details. Each day we had to take these dockets personally to the Carabinieri during their office hours (they were closed between 1 p.m. and 4 p.m.) where with all due solemnity an officer would separate the duplicates, rubber-stamp each one and sign his name over the splodge before handing a copy back to us for our records. We then had to keep it on file for five years. Twice a month we had to fill out Antonio's sheet summing up the details of our visitors – it amounted to 36 columns of statistics – and post it off to the provincial tourism authority's headquarters, at our cost.

Bruno and Gina had warned us about this when we had been staying with them all those years earlier and they had asked us for our passport details. We thought they were joking at first, but a story he told stayed with us for a long time. Apparently his neighbour's dogs had been barking all night, disturbing his elderly mother who was staying with them, and the man paid no attention when they asked him politely to keep them quiet. So they reported him to the police for causing a public nuisance. The man reported *them* back – for not having declared Mother's presence in their house. He was guessing of course: few Italians would follow the letter of the law to such a ridiculous extent, and he was right, they had not filled in a police form. The Carabinieri tried to fine *Bruno*, and he adamantly refused to pay. The Comandante, ex-cruise ship captain, aristocrat and bon viveur, spent the night in the local slammer instead.

The next surprise was that from now on we could expect all kinds of official busybodies dropping in and checking up on us. Many of these came at our worst time of day, around 9 a.m. when guests were paying their bills and checking out or asking questions about us and our background or 'how did you find this place?' It was extremely intimidating. We'd see an official uniform, an official swagger, and more often than not official guns whose effect on the guests I cannot vouch for but they certainly made us uncomfortable.

First through the door was a fat little man rather like Generalissimo Franco in a strange outfit we had never seen before: a tight-fitting khaki number featuring a yellow and red cap band. He resembled something out of panto, a Ruritanian Twanky, and he was pretty darned rude about our road signs. Actually, I'll go further. He was apoplectic.

'Why have you erected black and white signs?' he demanded huffily.

'Sorry,' we said. 'You are?'

He was the Comandante of the regional road authority, expressly empowered to supervise the sector of Chianti in which we had the misfortune to find ourselves. The same man who could be seen strutting down the road in spring and autumn alongside the tractor that strimmed the verges, flailing and shredding the white plastic marker posts and rendering them useless to motorists.

'What's wrong with black and white?' I bristled. We'd had enough of the darned things already. Now what?

'They should be black and yellow.'

'No they shouldn't. I actually went to the trouble of seeing the authority personally in Florence to get their guidance before having them made,' I said. 'Yellow is out now. It's black and white from now on.'

This seemed to confuse the poor chap. But he quickly went on the attack again. 'OK, what about your VACANCY signs?' he said. 'You have no right to put those up.' So it was him! He went away clutching a bottle of grappa which I just happened to have in the office for such emergencies. And we kept the signs.

After that we had quite a few official visitors. Two green-uniformed representatives of the Provincial Police turned up, fingering their holsters rather too nervously for our liking and explaining that their remit was to patrol all *agriturismo* activity in the area. What they lacked in charm they made up for in cheek, cockily passing comment on our guests (in Italian, in their presence) and sticking around until sufficient inducement had been offered for them to take their leave. I thought I was being generous enough when I offered each of them a pack of three bottles of wine. No thank you, they said, they preferred grappa.

We qualified for a visit from the Guardia di Finanza too. I suppose it was a raid; really, I'd like to call it a raid, I would, I would. Four gentlemen in dove-grey uniforms and with Berettas in their belts leaped out of their dove-grey Lancia which skidded to a halt in front of our office as we were telling a nice family from Pennsylvania how to get to Florence and where to park. They flashed their badges, interrupting our discourse, demanding to see our receipts and police reports, and got very nervous when other guests arrived, gathering round us in a protective circle like a corral. Twelve against four.

They counted the dockets, they counted the receipts. Everything tallied. They looked a little crestfallen, as though they had been expecting something different (Mafalda again?). Then:

'The family in the red Alfa that just left,' they said with an air of triumph. 'Why haven't you got a receipt for their stay, eh? *EH?*'

'Because they haven't left yet,' we said. 'They're on a day trip to Cortona.'

Does that qualify as a raid?

The visits we feared most were those of the health authorities, USL. We learned to pronounce that 'Oozlay' but it could have stood for useless, for all that we could see. USL were the people who decreed that bedrooms had to have minimum sizes and bathrooms should not be en suite; the guys who had given us sleepless nights over our bidets.

They made regular, most often unannounced, spot checks to make sure we were not cheating on our licence, which laid down specific occupancy limits per apartment. From her days in the travel agency Mira had been familiar with brochures that gave crafty descriptions of rooms that could 'sleep up to four' or 'sleep up to six' (often in shoeboxes where it must have been hard even for a couple to get any shut-eye), but we had to conform rigidly to the maximum they permitted. Often this was ridiculous, as in the case of one apartment that was patently big enough for four but they allowed to 'sleep three'.

We protested, but they said the second bedroom was half a square metre short of the size necessary to be classed as a double. We thought we'd box clever and gain that missing space by removing the door jamb from its position inside the room (the wall was half a metre thick) and putting it on the outside – 'With one bound, our hero was free' stuff. And sure enough, Renato's boys made short work of it, the result being rather attractive, we thought.

We invited USL back for an inspection and we failed again because the aperture in the 18th-century wall was only the height of the door and it did not meet the minimum headroom required.

On that occasion they had made an appointment and told us they wanted to inspect all the flats, so we had plenty of time to ask the nice Dutch girl who was in our smallest apartment with her boyfriend if she would mind very much hiding his clothes and shaving gear in the wardrobe when they went out for the day. She kindly obliged. Although the apartment was bigger than the first London flat we ever owned, USL would only agree to single occupancy.

In another apartment we had a new kind of problem: the room was too big for the size of the window. We had a clash of 18th-century architecture and 20th-century legislation in that we failed to meet the modern quotient for ventilation and light.

'The window's too small for a room of 18 square metres,' they said.

'We can't do anything about that,' we replied, 'there's a conservation order on these buildings.'

'Then we're sorry, but we can't allow anyone to sleep in here.' They were worried about the risk of asphyxiation, apparently.

As the bedroom in question was our own, this posed more than a small problem. We racked our brains for a while, then Mira came up with a question.

'Tell me, if we reduced the volume of the room rather than increased the window space,' she said, 'would that be an answer?'

They looked a little uncertain, not being used to lateral thinking, then got out their calculator.

'If you reduced it by 4 square metres, yes,' they said. So we got our bedroom back, complete with a nice big walk-in wardrobe.

Useless, all right. They even refused the grappa.

Naturally, as landlords we were very concerned that none of this percolated down to upset the guests. Their image of Collelungo as a tranquil haven had to be preserved at all costs, and we went to great pains to keep our official visitors hidden as much as possible or disguised as visiting 'consultants'. Some of our guests had enough to worry about anyway and we were amazed at the amount of baggage they brought with them (and I am not talking suitcases here). Having been keen travellers ourselves in pre-Collelungo days it was amusing to be static and watch the world with all its foibles dance across the stage we had created.

I've already mentioned some of the characters we encountered in our first season. We enjoyed their company and were genuinely sorry to see them leave, remembering the mistake Luca made when he wanted to compose an ad in English for the Grand Hotel Poseidonia. 'We say Hello to a stranger and Goodbye to a friend,' he wrote. No, I said, there's a nuance there you hadn't intended. 'Say goodbye as friends' sounds better.

After our initial disappointment over the Croquet Holidays deal our contract with the Whittakers brought us a small flow of interesting Brits, all of whom departed on the friendliest of terms. We had been worried about how to describe ourselves in their brochure, whether their clients would be comforted to know that despite our Italian name we were British (i.e. and therefore dependable) or upset that they were not going to be hosted by genuine everyday Italians. We thought about this for a long time before coming up with a solution of low journalistic cunning, a single phrase to fit both scenarios which was deployed with great success: 'Your hosts are Tony and Mira Rocca, who speak fluent English,' we wrote. They couldn't argue with that, though there were moments when my wife's Mediterranean countenance almost got us into trouble. 'Do tell us about yourselves and how you found this place,' was a favourite opening gambit. 'Obviously Mira is Italian, but where are you from, Tony?' I played my Manchester card carefully and rather than disillusion them, obscured my wife's origins by saying – truthfully – 'Oh, Mira has family in Milan.' All would go swimmingly until the phone inevitably rang as we were serving our Croqueters a welcome dinner their first night. It was my Ma-in-law, Baghdad-born but calling from Hammersmith, and it would have been very strange indeed if my missus had used any language other than Arabic to communicate with her mum. 'Is that Italian Mira is speaking?' I'd be asked. 'Yes, a very difficult dialect,' I'd reply.

The article that had appeared on the French Riviera brought us a bounteous supply of characters and a few comic turns. We recall with feeling the retired English solicitor who lived in Monaco and arrived in a beaten-up old Lancia with French plates (rather than Monegasque). It landed in a cloud of black smoke and he spent the best part of his holiday under its bonnet attending to leaking diesel injectors and a faulty radiator thermostat.

This meant the cooling fan was permanently on, even when the ignition was off, which drained the battery. So he determined to disconnect it every night and dirtied himself every time with a spanner I was pleased to lend him for the job. Why such an old car and the French number? It was a rental, he said, explaining that it is cheaper to rent in France than in the Principality. His own car was the very latest BMW and insuring it for unlimited travel would cost him 16,000 francs a year (about £1,600). He preferred to keep it garaged instead, and receive a 50 per cent discount for limiting his driving to 7,500 kilometres a year.

Another spendthrift from Monte Carlo came with a pocketful of those little aluminium coins that were in vogue in Italy a generation or two ago – the 5-lire and 10-lire pieces with a hole in the middle like a Polo mint. I had to break it gently to her that they had long since been withdrawn from circulation and sold as a job lot to the Japanese – for use, so legend had it, as back-buttons in the burgeoning rag trade.

We had a *Guardian* reader who brought his sense of social responsibility on holiday and asked me to fix up a visit for him to see inside a police station and a hospital during his stay. I said I would try my best and promptly forgot all about it until four days later when I came across a pile of traffic outside the public urinal in the village. Mr Conscience had crashed his rented Daewoo into a truck and was on his way to getting both wishes fulfilled without my having to lift a finger.

As you will have appreciated, cars featured prominently in our daily diary of accidents and near misses. A New Zealander was lucky to escape with only a few scratches when he totalled his Opel: driving on the wrong side of the road and seeing an oncoming car, he skidded and hit an oak. We even had pre-crashed cars arrive. A nice Blackpool Mercedes dealer and his family set out for us in a two-week-old model he was proud to be showing off. He had put it on the Motorail car-train in Calais for delivery in Livorno. The sight of it beggared belief.

Peter Standfield was a regular Motorail user. Rather than drive the long journey south in the heat of high summer with his wife Pat and their two boys he paid around £500 plus passenger accommodation and fare to let the French railways take the strain. The train entered a tunnel at high speed heading for Paris. 'There was a colossal whoosh of pressure as another train passed on the opposite track,' he said, recounting the story before an astonished audience in our bar. 'I was sitting with my back to the engine and when we emerged we were on a curve, so I could see our red car quite clearly. I thought it odd that the sun wasn't glinting off the back window so I got out my binoculars for a closer look. The glass had gone, and so had all the other cars' back windows. All the cars were piled into one another.'

It was surely the biggest nose-to-tail stationary shunt in history. No fewer than 37 cars were involved.

22

A Change of Course

❧

HAD things progressed as smoothly as we'd hoped with the British contract it is unlikely we would ever have entered the next momentous stage of our journey into Chianti. That deal with the Whittakers meant everything to us, and we had been banking on it to generate enough cash-flow to keep going. However, Mira had been doing the accounts and her conclusion simply confirmed what we both already knew in our hearts: we just had to have more income if we were to bear the loss of that revenue and carry on. Also, we still wanted to build a house for ourselves.

Already in the seven years that had elapsed since London our lives had girated 180 degrees; now we were about to set off again on an entirely new bearing. Contrary to everything we'd said about never wanting to become farmers, that spring we took back our vineyards and cancelled the rental contract with one of the big local winemaking companies that had been exploiting Collelungo at our invitation. We became grape growers.

Let me tell you right now, as a city boy who used to have trouble finding his way around his local off-licence, standing in the middle of one acre of vines makes the world look a pretty terrifying place when it all belongs to you. When you have 30 acres to go at and have just been told by your accountant that production potential with a good harvest could theoretically result in 85,000 bottles – that's over 7,000 cases – you may be forgiven for feeling it is all a bit over the top. Especially if you haven't the foggiest idea how grapes are grown, let alone turned into Chianti Classico, marketed and sold.

'Go for it if you want to, but only as far as grape growing,' I said when Mira gave me the news about our future vocation. 'Read my lips: We Are Not Making Wine Here. We'll just sell the grapes as a cash crop.' I was not looking forward to this at all.

It wasn't just the fear of the unknown. Quite apart from the agricultural Everest we would have to climb – and we were already in the foothills apparently – I was amazed that Mira seemed to be overlooking the new mountain of paperwork we would be letting ourselves in for. Had she forgotten: we had already done well to have come as far as this unscathed, given the tortuous nature of Italian bureaucracy and the convolutions we'd been obliged to perform?

Old Dante knew what he was doing when he sat down, an hour up the road from Collelungo, and penned the immortal line: 'Abandon all hope ye who enter here'. He was a Florentine, and things could hardly have changed much since the 14th century. Government offices were so hidebound by complicated, antique procedures and arcane language and terminology that it was a wonder Italy worked at all. The slowness of the state machine was exasperating at every level, with too many different offices doing the same job different ways and no apparent cross-referencing system. Each ran separate accounting systems that required separate means of payment. They couldn't even agree what time it was. Some closed at 1 p.m., others at noon, some at 11.30 a.m. Most (not all) never reopened in the afternoon. By then the civil servants had turned into civilians and gone off to their private afternoon jobs, cash down, no questions asked.

We had tried to keep as low a profile as possible, restricting our contact with officialdom to the barest minimum. Even so, the red tape had almost strangled us. Every time we made contact with authority it had to be in writing, in the form of a *denuncia* (declaration). To this, more often than not, we had to attach a *bollo* (stamp), a leftover from the *bulla,* or seal, that was attached to the Papal Bull of medieval times. (The price of this had already risen from 800 lire to 20,000 lire in the relatively short time we had been in the denouncing business). Worse still, after all that it still had to be notarised in those days. The problem was that for certain documents it may not have been thought necessary at *comune* level, but was essential at *provincia* level where it was sent for ratification. Once, we'd been so puzzled about the hold-up in one of our licences we made a special trip to see the provincial official concerned. His desk was barely visible under a sea of paper. 'Oh here it is,' he said after a search lasting 15 minutes. 'It's missing a *bollo.*'

Although it seemed that every functionary we came across had two telephones on his desk, an official one and his private mobile, neither could ever be used to inform you of the missing *bollo*; you had to discover your error yourself. And then our document would have to be rubber-stamped, sometimes in duplicate, triplicate or more. No Italian desk was complete without a wedding cake of rubber stamps on a carousel, their variety and number being a sure indication of the importance of the hand wielding the rubber. The mere act of stamping was not enough; each imprint then had to be signed by that same hand.

Come on, Mira! How could she forget that it took no fewer than 11 rubber stamps on one single A4 document, payment of 100,000 lire cash and an hour's pleading to get ENEL's agreement to reinstate our power when it was cut off due to a misunderstanding – plus a wait of three days to be reconnected? Had she forgotten what happened on the visit we'd already paid to the very provincial agricultural authority she now wanted to do more business with? We were registering land, as I recall, and were told our documents had to be in triplicate not just duplicate. (It was a sheaf of maps, licences and letters.) We used their photocopier and in receipt of our payment of 1,000 lire [37p] for this service a secretary had to lick a gummed stamp for each page, stick it on the back of the copies, frank it with a rubber stamp and finally sign over it.

I was savouring these arguments.

Had she, for example, forgotten there would be transportation dockets to deal with? We'd already had some experience of these when moving our olives around: nasty A4 forms that had to be completed in *quin*tuplicate every time you shifted produce from one place to another. For each shipment every single page had to be validated by Antonio, the village cop, if you could find him. Similarly, buying and transporting anything on behalf of our company required elaborate form-filling to include a description of the goods, the number (in figures and letters) of packages in which they were being transported, a description of the packages (colour, material), the precise time and date of dispatch, their origination and destination, the signature of the driver (and later the signature of the recipient), a description of the conveying vehicle, the vehicle's registration number, the recipient's VAT number plus the address of his registered office if different from the stated destination. This rule applied no matter how small your purchase, and because of the severe penalties incurred if you filled in the form incorrectly – in that 11-digit VAT number for instance – considerable delays could result at the cash register. You can imagine how intimidated some small shopkeepers felt by all this. On buying 2 metres of curtaining from Edouardo, who ran our village haberdashery with his Mamma, I found he had even added the number of the cash register itself – plus the maker's name to be on the safe side. As the writer Tim Parks has observed in *Italian Neighbours*, the creeping sense of paranoia resulting from all this means that 'you occasionally find that people have been imagining rules that don't actually exist, simply because they seem to be the kind of thing the government would invent to make life more difficult, and hence probably has.'

And she wanted to get more involved in *that*?

Apart from getting tangled in the bureaucratic Sargasso, I had been absolutely against the idea of making wine for two reasons. Not only were we totally ignorant of the mystical process; I could think of nothing more demoralising than spending a lot of time and money making a mediocre product and then not being able to sell it on a market that was overflowing with the stuff we used to drink in the Fulham Road. A new friend, Maureen, confirmed this prejudice by saying: 'You've got vineyards? Good luck to you!' when she bought a similar property to ours with no land attached and started turning it into a luxury country inn. And I remember right at the start the Comandante, Bruno, telling us that if we tried to work the vineyards ourselves we'd be lucky if we could get them just to break even.

As if further evidence were needed, we had recently received a letter from a complete stranger which convinced me the dangers were not at all imaginary. It was a curious missive I found in our Post Office box, addressed to Salimbeni, our old company, and mailed from the Haute-Savoie, France. A certain Madame Michèle Clin wrote to express her dissatisfaction with a wine she had just bought (label enclosed), which was, she said, 'nothing but coloured water with neither taste nor perfume'. She went on to administer the following *coup de grâce*: 'I hope it is not injurious to one's health.' The label bore our name, Salimbeni, all right, as well as the name of our village. Clearly someone was exporting Chianti of dubious quality and had alighted on Salimbeni as a name of convenience just as dear old Pepi had some years earlier. It was not a very auspicious start. We got Benito on to it straight away.

And yet. These misgivings were balanced by some cold facts. First, in order to stay registered as an *agriturismo* it was essential to show more revenue from agriculture than tourism. In the early days we thought we could fudge this by some creative accounting; we were told it was not a strictly limiting factor as figures were not properly checked. By 1996, however, *agriturismo* had become the latest wheeze; everyone wanted to jump on the bandwagon and licences were no longer being issued ad lib. We had to fill in a 50-page questionnaire every three years, proving our bona fides in painstaking detail. The second fact was that the price of grapes had gone up by 50 per cent since we had picked for Bruno and the price of bottled wine was up considerably too, commensurate with its quality. And thirdly, we had friends down the road, Roberto and Sylvie, who ran their *agriturismo* successfully by selling their whole production to their guests directly. Granted, they only had a quarter the number of vines we had, but it was encouraging.

Mira started to reason that if — in due course — we could make wine from our best grapes and sell the rest as a cash crop to one of the larger producers the figures would start to look a lot healthier and selling the little we produced would be a less daunting prospect. Class over mass, in other words.

These ideas crystallised in her mind because we had actually been approached by a Signora Barone from San Gimignano who was very keen to add a Chianti Classico to her repertoire. (She was well known for making a reasonably good, white, Vernaccia di San Gimignano as well as an ordinary Chianti.) Her proposition was that she would assume responsibility for the supervision and cost of building and equipping a winery at Collelungo and then provide staff to make the wine; we would split the profits. For this she wanted us to re-register the vineyards on a 50-50 basis.

To me the idea offered a neat way out: I was all in favour of avoiding a step into the unknown by ourselves, not having to finance yet another new project and letting someone else have the trouble of organising the work. More profit, no investment. The Monte dei Paschi thing was still festering like a sore and now we had 12 apartments to fill. We had to nurture that side of the business before we could take on anything more, and we were certainly not in a position to hire staff such as a manager or receptionist to free us from the hotel aspect of the business and allow us the time we needed to go it alone, winewise.

But Signora Barone's proposition filled Mira with disquiet:

it was easy to see that the overall value of the property would be diminished, and although we would not have to worry about day-to-day winemaking we would lose complete control over what was being made in our name. As for our lack of know-how, unknown to me Mira had been doing her homework on the quiet and explained how almost everything could be contracted out, or expertise bought in.

I gradually came round to her way of thinking: we should cultivate the grapes ourselves and leave winemaking to the experts. Even I, a dummy at maths, had to admit something was not kosher when she put the figures on the table. When we picked for Bruno, 100 kilos of grapes was fetching 100,000 lire. In 1996 this was up to 150,000 lire. In the meantime our contract with the winery that was taking our grapes continued to give us just 13,000 lire per 100 kilos – about 5p per kilo.

The name of the winery, funnily enough, was also Rocca: Rocca delle Macie (literally 'Fortress of the Cairn'). It made some nice wines but enjoyed the kind of reputation which good winemakers described as 'commercial', not a label you want to get stuck with if one day you hoped to project yourself as a serious player in the game.

If we actually went to the next stage and made wine, what quality could we produce? Italy was the biggest contributor to Europe's wine lake and what I feared most was that we would end up making unwanted, mediocre plonk after a lot of expense and hard work. We knew Lilliano, Giulio's Chianti Classico, was magnificent but it had taken generations to develop. On the other hand one didn't have to be wealthy and aristocratic and old-established in order to succeed: another friend, Stakis Aivaliotis, was making some superb wines without the benefit of ancestry – and moreover he had arrived from London at the same time as we had. Stak was a passionate Greek Cypriot with a huge and happy ego, convinced that he could make the best wine in the world. He had studied hard, invested well, and every aspect of winemaking came naturally to him.

Cancelling the contract was easily done and gave us great satisfaction. We'd never forgotten how surprised we'd been in the early days when we received our first measly cheque from them after much delay: it had Sellotape stuck over the hand-written amount. We questioned this unusual practice only to be told that it prevented anyone from tampering with the figures.

'*Cretini!*' Benito had boomed when we told him about it. 'Everyone used to do that in the old days but now is common knowledge – all you have to do is put the cheque in the freezer. When is frozen you can rip off the tape and do what you like with the sum.'

23

Heading for Trouble

My winemaking experience at that point was only marginally more advanced than my knowledge of grape-growing: back in our Ealing days I'd had a go with a Boots home-winemaking kit – all those crystals and things in the bathroom sink. The result was a disaster. Now I saw we were getting serious I didn't jib when Mira said she was going to invest in what she'd been told was the winemaker's bible: *Knowing and Making Wine* by Emile Peynaud. It is not a beginner's guide and costs considerably more than the average teach-yourself tome. Next came something more readable: *The Penguin Wine Book* by Pamela Vandyke Price which starts: 'How does grape juice become wine?' (much more my style). A picture book then joined the growing heap: *The Art and Science of Wine* by James Halliday and Hugh Johnson. I liked that even better because it had nice photos.

What was happening, I soon realised, was that Mira was slowly directing this whole venture in a way my instincts told me disaster lay. What I did not know was that Susan, an American friend married to an Italian farmer, was secretly encouraging her. 'Let me just find out how complicated it can be,' said Mira. 'There's no harm in asking.'

'Hey, come on,' I said. 'Let's just get on with growing grapes and leave it at that. It's a whole lot more than we ever wanted to get involved in.'

But where to start? Hiring a handyman, full or part time, to help run the estate seemed like a good idea. What we were looking for was someone who could turn his hand to the variety of work that our kind of lifestyle generated. He needed to be knowledgeable about grape-growing in general as well as olive cultivation.

The job description seemed never-ending. Harvesting, yes, he'd have to be good at that. Ability to drive a tractor? A must. He should also be prepared to look after the gardens and help bring the farm back to life, and be happy to tackle all manner of odd jobs when necessary. All this preferably with a cheerful mien and no bad personal habits such as smoking or spitting or doing anything to upset the guests.

Gigi Migliorini was an obvious choice. Not only did he know every centimetre of the land but he was also a professional tractor driver, lived locally, was a cheerful non-smoker and very likeable. But he was very concerned about his pension rights, which was a blow, and for this reason he had reluctantly disqualified himself. We could not persuade him that his pension could be protected by temporary employee status.

There was no shortage of people wanting to work for us 'in black'. Italy's famous black economy is worth a quarter of the national income, according to reports we read. It is the only way the country survives. But if you are running a place the size of ours without registered staff it won't be long before the taxman notices miraculous things about your accounts. So we put the word about with Daniele at the Consorzio Agrario that we were on the lookout for one or two young farmers who would agee to work on an official basis. He soon called me and said he had found two: they were not so young, 28 and 30, but were on the ball and extremely fit and active. Well they would be at that age, wouldn't they? I said. Contact was made, an interview arranged. But instead of the two young men I had been expecting I found myself facing two old codgers – one *born* in '28, the other in '30.

About three weeks later we were still no further forward when out of the blue a clapped-out Citroën 2CV clunked to a halt in front of us. Out stepped a grizzled little man with a squint, a single tooth and a smile as broad as the Straits of Messina, which he said he had just crossed in his journey up from Sicily looking for work. This was Francesco: a Sicilian forced to flee the island because of chronic unemployment and (he said, darkly) threats from the Mafia. In his time he had been a lorry driver, bus driver, ambulance driver, road repairer, farm worker, gardener and general labourer, most recently at his son-in-law's bakery. He said he was desperate for a job, having left his wife and three children in Palermo. He loved working with olives and vines; they would remind him of his youth spent helping his father in the fields. And although he was reaching pensionable age he actually needed regular, tax-paid work for two years in order to boost his pension rights when the time came. Best of all, he was staying with a relative nearby and didn't need accommodation. We decided he deserved a month's trial.

Francesco was a hard worker, all right. By the time three weeks had expired he had managed to impress us sufficiently for us to consider taking him on permanently and we thought his little mannerisms were quite charming. '*Ma guarda!*' he'd keep saying and we'd drop whatever it was we were up to and rush to where he was pointing out some exciting discovery or other: a bird's nest with eggs in it, a toad the size of the Mars rover, some fossils or a pair of scorpions frolicking in the pool. Then after a while these distractions began to pall and annoy. Raw nature was interesting enough but certain aspects of it just became a darned nuisance when we were trying to get on with our work. The hatful of giant snails the poor man left in the office by way of thanks didn't go down too well with Mira, either. They were the biggest, ugliest, slimiest snails you have ever seen, Godzillas of the gastropod world, worthy of a page in the *Guinness Book of Records* but not the kind of thing you want crawling over your Internet modem or up your trouser leg.

Francesco then developed another irritating trait, shouting 'Meestair!' every few minutes to draw our attention to the work he had done, fishing for praise. (We just hoped he was a better bus or ambulance driver than gardener: he was habitually going the wrong way and pulling up the wrong things.) Undoubtedly the low spot was when I saw him arrive late one morning and park next to the spigot at the edge of the vineyard. From the boot of the 2CV he pulled what looked suspiciously like a small wild boar (it was not the hunting season) and started washing the dead beast. '*Tasso! Tasso!*' he shouted to me – and when the smell reached my nostrils I had to grab the Kleenex as well as the dictionary. A badger! He'd caught a badger! (Aren't they a protected species?) And there he was, licking his lips and muttering something I only half caught about what a fine meat sauce it was going to make.

Where it came from we still don't know. We could cope with all of that: the snails, the badger, the Mafia. But a sneaking suspicion that we were being conned slowly began to dawn on us,

and when it came to the time for him to tackle the first real agricultural work we had our fears confirmed.

The wine books were proving a good investment. From our
newly acquired library we learned that by mid June the vines'
vigorous growth sends healthy shoots spurting merrily in every
direction and these have to be controlled, tied back by hand,
helped in places by a line or two of string or raffia, otherwise
the jungle will consume tractor and man alike and the bunches
of grapes will have nothing to support them. Here, then, was a
chance for our country boy to shine.

Sure enough, within days of starting the work the little Sicilian
had brought about a radical change to the top vineyard above
the houses, aided by two temporary workers who happened our
way by chance. Only there was something wrong. Instead of
leafy lines of abundant but tamed greenery such as we could
see all around on neighbours' farms, what looked curiously like
white trellis fences zigzagged up and down in line abreast as if
they were defying the plants to escape their cage. An elaborate
cat's cradle of string had created a corset around the vines – a
strange sight that provoked much amusement among the boys
from Big Blu and questions from our puzzled guests. It resembled a bandaging station on the Somme. Francesco looked shame-
faced.

Only later did we discover that he had been lording it over
the two part-timers working with him, local pensioners called
Alvaro and Anelio. They had literally been strung along by this
wily old fox who knew practically nothing about viticulture and
had been dragging out the job so we would have to pay more.
He had assumed the position of foreman over these two Tuscans
who had worked the Chianti vineyards all their lives and certainly
knew more than this lorry driver. Francesco resigned shortly

after this episode and Anelio took his place, having agreed to appear officially on our books, and we never looked back. We had found a true gem: a gentleman *contadino* who tackled everything we asked of him with equal enthusiasm and pride, never asking for praise. We were to come to cherish his resourcefulness and cheery manner, his friendship, and the many things we were to learn from him about the country and country ways.

One of the greatest shocks awaiting us in our love affair with Italy had been the discovery of how little Italians in general actually care about their countryside when environmental issues impinge upon the sacred cow of personal liberty. Following the principle that a citizen's right to do his own thing is greater than his duty to observe by-laws, too often the 'NO DUMPING' notice is interpreted as an invitation to do just that. When applied to a rural ambience such as Collelungo, where generations of poor sharecroppers had worked the land with self-preservation in mind rather than conservation, the result was remarkable. We had inherited a mountain of junk and scrap metal that had accumulated over the decades of decline. There was only one man capable of resolving the problem: The Pilferer, the gossips' prime suspect in the murder case.

'Better grab him while we can,' I had said with a grin when the nasty rumours started after the murder. And a few days later, just before our first guests arrived, the noise of his little three-wheel pick-up could be heard, phut-phutting up and down the estate in search of treasure.

Tuscany's Most Wanted (really?) looked like a cross between Desperate Dan and Steptoe as he scoured the vineyards scavenging for pieces we were amazed to see being retrieved from the most unlikely places. Rusty bedframes, spring mattresses, barbed wire, paint cans, oil drums, redundant piping, old machinery, abandoned bathtubs, a hot water boiler, bent old playpens, old taps, chicken wire, grids, grilles, the carcass of a freezer and a pair of garage doors were just some of the larger pieces that had adorned the property and we now managed to get rid of. Finally, I got roped in when he unearthed a massive metal pole the size of a lamp-post and tried to lift it onto the little vehicle by himself. The flat-bed, no bigger than a billiard table, was already piled high with a vast accumulation of junk and it was hard to see how the 6-metre object could possibly fit. But by combined effort he and I heaved the pole onto the wagon. The Pilferer managed to adjust it to his satisfaction, resting on his driver's cab at an angle of 45 degrees at the fulcrum with its front protruding a good 2 metres ahead of the windscreen. The whole assembly sank alarmingly about 20 centimetres closer to the ground with associated clatterings as the load shifted. Then off he clanked, sailing into the setting sun at the helm like Captain Birds Eye.

Now the estate in general was safe for our guests to walk around without tripping over any nasty surprises, but all the same there was still a lot of work to be done around the houses when Anelio joined us, and Renato brought us several truck-loads of good earth to throw over the area. Mira suggested we create easy-care patches and fill them with hardy native plants such as iris, lavender, sage and rosemary interspersed with roses and dwarf fruit trees, rather than anything touchy that required a lot of attention and water, like delphiniums and dahlias. Oleanders would provide a nice splash of colour all summer long.

We were doing all right with our iris-planting programme until we hit an obstacle far hardier than anything Big Blu's bulldozer could overcome mechanically: the Tuscan porcupine, lover of irises, tulip, indeed anything bulb-, tuber- or corn-originating.

The native porcupine is a bit of a prickly character, thick-bodied, and a grizzled black in colour. He can grow to a length of at least 60 centimetres, with some of his quills exceeding 30 centimetres, which is why his movement is restricted to a slow shuffle with his nose kept close to the ground. This tends to emphasise his quivering rump, making him look like a peram-bulating Pawnee headdress – but don't be fooled. This is one mean mammal; his body is a bush of ground-to-air missiles which can be fired whenever he perceives anyone or anything threat-ening him. It seemed there was not one but a tribe of these herbivorous rodents lying in wait for darkness to fall, when they would come out looking for their dinner and dig up all the rhizomes Mira and Anelio carefully planted by day.

'*Porca miseria!*' (pig misery) said Anelio, and for once the famous expletive sounded apposite although in this case it should have been porcupine misery. Anelio went on to impart some local wisdom: that these creatures only come out after midnight, are dumb, and can be dispatched with a quick clout from a sharp stick. All very fine, but we didn't think porcupine safaris by torchlight would be deemed politically correct by our guests. Besides which, they are a protected species, like badgers. Another solution had to be found.

First we tried to ring-fence our rhizomes with cuttings from our cactus (we had prickly pears growing in profusion). We thought their strong, sharp needles would put off any animal, but no chance. The next morning we found the cacti pushed disdainfully aside and a new patch of flowers gone. Mira tried another tack, planting some decoy bait – their own feed, some succulent potatoes – in the vineyard. They fell for it at first but the spud trick soon became boring and they came back to the iris.

One morning a nice German couple from Berlin, Christine

and Olaf Muller, asked me what kind of animal it might have been that they'd heard scrabbling under their bedroom window in the night. When we found the iris there had been tampered with I told them, and at my suggestion they searched the area and were excited to find a number of quills which they carefully collected to put in a jar in their flat – aptly called Porcupine after the *contrada* of that name. They said they thought the porcupine was extinct in Tuscany. No, I explained through gritted teeth. Not yet.

So were we back to killing them with sharp sticks? I might just have mentioned it in passing, for that night a number of our guests, alerted by the Mullers, organised a midnight vigil with torches and cameras with flash guns, all of which was totally unnecessary as the porcupines didn't appear.

That winter another possibility presented itself unexpectedly, on a visit to my parents in Devon. One of their neighbours mentioned a very effective repellent which he used against badgers and foxes. It seemed one sniff of it and they would run a mile. I eventually tracked down this potent product, called Renardine, noting that even a small can cost £9 and came with a big 'X' and 'highly flammable' warnings. By the time I met Mira in London three days later I must have dented it somehow, because it was already exuding a foul odour. We realised it would be dangerous to take on the flight with us so I wrapped it in a nylon bag, tied it securely, then put it in a Jiffy bag and posted it to myself in Italy. Luckily I was saved the embarrassment of explaining the smell because it was one of those London post offices where everything is done behind glass at arm's length.

We hadn't been back in Collelungo two days when I got an urgent message from our local postmaster to come and collect a parcel. Incredibly, for a place where parcel post from Britain can take up to two weeks, the precious package had arrived in under 48 hours – and so had the pong. It was evil. The can had leaked again and the Jiffy bag had been placed (with forceps?) in something like a forensic evidence bag lest it infect the European postal system and bring armies of sorting staff to their knees. There was a polite note from the English postmaster inside, apologising for damaging my package.

In the short journey home our Renault was turned into a stink bomb. But I followed the instructions carefully and our tribe of porcupines must have decided they had better relocate to sweeter pastures for we never had trouble with them again. Trying to explain the offending stench to visitors was quite another matter, however.

There! At last I'd been able to show Anelio that Tuscans did not have the monopoly on native ingenuity, and that we British could come up with a thing or two when roused. '*Cavolo!*' said our friend, and Mira giggled. It was the only swear-word we ever heard him use beyond *Porca Madonna* and *Madonna Santa* and seemed a little odd and lacking in depth of feeling to do justice to his emotions: it literally meant 'Cabbage!' We soon found out it had a hidden meaning too: it was a catch-all expletive, a euphemism for '*cazzo*', or cock, used for situations both good and bad.

24

Water Wears Stone

BARNEY and Bunty described their clients as 'PLUs', short for 'people like us' they explained, and the accuracy of that statement was never in doubt from the moment the first characters descended a little hesitantly from the minibus bringing them from the airport. They were cultured, well travelled, a little eccentric perhaps, and the majority well past their salad days and into the dessert course. We learned quickly on the job. The arrival of the Croquet party became the signal for us to go to action stations, and the welcome dinner for each incoming group became a rich source of surprises. I just prayed that we wouldn't be interrupted by phone calls too often and could gloss over our own provenance so we could discover more about our guests. Conversation was always guaranteed to be interesting when captains of industry, admirals and judges were at table and the wine was flowing. We even had some odd 'small world' encounters: the former colleague from *Sunday Times* days, the former news editor from the *Daily Mail*, the lawyer from chambers that were clients of Mira's travel agency.

Coupled with the 'Crocks' we also found ourselves being educated into how the West Germans disliked the East Germans (both Westies and Esties were often simultaneously present) and how charming Israelis can be when you get them away from Hamas and into hummus and horticulture. The Americans amused us. A New York couple asked for a cooling fan that cool, wet April; they couldn't sleep at night because of the total silence all around us and needed the comfort its hum could provide. Another city-dweller thought the call of the cuckoo was the beep-beep of 'a truck backing up'. A young couple from Michigan asked me to solve a particular mystery of Italian life: everywhere, they'd seen arrows pointing to a place called SENSO UNICO but never managed to find it (it means 'one-way street'). Everything for them seemed mysterious, from quaint power supplies to three-part Moka coffee pots. Our only fear was that they had little appreciation of Collelungo's limitations: the gas and water was not from city mains and the electricity was expensive and limited to 15 kilowatts. So water should not be wasted, lights should be switched off when not wanted and windows should be kept shut in cold weather. We also found to our chagrin that we did not have much spare time to chat. That was the worst of it. I sometimes felt squeezed like a sponge with all the questions about ourselves, the property, the wine business (as if I knew), life in general in Italy, why the washing machine was taking such a long time to finish its cycle. . . and so on.

The visitors were, however, charmed by Chianti and Tuscany in general, overwhelmed by the wealth of cultural and artistic beauty on our doorstep and generous in their expressions of appreciation for what they had seen. 'Awesome!' they said, and I had to sympathise. It must be tough, coming to grips simul- taneously with the towering majesty of the Renaissance, the realisation that a 110-volt hairdryer will melt if you run 240 volts through it and the grim reality of gasoline costing five times the price back home.

Everyone enjoyed shopping for food locally and bringing it home to eat on their balcony or terrace. The Co-op was a great source for cold cuts such as *finocchiona*, Tuscany's fennel-seed salami, *prosciutto cotto e crudo* (cooked and cured ham) together with sun-dried tomatoes, olives, fresh tomatoes, mozzarella cheese or pecorino made with fresh ewe's milk. Its delicious 'seven cereal' bread tasted even nicer when accompanied by our own olive oil which Mira spiked with garlic, chilli pepper and garden herbs, together with a bottle of Chianti Classico (other people's brands, she would insist on pointing out to me).

We settled into a routine, but all the while I suspected my wife was up to something, playing out her own fantasies about winemaking, determined to move on to the next stage of the process and drag us into the abyss. We hadn't even come to grips with grape production yet and there she was, answering questions about winemaking with an aplomb that amazed me. I thought I'd said No Wine. (Meanwhile, her ally Susan was egging her on: 'Don't give up. Just remember: water wears stone.')

She had absorbed those blessed books, reading well into the night when I was knocked out with exhaustion after parrying tourists all day. And, it later transpired, she had been pumping our winemaking friends for their advice. I woke up early one morning when she was still asleep, slipped down to the office and started rummaging through some papers on her desk, looking for the phone list. That was how I discovered how advanced across the Rubicon we were. Scribbled on an old yellow legal pad left by some American appeared what seemed to be a shopping list of extraordinary complexity. It made what little hair I had left on my head stand on end. Aghast, I read words like 'cuve', 'crusher', 'de-stemmer', 'de-stalker', 'speculum', 'hydrometer', 'press', 'high-pressure hose', 'barrels', 'pumps', 'tubes', 'hopper', 'fork-lift', 'tractor'. There were notes about something called 'malolactic fermentation', and 'chaptalisation'. Following this there was the annotation: Winemaker? Permits? Licences? Registers? And lastly, the word that troubled me most, in large block letters: WINERY.

'Let's look at this together sensibly,' said Mira when I confronted her with the evidence. It was a tone of voice I knew from experience meant there was no room for argument (she is a Taurean). So to humour her and keep the marriage intact I did what I had always done in such circumstances: I agreed to go along with her crazy whim, pretty confident that any fact-finding mission would soon prove me right.

Maybe it wasn't going to be so hard after all. The first stop was at the surveyor's, and his instant reply was that to get permits to build a brand new winery would take several years. But my smile vanished when Mira asked if we could reuse the old stables that were on the property, and he agreed. So long as we did not change their agricultural status and only did maintenance work we would not need to go through all the normal planning procedures. A simple declaration would do, like my anti-Mafia statement. Uh-oh.

Next stop was Big Blu. Could we convert the stables with simple maintenance work? Yes, said Renato, quite easily, but the floor will have to be reinforced and the walls insulated. However, there was asbestos in the roof which was illegal. My hopes rose again.

Next stop, the asbestos experts. They told us there were two options: we could either get permission to dismantle the roof and destroy the offending material according to the correct procedure (which would be expensive); or spray it with 8 centimetres of polyurethane coating to seal it inside like the filling in a sandwich. This would be less costly and give wonderful insulation. Let's call that love-all, I thought.

Finally we made contact with the man whose name we had most frequently seen on roadside hoardings advertising stainless steel wine tanks: Mr Cavalzani. This busy entrepreneur agreed to visit us and as we stood there in the ruined stables I felt sorry for what was so obviously (to me) a waste of his time. I kept very quiet as Mira explained her intentions, finishing by saying: 'And we would like you to equip it. Are you able to do this?'

'Certainly!' said Cavalzani. 'What would you like it equipped with?' Mira's answer was: 'Winemaking equipment for 12 hectares of vineyards.'

'But you have to tell me what equipment you want,' said the surprised businessman. Innocently, Mira said: 'Equipment for the whole process. Can you do that?'

At this stage, if not before, Cavalzani must have realised that she did not know what she was talking about. 'Your winemaker should be telling you what exactly he wants; you cannot second-guess him. Who is your winemaker?'

'We're interviewing,' said Mira, to my private delight. Now she was really winging it.

'Who are you interviewing? I can speak to him. I know all the winemakers in Tuscany.'

'Oh, you wouldn't know them,' said Mira airily.

Cavalzani gently said: 'Look, Signora Rocca. I understand. Leave it with me. I shall think about it and suggest some names to you.'

Within 24 hours he had come up with a list of three names, the first of which, Alberto Antonini, he strongly recommended. 'He's young, he's innovative, he's had years of experience with the biggest wineries and just now he is leaving his position as chief winemaker for Antinori to set up a consultancy.'

That was to prove the catalyst. Game, set but not quite match to Mira. But there was still the matter of who would do the paperwork – the registers, the licences, the permits – and be prepared to give hands-on guidance to two complete novices.

We found our salvation in the CIA. High in the garret of a medieval *palazzo* on the edge of Il Campo we were secretly enrolled with pigeons cooing above our heads and smells of onion, tomato, oregano and garlic wafting through the window from the pizzeria four storeys below. The ceremony was swift and painless, the official kindly and understanding. And as we signed on a dotted line and received our membership cards, things started to look much brighter.

The Confederazione Italiana Agricoltori was one of two main organisations dedicated to the protection and well-being of those who grubbed a living from the Italian soil. The other was a 'bosses' club', by nature a right-wing pressure group that lobbied for landowners, which Benito wanted us to join; but the CIA militated for the masses and hence bore different coloured plumage. Sylvie, our friend with the *agriturismo*, had told Mira about it; like many shrewd farmers she found it prudent to be a member of both organisations simultaneously.

Being quite used to dealing with illiterate *contadini*, acting on behalf of ignorant foreigners came as second nature to the people we met at the CIA, a nice young crowd with whom we became firm friends. These cheerful souls working under the bare terra-cotta rooftiles and skylights full of pigeon poo were quite prepared to take over all our paperwork for a token charge, filling in form after form and saving hours of our time and nervous energy. In duplicate, triplicate, quintuplicate.

Apart from being up to date with the constantly changing legal scene vis-à-vis the European Union and any grants that might be wheedled out of the Common Agricultural Policy, our guardian angels provided an important conduit to the provincial administration. They were dealing daily with people in authority, Communists themselves, on whom our future squarely sat.

We were, evidently, on our way to becoming winemakers.

25

The Country Year

THE best thing about the CIA was that it was so big it had
members everywhere and it was immediately able to bring us
together with a local grower who could solve two urgent matters.
The pattern of life in the vineyards was continuing regardless
of our lack of direction, and there was no spare cash for even
the most basic of agricultural tasks. We came to a deal whereby
he would take care of all the maintenance work, pick the grapes
and make wine in his own garage-*cantina*, and give us half of
the production. This came as a huge relief: it would spare us the
worry and responsibility, sidestep the need to learn another new
métier while facing the challenge of tourism, and we hoped
there would be some cash-flow from the sale of the wine. For
me, this arrangement more than satisfied my ambition but no,
my wife clung to her *cantina* dreams like a dog with a bone.

Whatever our differences, it was evident that our perspec-
tives were changing. The countryside was taking over our lives
and it was inevitable that they should become entwined with the

natural cycle of the vines. Once my daily existence had meant wrestling with deadlines, while Mira had been embroiled in air fares; now the seasons became our masters. I don't suppose our routine was so very different from the old ways, despite Internet and email entering the scene and revolutionising the way guests were starting to find us and make bookings. Anelio thought it amusing that I should be spending so much time glued to the screen instead of being outside in the fresh air. (Mira had set him to work clearing the impenetrable terraces near the houses armed with just hand tools and a strimmer and was deeply touched when she later discovered the dear man had made a little allotment for her, complete with tomato plants.) But in truth we both escaped whenever we could. We were at last starting to appreciate our surroundings, although we still had no off-road vehicle or tractor and the only way to get about was by walking.

Collelungo itself is tucked away on land that is invisible from the highway, discreetly hidden down a long and bumpy dirt road that snakes through the woods for a kilometre and a half. Guests marvel at the absence of even a distant hum of traffic. Just when you think you are lost, the view opens to 200 acres of dipping and curving hills covered with magical forests and vines that march like Sandhurst cadets on parade, right up to the saluting base where the farmhouses lie cradled in a fold. Our cultivated fields are for the most part quite small, following the matrix laid down by ancient farmers, along the edge of which runs a Roman road, long disused and overgrown (did someone once ride down here with dispatches from Britannia for Caesar?) We are only half guessing when we tell guests grapes have probably been grown at Collelungo since Etruscan times. We know for sure, however, that wine under the Collelungo name was produced briefly in limited quantities by Don Vito and the Pepi company at their own winery some 20 kilometres away until 1969 when the vineyards were first contracted out and the farm began its decline.

It had been a sleeping beauty for more than a quarter of a century. The Migliorinis had made some wine in the peasant manner for their own consumption, and even though the names Dina gave the various fields lacked poetic distinction we were determined to keep them for old times' sake – La Casa, Di Sotto, Di Sopra, Il Poggio, Rovi, Sotto Rovi, Sorgente, Bosco, Nuovo and La Capanna. Yet never in its entire history had old Collelungo had its own professional winery. What we were doing was breaking new ground. For the very first time, it would mean these vines could express themselves. In spite of my misgivings, I was getting keyed up. There was an awful lot that was positive about the project.

With altitudes ranging from 250m to 600m, on a clear day in Chianti you can see the Apuan Alps, 112 kilometres away to the north, where even now Michelangelo's marble quarries are producing valuable stone. North and east of us rise the Apennines, Italy's backbone, crowned with snow in winter when the north wind, the *tramontana*, whips glacially over our hilltop and freezes the trusty Renault. To the east, in the valley of the Arno where our geraniums were born, morning fog might swaddle the motorway, the same Autostrada del Sole that channels millions south in summer full of holiday hope and sunny expectation. At the same time we can be above it in bright sunshine, under a cloudless blue sky, looking down on the billowing candyfloss as if from a plane. If we glance to the west we can see Castellina with its turreted castle and unfortunate silo, and know that beyond them in the distance the skyline is pierced by the medieval towers of San Gimignano. When I first saw their outline I made the mistake of assuming another modern architectural horror had been perpetrated. The 13 remaining towers (once there were 70) still make a startling sight.

And so began our love affair with the vineyards. In winter, stripped naked and often dusted with frost, they spread like starched sheets hemmed by evergreen holm oaks. We awake on such mornings to see our valley filled with a theatrical mist that makes a swirling seascape of immense beauty, through which loom the castle and an archipelago of islands with infrequent vineposts protruding at odd angles. Before full daylight can break the spell the grey blanket billows moodily, revealing all the battlements of Castellina bearing down from the distant high ridge. Our little river, the Arbiola, holds the ghostly shroud in its clutches for hours before the sun can work its way round and burn off everything. The land is dormant, but there is no mistaking the activity taking place all around as we watch the work progress: an age-old schedule of pruning, tying back, mending supports, replacing broken end-posts. Then, at the end of each day, the mounds of vine prunings that accumulated will have to be set on fire. On frosty evenings when the moon is full we can easily believe the witches are flying when the farmhands light crackling bonfires to send the *sarmenti* up in flames, and their silhouetted figures dance against the blaze. We remember Dina's stories of family gatherings by the hearth and the fairy tales that beguiled the children . . . once upon a time.

In springtime when the days lose their bitter chill and the sun begins to warm the still-moist soil, the cherry, plum, pear, peach and apple trees studding the edges of the vineyards are bursting in pink and white blossom. The first of the wildflowers are also in bloom: cyclamen and violets, and dog roses which always remind me of rosehip syrup; any irises that may have avoided the porcupines' path; and later, scarlet poppies that stain the

Chianti countryside blood-red. Fields of rape add fluorescence to a palette that banks of broom have already dappled sunshine yellow. Honeysuckle, thyme, fennel, marjoram and pine scent the air. Frogs and lizards come out of hibernation. Pheasants patrol our white road, often with a platoon of chicks in tow. Crested hoopoes swoop ahead of the car like dolphins before our bow. Goldfinches and blue-jays pay frequent visits. Hare nibble at the young shoots of our vines. Scorpions, wasps and other products of nature overlooked by the guidebooks (such as adders and grass snakes) make their appearance. We see the occasional viper, doubtless descended from helicopter-borne progenitors. Anelio introduces us to a man called Aldo who appears in a white biohazard suit straight from a Spielberg movie and sprays foul-smelling insecticide around our buildings to protect us all instantly from mosquitoes and tiny biting things. Later he will come again with a higher-octane brew to zap the horseflies and hornets that we shall have to contend with towards the end of summer.

It is the start of the growing season, a time of great anticipation and concern: from now on everything that happens will influence the health and size of the crop. The sap begins to rise and droplets glint like diamonds on the tips of the vines. We learn that as the buds swell and open we must spray and dust to guard against mildew and other diseases. Crucial to the vines' well-being is that old standby, Bordeaux Mixture, the copper sulphate remedy that tends to turn fence-posts blue along with anything else (such as a white Renault) that happens to get in the way of the tractor. And by May the vines are indeed growing prolifically, their leaves shining green-gold with clusters of tiny white flowers that will eventually turn into grapes.

This is *The Good Life* on an amplification scale that knows no limit. There are so many things to learn, first among which being the extent of our ignorance. Anelio constantly impresses us with his intuitive knowledge, carefully hidden behind a modesty that is quite easily mistakable for shyness. He tutors us in local ways that seem so simple and logical, making me think 'now why didn't I think of that?' every time (such as when we stuck a big mirror on a pole on our access road to help visitors see hidden traffic. I'd forgotten to bring the spirit-level to check it was precisely vertical; he cut a long spike from a clump of broom, tied a small rock to it and held that up as a plumb-bob.) He has made his own ladder for inserting into the olive trees, of such design that it will not damage the branches. Later we see him apply his carpentry skills to an even greater invention: a massive rake which he fashions to haul the grape-skins out of the wine vats. It has a knotty handle 2 metres long and a head of beautifully turned teeth that could do credit to *Jaws*.

What we cannot pick up from books we are taught by Manuela, our consultant agronomist from the CIA, a great pal from the Goose *contrada* who explains the principle of 'canopy management' – tying back the foliage so that the fruit can be correctly exposed to sunlight. We also begin to appreciate that we have a choice of ploughing between the lines or leaving the soil untilled, simply relying on weedkiller to control unwanted weeds or excessive grass growth. We are trying to go the organic route; 'Manu' wants to encourage a variety of plants to grow there to add nitrogen to the soil and create a micro-climate. But there is an argument that a light ploughing would be better, in order to prevent rain run-off and conserve moisture. Too much vegetation between the vines could rob the vines of their sustenance as well as make the vineyards look unkempt, and appearance is also important. I learn something else in this last respect: planting a climbing rose at the end of every line of vines is not just for prettiness; it serves as nature's early warning system of bugs, mildew or airborne disease. The sensitivity of its petals and leaves is so much greater than the sturdy vine that it acts as a telltale, like a canary down a mine.

We are building up to summer, another favourite season. With most wildflowers gone the yellow cactus flowers on our prickly pears fade and the grasses are turning brown, leaving only bright blue thistle and chicory in their wake. It is as if the house lights are being dimmed, preparing us for a spectacular theatrical event – and suddenly here it is. Right on cue, the fairies come out. There are *fairies* at the bottom of our vine-yard! True, they may be disguised as fireflies but it is no less a spellbinding discovery as they fill the night with winking pinpricks of stardust on velvet, all in total silence. Vittoria and Mirella's ephemeral *lucciole* are still here after all the years, signalling to each other in a mating ritual unchanged by time. The wills-o'-the-wisp dance from place to place, now flashing coded messages, now vanishing in black holes in the firmament. Sometimes the bravest appear to tease us by alighting on our bodies; we can hold out a finger and if we are very lucky one might land and wink before being dispatched to join its pals in the Nescafé jar we keep for the occasion. I confess, the sorcery is so powerful that for a moment we are children again, transported from our world of worries. We can almost believe we are capturing moonbeams home in the jar . . . and the prize is our very own piece of moonlight to put by the bedside.

Enchanted, we nevertheless take the precaution of pricking the lid to let the air in, for their existence owes more to biology than mythology. All that any of these little creatures can expect is a few short weeks of life – they are destined to die of old age when the season is over – but there is no point in hastening their departure, so when morning comes we release them and they fly away having performed their night vigil. We are entranced, never having experienced anything so lovely. Childhood holidays for me were made captivating by the discovery of glow-worms spreading their lantern-light on evening walks over Beer Head in Devon in the 1950s, but nothing will ever shine so brilliantly in our minds as the full force of bioluminescence witnessed in the vanishing hours of daylight at Collelungo. It is impossible not to think of fairies, witchcraft and enchanted forests. *Firefly, firefly, come to me!*

The fireflies are a prelude for a season that brings the quintessential icon of Tuscany, golden fields of head-turning sunflowers, stretching as far as the eye can see. The screech of cicadas is all about. They go at it all blazing day until that wonderful twilight moment when tiredness overtakes them and their chorus is picked up again on a different octave by the scratch of crickets. The percussion section works a night shift that produces an overlapping continuum of insect whistle, throb and hum, punctuated by evening songbirds and the odd owl hoot or bark of a distant dog. Offstage, too, we can hear the snuffles and grunts of wild boar, and on occasion catch sight of a family taking their nocturnal constitutional under the moon. That is when the New York couple would really feel at home; we appreciate a ventilator then to keep the air cool, not for the noise that it makes.

We have such an abundance of butterflies that one British guest who stayed two weeks with us identified no fewer than 36 species – and in the same two weeks another Englishman gave names to an equal number of birds. We are especially entranced by the swallowtails dancing and floating around the vivid blue lavender hedge we have created from La Ballerina's plant drop. Botanists marvel at the amount of lichen encrusting our rooftops, a sure sign of healthy air, and worts long vanished from English woods become the subject of animated conversations. Bird-lovers

exclaim how long it has been since they last heard a nightingale
or nightjar. We are assured by Celia Haddon, a good friend and
passionate gardener, that no fewer than seven different types of
orchid are happily resident upon our land and enjoying our
company.

High summer in Chianti is when the vineyard workers start
their jobs at 5 a.m. with the sunrise and go home after seven
hours without a break. By 9 a.m. it is already very hot and we
are looking for shelter; we cannot believe they can still be at it
without any shade, yet no matter how blistering it gets by midday
there is no interruption to the pace of work. It is cruel in the
circumstances to have to ask them to keep their voices down,
yet no Tuscan fieldworker seems able to talk at what we consider
to be normal volume, and their foghorn voices carry across the
dawn with enough force to raise the dead, let alone awaken
slumbering tourists. We compromised with their agreeing to start
their early work in the vines furthest from the apartments.

Predictably, heavy rain will arrive with the end of August,
greatly reducing the risk of forest fires that have been our big
concern since the heat-seared countryside turned tinder-dry
across Chianti's 777 square kilometres. Now we pray to be spared
thunderstorms, lightning, and above all hail, which can puncture the skins of the grapes which have turned black and are
delicate. This is the process known as *veraison* which marks the
beginning of ripening. (The berries start off green and hard,
then they change colour and soften as sugars and volume increase
and acidity decreases.) Our 'white roads' are mired, turning
very brown and muddy and needing rapid repair if the guests
are not to be inconvenienced (though the Dunkirk spirit mani-
festly lives on among the British). The nights are alight with
lightning flashes of far-off storms, the distant rumble of thunder
and the persistent *thok, thok* of the machine our neighbouring

vineyard has installed to scare off voracious boar and deer. Our gardens are enriched by the persistence of a plant known as *Bella di Notte,* or Beauty of the Night, an amazing species that defies all the rules by growing prolifically on the poorest soil and blooming in purple profusion to scent the night when the sun goes down. It is visited every evening by giant moths that puzzle our visitors, who have trouble coming to terms with an insect that behaves like a dragonfly and looks like a humming-bird.

Sun and cloud continue to play hide and seek. The beautiful September light gives way to October. The air is pregnant with anticipation of harvest, which we know usually takes place at Collelungo around the first 15 days of October, later than usual on account of our high altitude. And it is the busiest time for tourists.

By now Chianti's mood has mellowed. The breeze carries woodsmoke and the scents of grape juice mixed with tractor diesel as all the hard work of the year starts coming to fruition. The Sangiovese vines are heavy with juicy black grapes that could be graded A1 at Harrods, as ripe and sweet as can be and veiled with purple bloom. The moon is going into the right phase, waxing nicely, so there is nothing to say the *vendemmia* cannot soon begin.

26

First Harvest

10 October, 1996. An official letter. Apparently we should not be in business and have no right to be carrying on this activity. It is signed by the *vigile*, Antonio, who says the documents we presented back in April before opening to guests were not *in regola* as they were out of date. This is an interesting point to which he has somehow failed to direct our attention on the dozens of occasions we have been regular visitors to his office in the last six months. I say ignore it. Mira says file it. We both wonder if it is the work of You Know Who?

Heavy rain and landslides bring chaos in Piedmont and around Bologna. Massive hailstorms in the south leave a 20-centimetre ice layer in some parts. But it's warm here, with watery sun. Will the grapes increase in sugar and reduce in acid in time for picking? Our CIA partner, Nicassio Perna, says he'll start on Monday and bring a team of 30. 'It should take four days.'

12 October. There is still no sign of rain, so Perna is still optimistic. Now the hunters are starting to annoy us. We get lots of questions from guests about their dogs running everywhere, barking. We keep bumping into men with guns walking through our place as if they own it. One marched past the office just now with a shotgun over his shoulder. There's not much comfort from Benito: he says they are not allowed to fire within 150 metres of an occupied dwelling. There are supposed to be as many as 10 million licensed guns in Italy; all you have to do to obtain a permit is demonstrate that you are a reasonable shot and able to recognise various species. But the licence applies to the user, not to the gun, so one licence can mean as many guns as you like, providing they are of the same calibre. A licence gives the holder the right to walk on any part of Italian territory, even someone's back yard. There's no law concerning the respect of private land and trespass. The established precept of Italian law is that all land is ultimately vested in the State, therefore the State can give permission for its lands to be walked. It's Liberty Hall here. So much for an Englishman's castle.

Anelio brightens our gloom with a present of fungi. There must be about 2 kilos in his basket, all picked only a few hours earlier. But we are concerned. Are they edible? *Madonna Santa* are they edible! Ones that look like toadstools are OK because they have a thick stem. Ones with small dome shapes like the head of an octopus are OK because they have a collar like a Victorian ruff. The bright yellow ones with delicate heads on long elegant stems are OK as everyone knows they are *giallini* (the name means yellow). And last of all something we recognise: big *porcini*, THE famous Tuscan mushroom (like French *cèpes*). Pig mushrooms. *Porca Madonna!*

13 October. Here is the weather forecast for Tuscany. Monday: fine and sunny. Tuesday: showers. Wednesday: stormy. Thursday, Friday, Saturday: return of good weather. It's a go.

* * *

Because it was a nature-lover's paradise it was inevitable there would be a serpent or two in the Garden of Eden. The problem began in late August. The general hunting season for anything other than boar did not officially start until 17 September, with open season on the beasts being declared on 1 November. But following 15 August – *Ferragosto*, the biggest holiday of the year – it was the right of any hunter to train his dogs wherever he fancied. 'Train' was hardly the right word. Kennels bred special hunting dogs that were often bought in bulk, stuck in cages and trailed behind off-road vehicles into the woods before being freed for their baptism of fire.

We knew of two or three of these breeding factories in and around Castellina and the noise the hounds made, especially at night when you were trying to sleep with your windows open, made you yearn for the simple life of the city. Luckily, we had experienced this early in our agricultural career otherwise we might have been tempted to accept the local hunters' request to establish one in our spare woodland when they approached us, most amicably. We just wanted to keep the woods as they were, and had already disappointed our friend Nora Kravis who wanted to graze a hundred cashmere goats there (she has quite a business, making woven articles and skin-care products from her herd's wool and milk). For a while I also toyed with the fashionable idea of breeding ostriches to gain some quick income. That one soon got nipped in the bud – fortunately, I'd say, considering the resilience of the local market to new trends in the food chain.

The hunters' dogs were no loved Labradors or Lurchers. After being caged and kennelled for a long time the scent of the countryside was too much for them. Sniffing, snarling, scrabbling to be free, they leaped off their trailer and vanished in the kind of barking frenzy I imagined Battersea Dogs' Home might suffer on Open Day. Disturbingly, their accompanying masters seemed to have scented blood themselves and emitted a primordial barking squawk – '*Qua! Qua! Qua!*'– which carried across the valley at irregular intervals. It was a curiously penetrating noise, which impressed us at first. We thought it was some kind of special command, a gifted means of communication with the animal world such as we'd seen at sheepdog trials on TV, and thus to be admired. But we soon discovered it was simply a Tuscan way of shouting 'Here! Here! Here!', trying to call lost dogs to heel. To no avail, of course: no self-respecting dog would have any intention of responding when its nostrils were flared and filled with exciting odours of juniper and broom, porcupine and hare.

The dogs also had tinkling bells around their necks which could be heard hundreds of yards away even with the wind blowing in the wrong direction. The noise of these bells was intended to flush out their prey well before the dogs' own scent did, making it impossible for a hound ever to catch anything. The bells served a further useful purpose when the hounds got lost, which was nearly always, for then *they* had to be hunted by their owners.

Now we could add rural terrorism – i.e. dogs – to our list of concerns. Would the weather hold? Would all the pickers Signor Perna had recruited show up? Would Anelio cope? Would Mafalda, strangely quiet since my Internet attack, pick this moment to revive her mischief beyond meddling with the *vigile*?

That Sunday night before harvest we went to bed early to get a good night's rest, knowing how hard the next day was likely to be. But around 4 a.m. loud barking and bell-jingling shook us out of our slumbers. Two dogs that had become detached from the rest of a pack had spent the afternoon running wild through the vineyards and were evidently still on the loose, probably chasing a hare or some other delectable object near the swimming pool and disturbing all our guests (we had a full house by then). I stumbled out, pulling jeans over pyjamas, only realising when I reached the white shape that was our car that visibility was down to 20 metres and we were wreathed in a bank of low cloud.

From the vineyards I could hear snuffling noises that could have been either a dog or a wild boar, so keeping my voice soft for fear of waking our clients, I tried a tentative 'Here, boy!' in best Barbara Woodhouse '*Walk*ies!' style. Two black shapes shot past me in quick succession then turned and ran back the way they had come, barking, whining and tinkling their bells. That did it. '*Qua! Qua! Qua!*' I shouted at the top of my voice into the floating mist, casting discretion to the fog. But I might as well have been addressing the hare. Fifty minutes later, after patrolling what I could see of the vineyards in the Renault with its foglights piercing the gloom, I gave up. Of the mutts there was no sign. The bells sounded distant. It was time to go back to bed, where I kept wondering where the dogs might be and how frustrated, tired and hungry they must be getting. By 6 a.m. I had drifted into a fitful sleep and by 7 a.m. Mira and I were up, ready for harvest. That morning a guest enquired why it was we had decided to leave our dogs loose at night.

And so our first harvest began, watched by men with guns and an audience of fascinated guests whose offers of help we reluctantly had to refuse as we were loath to let them loose on the secateurs for fear of accident. All workers had to be regis-tered: as you can imagine, copious amounts of paperwork were needed before you could snip one grape and we did not want to get Signor Perna into trouble.

As it turned out, Perna's pickers numbered 16 rather than 30. Before we could say 'Knife' they started in the wrong field (it was Il Poggio at the top that was ready to pick, not Di Sotto down below). And the weathermen had got it all wrong: we worked all day beneath black lowering skies that could have graced Salford. It would probably rain tomorrow.

But we had hauled a fair amount of grapes up the hill by 5 p.m., the hour all Italian workers know instinctively it is time to down tools despite our pleas to keep going to beat the barometer. I had established a nice working relationship with one Emilio, who spoke good English and astonished me by saying he'd worked in Sainsbury's for 10 years before coming home to Castellina to retire. This was his 14th *vendemmia*.

'How are the grapes?' I asked him.

'Really juicy and sweet,' he said. 'You'll make a lovely wine.'

Another picker walking by added a happy note. They were, he said, '*buone, sane* and *discrete*' – the ultimate accolade. Good, healthy and reasonable. That seemed fair enough to me.

Hunters, it seemed, were after three types of life form: things that flew, things that ran and things that went bump in the night, to wit wild boar. Somehow we would have to deal with this phenomenon.

It had seemed funny at first. Right at the moment when our tourists, embalmed in Ambre Solaire, started turning pink/ brown/bronze by the pool and vines, heavy with promise, were working their way towards purple/blue/black we could walk into any clothes store and be lost in a sea of khaki/olive/tan. This was due to their owners' foresight in stocking them well with military-style jackets, jerkins, waistcoats, parkas, leggings and boots – precisely the kind of desirable attire no self-respecting hunter could afford to be without. And this, well before the autumn rush; for above all the Italians' innate sense of costume drama and love of dressing in uniforms has to be satisfied. No expense is spared; everything must be sacrificed in the name of *bella figura*.

We knew our wild boar were being fattened for the kill when we caught one of the local woodsmen driving a van across our land and I followed, to find that he was dropping piles of restaurant waste at what were evidently strategic sites. Apparently this routine had been going on for some time, under our very noses. They loved their little piggies and could not bear to let a day go by without giving them their handout of tuck. This was not good news. Something had to be done.

Theoretically, by erecting a continuous length of chain-link fencing 1.4 metres high around the entire perimeter and declaring our land a *Fondo Chiuso*, a private hunting domain, we could prevent anyone from outside coming in and troubling us. However, the expense and paperchase this involved can be imagined. Also, the attendant alienation of the locals would doubtless cause us even more difficulties in the long run. Then again, how could we be assured that in ring-fencing our cultivated lands we were not corralling whole families of boar, deer, porcupine and hare within and thus creating a *tavola fredda* of our precious crops for them?

There had been numerous attempts to have the tradition of zapping little birds banned, but all failed and Chianti's primeval woodlands in general were blighted with jerry-built shacks that the sharpshooters created and used as hides. We were told by sympathetic friends that we had the right to destroy any we found in our woods, but it would have taken a brave or foolish person to incur the wrath of the hunting lobby. It was not just that such action would be considered provocative and likely to inspire costly and unpleasant counter-measures. Doggie friends warned that if we antagonised them they might spread poison around our place and kill any domestic animals we might have.

The threat was real enough: about 150 cases of dog poison-
ings a year were being reported to the Carabinieri in Tuscany.
Several *contadini* used poison liberally (but illegally) to protect
their allotments from predators such as fox and porcupine, never
bothering to place warning notices for those walking their dogs.
Not that, in the countryside, anyone bothers to keep a dog on a
lead. The more we looked at this the more alarming it became
and we counted our blessings for not having any pets ourselves.
Mira convinced me she was not the only person in the world
who disliked dogs – in the Middle East they are seen as carriers
of disease – so they would be a turn-off for as many guests as
they would be a turn-on for those who liked them. Such as me.

The fact was, dogs were dying horrible deaths wherever we
looked. The product of choice was nearly always strychnine,
access to which was not difficult, though lately cyanide had entered
the picture. In next-door Umbria hunters were killing each others'
animals almost indiscriminately in a self-destructive race to find
increasingly rare truffles. On the roads, abandoned dogs were
being run over in their thousands, causing an average 4,000 accidents a year in which 20 people would be killed and 400 injured.
(The statistics are terrible: annually in Italy, 130,000 dogs and
cats are abandoned during the holiday months, a figure increasing by around 20 per cent a year.) Even in the short time we
had been in Chianti we had personal knowledge of two canine
poisoning tragedies: our friends the Baldinis had lost a great big
bow-wow called Goliath, of aptly large proportions and friendly
character. Willi and Antonia took in a sorry stray called Ambra,
who swallowed something evil and was brought back to life only
by the swift intervention of Nora, our goatherd friend who is
also a fully qualified vet. Six months later Ambra was ill again,
having guzzled a mixture of strychnine and broken glass. This
time she did not survive.

This was not only awful for animal-lovers, it was bad for tourism. Apart from the killer *contadini*, who were these maniacs who might stoop to deliberate canicide? Hunters came in two species: the 'outsiders' who might act in spite and the 'insiders' from our local community whose respect for fellow citizens and civic rights was somewhat more advanced. It was the former who posed the risk.

We had to watch our step with the local lot all the same. Mira pointed out to me that those same crack marksmen (often as not, they missed) could be crucial to our future. Behind the Che Guevara fatigues and designer stubble and mandatory Ray-Bans there could have been lurking an important member of the village planning committee, or the nephew of the mayor, the bank manager or the friend of some heavyweight politico, whose paths it would have been suicidal to cross. We underestimated the power of patronage at our peril. Softly, softly was the watchword, no matter that when the shooting season for wild boar started it seemed as if we were living in the trenches.

It occurred to us that it might be a good idea to consult Renato, our friend from Big Blu whose face would crack up like a porker with an orange in its mouth at the mere mention of *'cinghiale'*, the word for wild boar. He had told us on numerous occasions how proud the *squadra* of hunters from Castellina was of its professionalism and prowess – the same chaps whose request for an *allevamento* we had turned down. Maybe there was a compromise, he said. If we declared the land around the cultivated areas to be off limits in this way and left the rest of the estate free for hunting, honour could be saved. Make the fence, but cut a new through passage around it for the hunters from Castellina.

My current thoughts about the defences of Collelungo already revolved around a cattle grid (an alien notion: I had failed to find anything like the common-or-garden English variety on sale anywhere and had commissioned Graziano, the village blacksmith, to make one to a design I sketched on the back of an envelope). So this is what happened. We did the paperwork, got planning permission, paid the fees, paid the workmen, paid for the requisite signs to go up, and built our ring fence at a cost of about £20,000. Once Renato and his mates were happy that their dogs would not break their legs in the cattle grid's bars we invited the entire *squadra* into the forbidden zone to beat any trapped animal out.

We had seen how a *battuta* worked. The men joined up in teams, beating the forest and yelling as loudly as they could to drive out their quarry. As up to 30 beaters converged, in touch with each other by mobile phone, the hills would ring to the sound of harsh cries that made '*Qua! Qua! Qua!*' seem like a lullaby. A crackle of shots might rip through the air. Another Tuscan tusker would bite the dust.

Renato turned out to be one of the best marksmen among the villagers. I'll never forget the look on Mira's face when he appeared at our door the day they beat up Collelungo. He carried in his arms what would clearly in normal conditions have been considered a generous peace offering: half a side of freshly killed wild pig. Thanks but no thanks, said my Jewish wife. Boy, was she wild.

27

Made in Tuscany

THE Chianti region consists of around 150,000 acres of vine-yards stretching inland from Pisa in the west to Arezzo in the east and from Florence in the north to Siena in the south. There are seven distinct zones, but it is Chianti Classico, right at the heart of Chianti with 17,000 acres, that produces the finest wines and can also lay claim to the geographical name. Where that name comes from is open to debate. Wine has been made in Tuscany since pagan antiquity, and nobody can say whether its true roots lie in 'Clante', the name used by both the Etruscans and Romans, or the Latin *clango*, which has something to do with the blowing of horns.

It's all a bit academic. However, the place name can definitely be traced back to 1211 and the earliest record of 'Chianti' as a moniker for wine dates from 1398. As early as the 16th century, hogsheads of Chianti were being exported to England as a highly prized commodity and in our time it can claim to have become Italy's most famous – some might say infamous – red wine. That negative reputation is now thankfully also a thing of the past, but not so very long ago wine writers dismissively described it as thin and acidic, thanks to the disgraceful amount of cheap plonk from elsewhere in Italy that used to be palmed off eponymously.

What we recognise today as Chianti was invented behind Medici-fortified walls in the middle of the 19th century – practically yesterday in the 4,000 years of winemaking history of a country the Greeks called Oenotria, the land of wine. The man who set out the basic formula was Barone Bettino Ricasoli, the 'Iron Baron' who became the second Prime Minister of a united Italy in 1861 when my Great-grandfather Louis was hitting the immigrant trail. Looking east across the woods and vineyards from Collelungo we can just see his Castello di Brolio where he mixed red Sangiovese grapes with the other varietals we had come across when picking for Bruno back at the start. His descendants are among the 40 or so families that have remained attached to their lands for more than 800 years, living in Chianti and selling their wine under the imprimatur of their own coats of arms.

Somewhere along the way, Ricasoli's formula for a wine of distinction managed to get corrupted and became the basis for a hangover-inducing brew guaranteeing a birdcage mouth. By the 1960s when we took armloads of it in bulbous flasks to parties it had been stigmatised as a cheap supermarket staple, thanks to the absence of quality control and doubts about its provenance. Which was why the first wave of foreigners could acquire homes here so cheaply and find whole vineyards thrown in as a bonus.

But something else was happening. At the very moment the generic name Chianti was starting to acquire its jug image a 'Super Tuscan' wine revolution was electrifying the cognoscenti of the wine world. Sensational reds were emerging from vine-yards planted with Cabernet Sauvignon from France, then alien to Tuscany, which went on to be blended with the native grape. By the late 1980s the names Sassicaia, Tignanello and Solaia were on every connoisseur's lips.

And for the following years attention remained focused on the Super Tuscan arena where the idea of ageing the wine in new oak in the form of small casks, Bordeaux-style *barriques*, rather than traditional oak vats was gaining passionate support. They add structure and body and a rich vanilla flavour to the wine.

Bruno had told us about these new vinification techniques, and the way stainless steel tanks were taking the place of old cement vats, which helped to explain how Chianti Classico was beginning to be treated with new respect by the wine trade. Producers had watched the Super Tuscan success story, thrown out equipment that had been creaking and leaking for centuries, started timidly to grub up a number of bad vines that had been bulking out harvests with lifeless juice, and begun replanting with nothing but the best strains. Finally, the old Ricasoli formula was scrapped, even permitting a Chianti Classico to be made purely from Sangiovese grapes. For over a decade now the tall Bordeaux bottle, with its nuance of quality, has almost entirely replaced the flask in its jacket of straw which Leonardo da Vinci is credited with having invented to stop the glass smashing during transportation.

We had no coat of arms, no noble background and no family connections going back centuries. We were simply two foreign sky-divers who had plunged gaily into this crazy drop-zone and had only recently furled our parachutes. The project facing us involved taking an ancient wine farm and bringing it up to these exacting standards, all with a lack of the requisite capital and an adversarial bank at our throats. We were total novices in the world of wine. We would be competing for a share of a market dominated not only by the local aristocracy but also by other newcomers who were busily getting in on the act, notably foreign bankers, American and Italian business magnates and even pop celebrities such as Sting. Of course we would have to concern ourselves eventually with the daily routines of field work, work in the winery, the techniques of harvesting and the business of bottling and marketing our produce – all the nitty-gritty which I never lost a chance to remind Mira of. But staring us in the face right then was the job of building and equipping a winery, plus (to my sudden horror) the news from Alberto that if we were to have any chance of succeeding commercially we would need a redevelopment plan. Our vines needed rejuvenating.

'Rejuvenating?' I gasped.

Mira and he exchanged glances.

'They need grubbing up and replanting,' said the grape doctor, delivering the prognosis in the sepulchral tones surgeons reserve to tell you your beloved has terminal cancer.

Oh great. This was just the kind of thing I wanted to hear. We must be mad. Lobotomy would have been a simpler option.

28

A Late Delivery

THE *cantina*, our winery, came into being in 1997 thanks to an improved cash-flow, the sale of the 1996 wine (now fetching 300,000 lire per 100 litres) and a loan from a new source, the Banca Nazionale del Lavoro. There was also the promise of an EU grant for investment in improving agricultural buildings. Here again we were guided by the CIA and Alberto. Not only was he a true expert, he also spoke Tuscan-American English so we got on like a house on fire and it wasn't long before we became close friends. I could even forgive him for suggesting we should tear up the vineyards and begin again.

For us the big thing was that he had an open mind, unlike many of his dyed-in-the-wool contemporaries, and was familiar with winemaking techniques in the new world, therefore aware of the broader horizon. Plus, he had agreed to throw in his hat with us when Mira told him his services were too expensive. 'Oh really?' he'd said. 'Then I'd better come down in price so we can get going.' Both he and his colleague, Paolo, had unlimited patience and managed to imbue us with something of the passion they felt for wine and the art of winemaking.

I always think of poor old Pepi and his racehorses when I recall the moment Alberto joined us, for the role of a wine-maker is rather akin to that of a jockey or trainer. A syndicate might own a racehorse, loving the sport but not knowing a thing about the animal, how to ride it or look after it. You need a professional for that, the better the jockey the surer the win, and we were sure we had backed a winner. The synergy was perfect. We were absolute beginners, with no prejudices about how wine should be made because we were totally ignorant and were not embarrassed to admit it. He was setting up for himself in busi-ness, and was handed an empty building with an invitation to equip it to his design, with no restriction other than budget. Another good omen was that his wife Alessandra gave birth to their first baby, Angelica, that autumn.

The *cantina* started life as a piggery in the 1960s: a shell of a building made from perforated brick, steel girders and asbestos roofing which Pepi had used as a horse barn. The transforma-tion to winery was brought about by a little architectural sleight of hand, the skills of Big Blu and the procurement of a letter from the provincial authority in Siena conceding, indeed, that no planning permission would be needed as the end purpose of the structure would remain agricultural. No 'new build' would have been permitted.

To begin with, that year, the 30-metre exterior length was left unclad. Alberto quite rightly said it didn't matter at all. We protected the underside of the roof with rock-wool, sandwiched the asbestos in a false ceiling of aluminium slats, and sprayed dark red gunk all over the outside. We lagged the walls, the better to deal with extremes of heat and cold, and panelled the inside with plasterboard. The old concrete floor, designed to take nothing heavier than pigs and horses, was now anchored with load-bearing iron grids and covered with a smooth industrial surface with special attention to drainage. A stockroom, kitchen, office and bathroom materialised amid all the chaos. As our second working year arrived, with some trepidation we went ahead with ordering the equipment we needed to get started.

If we had to save money, Alberto's advice was to buy a reconditioned second-hand press. An old Vaslin, a famous French make, would be ideal. However, he insisted that we go for state-of-the-art machinery for the de-stemmer/de-stalker, the three pumps we needed, each for a different job, and the high-pressure hose for steam-cleaning. There were assorted pipes, clips, connectors, ladders, plastic containers, buckets, jugs, funnels, demijohns, measuring vials . . .

The shopping list made stomach-churning reading. It included seven stainless steel tanks 3 metres high and 2.5 metres wide, each with a capacity of 100 hectolitres (10,000 litres, or if you prefer 13,500 bottles); 25 *barriques* – 225-litre oak barrels – at a cost of around £600 each; and a custom-made hopper to receive the grapes, complete with auger – the Archimedes' screw that pushes the grapes along into the de-stemmer/de-stalker. This, we discovered, was a machine resembling a small aircraft engine which would use centrifugal force to complete its task. It cost £8,000.

Finally, with Alberto's help we found a specialist company that would contract to do the field work to save us the expense and worry of staff and the machinery we knew would be needed – a tractor with all the bits that get towed behind it such as the sprayer, the plough, the rake . . . a list that seemed endless.

The year progressed. We ordered all our bits and pieces as well as the major items that needed time to be made to our design. The tourists returned, with the swallows. The Whittakers renewed the Croquet contract, saying how satisfied their clients had been. We had further interesting incidents, such as guests either putting diesel in their petrol tanks by mistake or bashing their doors in our car park or locking their keys inside their vehicle and having to have our Renault garage mechanic come and drill holes in their bodywork. Meanwhile the building work forged ahead. The weather turned mild and dry in contrast to previous years when crops had been plagued by excess rain.

We put in the order for the steel tanks and the hopper in May, five months before a likely date for the harvest. June turned to July and a time bomb started ticking in my head. What if . . . ? All of Italy goes on holiday in August and often life gets disrupted long before that. Mr Cavalzani had promised to have the tanks ready by the end of July so when I called in mid-month to see how our order was progressing I was dismayed to hear that he had run out of large sheet steel. 'Don't worry,' he said, 'I'll have them with you by the start of September.'

Manuela noticed it first: our vines were starting to bud 10 days ahead of time, giving them a longer growing period – and when the sun came out it stayed out. As the weeks and months passed and I agonised over getting the winery finished it rained only a little and just at the right time. Big Blu completed their work, leaving a vast empty space like a small airport terminal – water rigged up, electricity connected, drainage installed and tested. All around it, the grapes were maturing beautifully. Prematuring, you might say. It was going to be an early harvest! I started to panic at the prospect of bringing them in to an empty hangar, for we had one feature that made our winery unique: a total lack of equipment.

On 9 September Mr Cavalzani called to say that he was sending us our tanks the following day. This was not a moment too soon, as the agricultural cycle was accelerating daily and the grapes looked like beating the tanks to the winery by a short head. The press was now in place and the hopper had been delivered. At last we were able to phone the hygiene people, USL, and ask them to come quickly because we intended to make wine within a few days and needed their authorisation.

At 10 a.m. the next morning two lorries bringing the tanks arrived and got stuck on our white road. '*Impossibile!*' said the driver of the lead juggernaut, trying to extricate himself from the tangle of greenery through which a wall of stainless steel glinted in the sunshine. 'This is as far as we're going.' And with that, 300 metres from the winery, the tanks were offloaded on a hilltop which quickly took on the look of an oil refinery. These things were enormous, standing there with the sun dancing on them. Which is how the USL inspectors saw them when they responded to our call with unusual alacrity two days later, and were somewhat surprised at the novelty. Mr Cavalzani sent a smaller truck to ferry each tank individually to its new home. We pressed more grappa upon the USL and spent another nail-biting week waiting for them to come and inspect again, 'for real this time'. It was almost harvest time.

All of September was hot and dry and it became evident it was going to be a good one with the grapes having unusually high sugar concentrations, which promised higher quality. By late in the month when we finally got the health certificate and the pumps and hoses were assembled in anticipation of the coming action even the experts were dumbfounded by their perfect condition. The *cantina* was ready, under starter's orders and resembling the engine room of a great ocean liner. Alberto said: 'If you have any money at all to spare, I beg you to buy as many more *barriques* as possible.'

Hardly were the words out of his mouth when the earth shook. On a Friday before the *vendemmia* the whole of central Italy was engulfed in violent tremors when two earthquakes hit. They were centred on Assisi, about 120km from us, where they toppled stone houses and medieval bell towers and sent parts of the vaulted inner roof of the 13th century basilica of Saint Francis crashing to the ground. The quakes were felt as far away as Rome to the south and Venice to the north. Nine people were killed. Thousands of houses were damaged if not destroyed. Tent cities sprang up and caravans and campers for thousands of people were made available for those forced out of their homes.

Nothing like that happened at Collelungo, thank God. The *cantina* held. The apartments remained intact. The whole of Chianti escaped with merely a trembling and a skittering of stones. We had known we were in an earthquake zone because right from the beginning we had been obliged to take anti-seismic precautions in the rebuilding programme, and we were relieved too that our new water emplacements had survived unscathed. But it was a close call – a reminder of how vulnerable we were. The moment was all the more emotionally charged as it was only three weeks since the news of Princess Diana's death had left us badly shaken, along with our guests. We heard about it on a BBC World Service bulletin at 7 a.m. and had to find words to tell our houseful of British and American visitors. As someone who used to report the news I was accustomed to delivering the written message. When it had to be delivered in person it was quite another thing.

We ordered another 14 *barriques* a few days later when the wine experts said it was going to be the vintage of the century. We were determined to be ready for it, my Destiny and I.

29

Total Immersion

WHEN we were picking grapes for the Comandante it took half a week to clear his vines and that was that. Each evening as night was falling we would load the day's rewards into an ancient lorry that bore the weary look of an old workhorse. Then we jumped up and down on the load in our gumboots, crushing the grapes to squeeze more in, and finally embarked on a perilous journey to the wine co-operative *cantina*. That was how it had always been done, said Bruno.

It was a hazardous enterprise for several reasons: the road twisted and turned through hairpins for nearly 5 kilometres and we were seriously overloaded with four of us squeezed in the driver's cab, plus far more cargo than the makers ever intended. The asthmatic engine gave a passable imitation of conking out on every bend and rarely accepted second gear without a fight. Twice we suffered the ignominy of a puncture, the whole truck keeling over with precious grape juice pouring out over its sides. Eventually we would arrive at the winery to join what resem-

bled a French farmers' blockade: a long line of creeping trac-
tors, trailers, pick-ups, carts – vintage vehicles such as our own,
belonging to private growers like Bruno with smallholdings that
did not merit the investment of their own winery.

Then the last stage of the operation could begin: manually to
transfer our load with shovels and pitchforks into a giant hopper
containing an outsize horizontal corkscrew (the auger) with
menacing blades that glinted as they turned under the glare of
arc lights. We slipped and slithered in the sticky-sweet juice,
trying not to become part of the vintage ourselves by being
pulped in the masher. I admit, this became such an obsession that
what happened at the other end of the tube into which our grapes
had vanished held no interest for me; that 'wine' did not simply
emerge, all ready for drinking, was someone else's affair. The
process of converting the glutinous mess of black and green grapes
into the red liquid called Chianti Classico could remain a mystery.

Now we quickly had confirmed what we had long suspected:
that the system of harvesting grapes favoured by Bruno –
jumping up and down on them in wellies and cramming as many
as possible into a wagon for a long drive to the winery – was
not the ideal way to handle them. If the fruit gets mashed the
juice will oxidise and can set off spontaneous fermentation, which
is most definitely not desired. We must have delivered tons of
macerated mulch to the co-op *cantina*, not knowing any better.

With Collelungo, because so much was at stake, the grapes
had to be handled reverently. Alberto insisted that the contrac-
tors use the smallest trailer on the market, as it was better to
haul many small quantities the short distance from the fields
(where Franca and her daughter Fabiola joined the team picking
everything by hand) rather than fewer, bigger loads. We roped
in as many of our guests as possible now, as this was our responsibility not Perna's, and aching backs apart, all said it was the

highlight of their holiday. Anelio was on hand to receive the grapes which then started their journey from the hopper to the crusher/de-stalker, which had a cylinder with a slow-turning perforated sheath on the outside and rubber-tipped paddles on the inside that rotated at fearsome speed. The paddles knocked the grapes off the stalks and pushed them through the holes in the sheath and into another, smaller, hopper. The stalks were too big to follow, but even if they wanted to, the centrifuge drove them out at the end of the machine, where they piled up in a heap. Picked clean, as if by mouth.

Mira and I stood there, sticky from picking, with our mouths open. Everything worked! The crushed grapes were eased through a piston pump that clunked away as the juice and skins were pushed through a red PVC hose the diameter of a football and into one of Mr Cavalzani's large stainless-steel fermentation vats. The vast quantity each was capable of holding was a heady thought for the two former patrons of Safeway and Victoria Wine. Only once, with the very first surge, did anything go wrong. We badly underestimated the force of the pump and the hose bucked wildly, spraying everything in range including us. '*Battesimo!*' shouted Anelio. A baptism was a good omen. Even the damage we thought we'd done to our hands, which were hard and rough and stained black, on the palms as well as under the nails, proved less than the life-threatening disaster it first appeared. Rubbing them in powdered citric acid had them as pink and smooth as a baby's bottom in no time.

Two weeks later, in mid October, Alberto gave the go-ahead to start a second harvest – the choicest bunches we had left on the vine that were destined to make a Riserva. We were unbelievably lucky that it hadn't rained in all that time, and when those grapes came in even we could see they were luscious. Simply de-stalking them and pumping them into the big vat to ferment was already giving out such heady aromas. And then, to our horror, Alberto said: 'Now take out 20 per cent of the juice and pump it into the wine you'll be selling in bulk.'

'What? But why?'

'Trust me,' he said. 'It will make what's left more concentrated and enrich the Riserva. More skins and less juice will give you a deeper colour and more aromas.' He could see we weren't convinced, so added: 'It's what the French do to their premium wines. We are conducting a *saignée*, a bleeding.'

Reluctantly we followed our orders. It was to prove to be one of the best things we ever did. But at the time we were doing all this we were just going one step at a time, not knowing why, not knowing what came next, apprentices blindly obeying the instructions of our tutor. The system worked well, most of the time. Once, when Anelio noticed that some wine had taken on a soupy, silvery look which he couldn't understand, Mira asked Paolo what it meant. He glanced at the soup and said: '*Oh, è emozionato!*', which Mira took to mean something nice. 'Isn't Italian romantic?' she said to me. 'They even talk about wine as if it has feelings. He says it's feeling emotional.' We suffered this delusion for days before realising he meant emulsified. The word was *emulzionato*.

It had been a brilliant harvest and things had gone remarkably well, the only accident being that moment when we sprayed the pristine winery with red juice. The time that followed saw a learning curve verging on the vertical. Guided by Alberto and Paolo we prepared a work schedule that was to involve us in three weeks of intensive labour. Quite how much physical work was likely to be involved came as a shock – especially the business of 'pumping over' the grapes as the skins formed a cap inside the tanks and needed to be broken up.

We started the fermentation process using purchased laboratory yeasts. You could hear the gloup-gloup of the juice quite clearly, the signal for Anelio or me to clamber to the cone-shaped top of each vat, carrying a heavy hose which we pushed over an opening the size of a manhole and secured with a cord. At the foot of our rickety 3-metre ladder this hose was fastened with clips like handcuffs to a big pump, from which another cuffed hose led to the base outlet valve on the same vat. The trick was to get the juice flowing from the bottom of the vat, into the pump and out again up 3 metres of vertical hose while opening and closing valves and remembering which way the switch went – was it left or right for forward or back? After that it was simply a matter of having to sit on the sloping top of the vats, hosing the fermenting mass with pressures that were surprisingly fierce, up to 30 minutes per tank, morning, noon and night, seven days a week. Now we knew why Alberto had chosen short, wide tanks instead of the long tall ones favoured by our neighbours. The dense cap of skins that rose to the top was over a metre thick and had to be kept moist, our professors said, and this was much easier if we had a wider volume to deal with rather than a deeper one.

So we pumped and pumped, the juice travelling back and forth over it in order to draw out colour, aromas and tannins – all the sought-after elements whose extraction underpins a good wine. It was a crucial moment; after that it would be too late. It sounds easy and so it should have been, but the exertion of holding a hose under considerable pressure while balancing on top of the tank on an incline for long periods was quite a physical challenge. Pushing the jet of precious liquid into the corners of the cone meant stretching one arm to full extent while holding on with the other. We had to punch through the cap without stopping or losing our concentration for even a second. Not only that but as the sugar turned to alcohol the fumes made us giddy and turned our cheeks bright red. For it was hot – powerfully hot. During full fermentation carbon dioxide was released and temperatures in the winery were nudging 35 degrees Celsius. Not so long ago, said Paolo, workers used to get into the vat to break up the cap. How they came out alive beats me.

The very high temperature was a big concern. It should have been much lower, and if it went up any more we would be making jam. Without the sophisticated cooling tanks of a major winery we had to improvise with a garden hose that I turned into a ring, which I then pierced with a skewer and draped around the head of the tank. Water dribbled down its sides and, left overnight with the winery windows wide open, the mass had cooled a vital degree or two by morning. Not so the blood pressure of our guests, however: our constant watering had made the spring run dry and we had a crisis on our hands. The *agriturismo* was just waking up and 31 people would want to flush lavatories, take baths or showers and run water in the kitchen. A brave man it is who tells an American citizen he has been deprived of his inalienable right to shower. 'You go and tell them,' I said to Mira.

Another heart-stopping moment came that first harvest when we filled one of the vats a little higher than the rest, added the yeast and went to lunch. Mira returned a mere 25 minutes later to see how the brew was developing and was met at the door by a foaming mass of rivulets like lava, pouring from the top of the tank. This pink sticky goo was straight from *Quatermass*, its tentacles advancing menacingly through a fog of fumes having clearly taken on a life of their own. She came running back to me, as if I knew what to do. It was our hero Anelio who came to the rescue. In his usual calm way he cured the problem with only a turn of a valve, a big basin and a mumbled *Porca Madonna!*

Regularly, Mira would use a hydrometer to check the vital sugar content of the grape-must, monitoring its conversion into alcohol and ensuring the fermentation process was not getting stuck. To be within the Chianti Classico consortium's parameters we had to have a minimum of 12 per cent alcohol; below this we were in danger of being downgraded to table wine, with attendant financial consequences.

We followed this routine for what seemed an age. Then it was time to pump out the new wine and ease open the vat doors. The quantity of glistening ruby skins was huge! It all had to be shovelled out (here's where Anelio's rake came in), dripping blood-red, then pumped into the wine press. This was something like a Keystone Kops fire engine with a huge horizontal rotating drum programmed like a washing machine with crush rather than spin. Hoops and chains and a central screw worked a concertina action on two metal plates at each end, drawing them to the centre to extrude the juice. Finally we transferred the best young wine into our oak casks for ageing, and put the bulk wine we were going to sell back into the cleaned-up steel vats.

The process did not end there, however. The vats had to be constantly monitored and topped up to the correct level as the wine expanded and contracted according to changing temperatures and atmospheric pressure. It was extraordinary how capricious a big volume of liquid could be and how many times I had to run up and down that ladder clutching a bottle and funnel. Then the wine had to be racked every so often on Alberto's orders – that's transferring wine from tank (or barrel) to tank and back, to clear it of its lees and sediment. We gave the precious *barrique* wine as much care as a newborn baby. It was absorbing the aromas of the French oak and was burping away merrily in the process. Wine actually does burp CO_2 when it goes through its second, malolactic, fermentation and the noise in the winery was wickedly enjoyable, indicating we were on the right track.

What a completely efficient operation it was. Nothing was wasted. The pressed grape skins and lees went to the distillery to make grappa and pure alcohol for medicinal or culinary purposes. The grape stalks were used as mulch in the vineyards until the cost of labour – spreading them about was a time-wasting business – became prohibitive. Our neighbour Betty, the American university don, was happy to take them away for her organic garden, setting new world records for the amount that could be squeezed into a Fiat Panda.

Even the waste water was recycled for irrigation. In line with everything else, Italy had adopted new EU standards with its usual brio and Tuscany's environment protection agency made it a condition of our operations that we should not risk polluting the woods around the winery.

I was musing on this in the bathtub with my big toe up the spout, content after a day's hard work in the burping department, when Mira shouted to me: 'Did you remember to add the sulphites?'

'Yeah, no problem!' I replied, putting down the loofah. Paolo had explained that sulphites were needed to stabilise the wine and kill bacteria.

'How much did you put into each barrel?'

'Like Paolo said, 45 grammes a barrel,' I sang out joyously.

Suddenly Mira was in the bathroom with me. 'FORTY-FIVE grammes a barrel?' she shrieked.

'That's what he said, isn't it?' I asked innocently. But I had a sinking feeling, a premonition my maths had let me down again.

'No! It's FOUR POINT FIVE per barrel. Four and a half grammes,' said my panic-stricken wife. 'What he said was two grammes per hectolitre.'

'But that's less than a pinch of salt,' I said, bursting out of the water like a whale as my worst nightmare was confirmed. I had just gone and ruined our best wine, the Riserva 1997.

Paolo came at the double but he was flummoxed. He didn't say it, but the words 'how could you?' hung in the air. He called Alberto on his cellphone, waking him in the middle of the night in Australia. Once the maestro had grasped the problem he came up with what he said was the only possible answer: to expose the wine to air by leaving the bungs off, allowing the sulphites to dissipate. This was quite contradictory to the normal practice of preventing air coming into contact with the wine to avoid oxidisation. Crisis management *in extremis*, akin to staunching a wound by opening it to let the germs in.

Curtains closed around us. Black images swamped every moment: *Titanic* hitting the iceberg; Chernobyl exploding; Mussolini – or was it me? – being strung up from a lamp-post. I talked to the wine, saying sorry, sorry, *mea culpa, mea maxima culpa*. That was before I was led away and banned from the *cantina*. Over the following weeks we beat a track to the laboratory with samples we treated as carefully as if we were taking gold to be assayed. The wine was in intensive care and we were nursing a critically ill loved one back to health.

How had we done? Frustratingly, it would be months before we could expect any true indication. When Alberto came to inspect us shortly after Christmas he dipped the long glass pipette known as *il ladro* (the thief) into a bunghole to draw a sample. He squirted it into a glass. He sniffed. He tasted. And the smile on his face said everything.

30

A Banned Substance

It is just before the burping stage that supermarkets mysteriously run out of sugar in wine-growing areas. But it is a mystery only to tourists and city-dwellers, as we had been until then.

The principal method of increasing a wine's alcoholic strength is to add sugar, a process known as *chaptalisation* after Napoleon's minister of agriculture who gave it the go-ahead almost two centuries ago. It is purely natural and there is nothing dishonest about it: wines are sweetened during fermentation but are not made to taste sweet as the sugar is completely fermented. The sole purpose is to improve the quality of the wine, which is why its use is common in some of the best wineries in Bordeaux and Burgundy. However, while the level of 12 per cent decreed for Chianti Classico was higher than French wines, this route was not open to us. The EU banned it in warm southerly parts of Europe while permitting it in the coldest, most northerly regions, and condoning it in moderate zones such as France. Also, in order to boost the flagging fortunes of grape-growers in Italy's impoverished south, where over-strength wines of up to a hefty 16 per cent alcohol content were common, the government was promoting the use of their must concentrates as an alternative to sugar. The trouble was that it involved yet more paperwork, careful calculation and precise timing. At least 24 hours in advance you had to send a telegram to the Fraud Squad, the 'Ripressioni Frodi', informing them of time, date and place of the operation, thereby inviting them to poke their noses into your business. Finally, there was the cost to consider: sugar was far cheaper.

But how much sugar? We were told you need only 17 to 19 grammes of sugar to raise the level of alcohol of one litre of wine by one degree. This doesn't sound much until you multiply it by 10,000 litres and get 170 or 190 *kilos* which is what we would need if we ever had to doctor just one of our tanks. To prevent people doing that the Guardia di Finanza insisted that anyone buying more than 30 kilos of sugar must have a *bollo* – that transportation docket that can be inspected, together with the contents of your vehicle, at any snap roadside checkpoint they care to establish. Which is why most canny souls started hoarding sugar as soon as the harvest was over, in preparation for the following year, and did not leave it imprudently to the last minute as a friend of ours did in his debut harvest.

Well, about this German friend. Realising that his load of fermenting wine – all 30,000 litres of it – was falling short of the magic figure, he panicked. It was a Saturday afternoon and having made his calculations he launched himself on a mission to find 500 kilos – that's half a metric tonne – of sugar in as short a time as possible. Fermentation was already well advanced, so it was going to be a race against the clock. But everywhere he looked, the shelves were bare.

He was driving his old Audi, hoping his German number

plates would minimise the risk of ambush by the Finanza. Clearly, he had to avoid his local Co-op and his local Consorzio Agrario where he was well known. So, in ever-widening circles, he spiralled his way through Tuscany, passing all the famous cultural sites, sweating, cursing the tourists in his way, desperately seeking sugar. Alas, everywhere he looked the shelves were bare, stripped but for a few broken packets in what had evidently been a wave of panic buying.

Light was fading, finally, when he found himself in Poggibonsi at a discount store his company had done business with in the past. And yes, they could help him; would he care to bring his car round the back?

Only then did it dawn on him to ask himself what half a metric tonne would look like. It was nearly the combined weight of half an oompah band. He managed to load 300 single kilo bags into the boot and onto the floor behind the front seats before deciding any more could harm the car's suspension, then he paid in cash and said he would be back on Monday for the next load.

Skulking home in the dark, the car was so overloaded it was barely driveable. He kept imagining Guardia di Finanza officers behind every tree, a roadblock at every junction. Worse, his route took him through a village whose entire population was lining the main floodlit street to watch a veteran car rally that was about to start. The crowds pressed against the sides of the Audi as he was forced to slow. Hundreds of curious eyes bored in as he dropped to walking pace, horribly aware that the familiar red, white and blue packets that were showing from beneath the rug he had casually flung across the back were blatantly obvious. 'Ah! A foreigner!' someone shouted. And the cry was taken up along the line of bystanders. He lowered his window and just smiled and nodded and saluted as the Red Sea parted and he was allowed to proceed.

Two days later, worried about how much longer he could remain incognito, he went back to the supermarket and loaded up with the remaining 200 kilos. Only this time the operation was not so clandestine: it involved passing the checkout seven times with his loaded trolley, for the store manager was present and insisted the 30 kilo rule had to be obeyed. There was some confusion as the cash register was rung up seven times for a total of 290,000 lire (£103), with other shoppers in line behind him threatening to make a scene, so it was hardly surprising that by the time he left he felt the stirrings of fermentation himself.

Back at the farm he and his farmhand locked themselves in the winery with all the sugar and performed the operation, running the pumps and mixing 500 separate packets as fast as they could. All the time he was dreading hearing a knock and finding the Fraud Squad, come to pay their respects – or inquisitive punters come to buy some wine; but all went well. Except that then it was a question of getting rid of the evidence, all 500 red, white and blue 1 kilo paper sacks that were marked SUGAR in big black letters. His helper was all for burning them, but it was a windy day and he feared the charred pieces would flutter off like black parchment crows with the dreaded S-word still visible, only to land in the vegetable patch of the local constable. He packed them into bin bags and set off on his rounds of Tuscany once again, depositing them in strategically chosen dumpsters in three separate municipalities.

The phone was ringing when he got back. The supermarket! The astute checkout girl had found his number, had recognised him even and remembered his company's name from previous transactions. She said her register was 'out' by 45,000 lire, which happened to be the price of 30 kilos of sugar. Could he possibly have made a mistake?

Mortified to have been identified so easily and not a little worried about the consequences if he said no, he knew better than to make a fuss. 'I'll be right there tomorrow with the money,' he said, thinking £20-odd a small price to pay for peace of mind – even if the store was wrong.

But when he went back to Poggibonsi as promised, he found the problem resolved. Another client had admitted owing them the money, for a pile of sugar he had bought 'for his wife's jam-making'.

31

The Earth Moves

By the spring of 1998 Alberto felt confident enough to take some samples of our wine to Vinitaly, the big wine show that is held every year in Verona. It regularly attracts over 4,000 exhibitors and is considered a crossroads for the trade, of crucial importance to producers and professionals from all corners of the business. Up against this, what chance did we have with our little bottles that bore handwritten labels like home-made jam? According to our man, they 'stole the show'.

Two American visitors who had tasted our precocious efforts were particularly impressed, to the extent that they left Verona prematurely and came straight to see us at the farm. 'We tasted every Chianti Classico in the show till our tongues and teeth turned black but to our palates there's nothing to touch Collelungo. This is going to be BIG!' they said.

We were chuffed that they were being so fulsome and open in their praise, having become used to people playing their cards close to their chests. Not only that, they were actually prepared to pay us in advance for as much wine as we could promise them. Soon afterwards our Greek-Cypriot friend Stak introduced us to his British importer, Roy Richards, who said he was looking for a new Chianti Classico and to our further relief *he* was willing to pay in advance too. We were not the only ones amazed; this was almost unheard of in the business – and twice in one go, as it were. Our luck held and a Japanese importer arrived on the coat-tails of the Americans, so it wasn't long before our first year's production was sold out.

We were talking to Jon, our London advertising friend, about a design for our label and he had come up with some elegant ideas. The Americans wondered if we should also have a name for the wine, apart from Collelungo, and we were tossing a few ideas around in the winery when one said: 'We are taking seven barrels. The magnificent seven! Doesn't *sette* mean seven and *bello* beautiful or magnificent?' We had to agree he was on the right track. 'Then let's call it Settebello!'

'Fine,' I said, 'but I think you'll find the name's already taken.' It was a brand name for condoms. We agreed to stick to 'Collelungo'.

By chance, one of our guests at that precise moment was a boyhood friend from Manchester, Mike Ajello, whom I hadn't seen for over 40 years. Mike was a patent lawyer and volunteered to register the name with the European Union, as well as 'Roveto' which we later invented for a grand cru. A short while later another guest, Randolph Schum, revealed himself to be an attorney from Illinois and expressed himself willing to file the trademarks in Washington for us.

With all those advance payments even I began to feel more confident about our decision to make wine, though the need to 'rejuvenate' the vineyards still filled me with dread. With Alberto we had agreed on a cautious winemaking approach, making only

Chianti Classico (and its Riserva), at least at the start, leaving the question of a Super Tuscan for consideration in the future. That way, as new boys on the block, we were able to count on the support of the Chianti Classico consortium which was to give us invaluable help. But our weakening grapes still had the Ricasoli ratio of white-to-red and also included some of inferior quality that we did not want in any wine bearing our name. Even I could see that this was not a good idea.

The trick in the short term was to select the best of the crop for the prestige wines and vinify the rest separately for sale within a few months to get cash-flow. The price of grapes had doubled again, and consequently so had the wholesale market for bulk wine. We sold 20,000 litres in the spring this way to a local producer to blend in with his own wines for a large order from Marks & Spencer. (It went without saying, I had to take our transportation documents to be completed in quintuplicate in front of Antonio the *vigile* whenever we shifted our produce, in fruit or liquid form.) I was amused that it was going into Britain's high streets and wondered what any M&S consumer might think, knowing a fellow Brit had toiled in the Tuscan sun to help bring this elixir to their table.

But the long term was what counted and only now could we contemplate the kind of spending we knew was coming if we were to programme the replanting. Anything 'incoming' was soon 'outgoing' though. With every cheque I wrote I could see my dreams of moving to a proper home of our own being pushed even further back (we were still in our bunker).

We sat down with Alberto and asked him to explain, in words of as few syllables as possible, what it was exactly we had to do.

Well, he said, our vines were getting tired, suffering from neglect and exploitation to the point that they were drained of all they could give. We had inherited a typical sharecroppers' mishmash, planted according to the old Ricasoli formula with little attention to clonal selection, rootstock, vine density or site suitability – big words we were hearing for the first time. Exposure was important for the maximum concentration of sunlight so the grapes could ripen well. (Great; luckily all our fields were south-facing.) Drainage was vital so that the roots would not become waterlogged. (Fine; we had rocks and shale coming out of our ears.) Density came next in importance as the goal was a smaller, more concentrated crop from the most suitable clones of Sangiovese; instead of 2,500 plants per hectare, which was traditional, we should go to 5,000 (6,000 would have been ideal but our land was so steep and stony it would have led to other problems). The object was to make them struggle more to get their nourishment and give the fruit more complexity. It would also lengthen their lives.

When a guest at Collelungo looks out on a vineyard from their bedroom window he or she sees predictable, familiar details of vines, grapes, with a scattering of poppies in spring, blue cornflowers or yellow and white daisies, plus a whole lot of rocks. We see a more primitive picture. Our X-ray eyes bore into the soil and see plates of solid rock lying just beneath the surface and recall how much effort goes into preparing the land before you can even think of planting anything in it. We engaged the services of a wizard with a power shovel, Valerio Valeri, and his father who drove an old bulldozer that pumped out evil black fumes from a smokestack borrowed from the *African Queen*. And this is how we started. Together we made the earth move.

Mira, whose gardening experience with window boxes had clearly given her a head-start, immediately identified with Alberto's philosophy that we had to make the vines work hard in order to get more concentrated extracts from the grapes. 'Ah, you mean treat 'em mean and keep 'em keen?' she said. (It is one of her favourite expressions and she knows it works when applied to me.) Just then we had an eminent Israeli agronomist who specialised in strawberry production staying with us. He took one look at the fertiliser we had ordered for the rest of the vineyards and asked in amazement: 'Is this all you're going to use this year?' When I said yes, he said: 'But Tony, this is hardly enough. Don't you want big, fat, juicy grapes?' I said no, I wanted small, rich ones because it was the skins that give the wine its character. Even I had learned the lesson that less, but richer, juice was better.

We needed at least 80–90 centimetres of broken earth so that any new rootlings could get established before burrowing down to bedrock in search of moisture. Simple, we thought, until the quarrying began. Valerio and Dad set to with a will and imme- diately we heard a noise such as a ship might make when hitting a jetty – a bang followed by a kind of primal groaning as the powerful Fiat-Hitachi shovel tore into tectonic plate, up-ending a giant piece of limestone the size of a crofter's cottage. Block after block surrendered to father and son but not before a mighty struggle that left the place looking like a war zone after only one day. The whitish rocks resisted like teeth refusing to be pulled, only to give way with such sudden release that the jib of the shovel would leap up and risk the cabin toppling over. Where stubbornness prevailed Valerio had to swap the shovel attach- ment for a hammer, a long steel spike which he placed vertically and started *chacka-chacka-chak* percussion work until a fissure became a split and a chunk would break off. Then it was on to the next bit, his tracked vehicle climbing precipices and travers- ing canyons in the new, raw landscape of his making while Dad steamed along belching black diesel behind the big blade of the 'dozer, sweeping up behind.

We noticed much of the rock was coming out with surprisingly chiselled edges, as if mitred and cut like building blocks, and had asked Valerio to look out for any piece that could be suitable as a picnic rock placed strategically elsewhere. He called us excitedly one day: 'Come and see!' In the middle of the field he had found two blocks, which now stood upright, like sarsen stones at some medieval monument and so big their shadow threw our south-facing slope into darkness. The poor chap seemed crestfallen when we gently explained that it was not our intention to recreate Stonehenge in Tuscany and we would like them destroyed. He thought this would need dynamite – a terrible idea as a permit would take weeks to get – but managed the job after a great deal of trouble by probing for the friable rocks' weak point and cracking them steadily by dropping another block from a height, each time reducing the multiplying objects until they were small enough for Dad to move in.

It was not what one thinks of when imagining the lovely agricultural hills of Chianti. After a few weeks the pile of rocks had grown into a makeshift mountain, about 100 metres long, 5 metres high and 10 metres deep. After six months – the amount of time it took to rework the levels, build a retaining wall, lessen the angle of slope and plough in some basic fertiliser having taken soil samples to see how defective it was – the accumulated mass had achieved such spectacular proportions it was no doubt visible from outer space. It was only then that we could start trucking it away and think of the next stage: planting.

Alberto was mortified to discover that the vine nursery we had entrusted with our order for a whole new mass of rootlings of the specific Sangiovese clone that he wanted had sold them to a richer and more prestigious customer (not hard to find). It was symptomatic of that period when everyone was rushing to replant in the wake of the Super Tuscan revolution, and such is the way of business in Italy: someone had made an offer that someone else could not refuse; in short, we had been gazumped. Our phone was white-hot for days before Alberto traced a few one-year-old rootlings that met his exacting requirements tucked away in a refrigerator in Pisa (cryogenics at play: their tips had been capped with wax to halt growth). The deal was I had to rendezvous under cover of darkness with the new nursery's van driver, half-way along the superstrada, where the transfer of the booty would take place. There were more than 700 of them, sticks about a centimetre in diametre and a metre in length, bound together in hundreds and bundled in huge black bin bags with their roots sticking out like lengths of human hair. They just fitted in the Renault and I limped home, relieved but not a little worried that someone might mistake me for a bodysnatcher. But these were hardly enough – we estimated we needed about 6,000 – and we had to look further afield. In the end another friend of Alberto's came to our rescue with 3,000 more and we found a supplier in France willing to send a truckload of propagated cuttings. At least I was spared any more hush-hush work.

By now we had engaged the services of a professional team of farm managers called Tecnovite who had all the latest gear for planting. Valerio and Dad had left a canvas for them to work on that hardly showed any sign of their labours; to my despair it even looked worse than before with its stones, rocks and boulders and I could hardly see any soil. It was not an auspicious start, the more for the fact that we were now into June, rather than April which is the ideal month for planting. It had not rained in over a month and the sun beat down with blistering ferocity as the team set up sight-lines by theodolite to make sure the vines would run correctly up- and downhill. Once the correct angle was agreed their next trick was to fix a beacon on a tripod at the foot of the slope, transmitting a laser beam up the hill. At the top a tractor equipped with outrigger arms stretching 2.5 metres from left to right, the width between lines, pointed down-hill. Each extremity had laser receptors to focus on the beam's point of origin as the tractor moved towards the tripod, thereby ensuring the driver kept a perfectly straight line. If he wandered an alarm sounded, an agricultural version of the 'Pull up! Pull up!' pilots hear when flying too low.

All this hi-tech state-of-the-art stuff was fine, but what came next was even better. A trailer attached to the tractor was skil-fully designed with two steel wheels angled towards each other to form a V so that with forward motion any surface rocks that remained would be knocked out of the way as it passed. Behind the V was an axle to which a dibber, a long metal probe, was attached. This could be calibrated to plunge into the ground with every revolution and was set to make a hole every 80 centimetres. Into this a workman sitting with his back to the direction of travel would drop either a plant or a rootling that had been submerged in water for at least 24 hours prior to going in, then another pair of vertical wheels would propel the earth back to cover all evidence of the ensemble's passage. Unfortunately, while the hi-tech laser wizardry worked well the dibber was no match for the Collelungo challenge. The whole mechanical enterprise had to be abandoned and the job finished off by hand. Finally another tractor with a water bowser had to pass and deliver a litre of water by hose to each little baby in its new home.

That's how you plant a vineyard. Now all you have to do is stake up each plant with bamboo; spray gently to ward off disease and mildew; water when necessary and keep your fingers crossed that hare, boar and deer haven't noticed your activity. Then you put in posts 3 metres high buried 50 centimetres down every 5 metres on every line and string five rows of taut wire between them for the plants to train up. Next, when the plants start showing vigorous growth you have to pinch out all surplus greenery to leave only two branches (later reduced to one). And that's just the first year. You must also learn to cultivate patience and find new ways to keep the bank manager at arm's length, for the plain fact is that even if all goes well it will be four years before you can expect to see anything that resembles a reasonable crop and six years before you have any wine to sell.

32

Estate Bottled

LATER, after the 1998 harvest, we said goodbye to the Tecnovite team that had been doing our contract field work. We had learned much from them in two years. Now it was time to buy a tractor for ourselves, with an agricultural loan at 2 per cent interest, and to our great relief Anelio proved to be a proficient driver. We even acquired a small Toyota jeep and chose one with automatic transmission so Mira could feel confident driving it. However, I am happy to say even she baulked at spending money on a bottling plant in the new winery. Contrary to character she didn't want to learn any more new tricks and we had heard we could call on the services of a company that sent its truck – a mobile bottling unit – around all the Chianti farms. It was a neat idea, allowing you to call your wine estate bottled ('truck bottled' would hardly have the same cachet, I suppose). So that's what we did as Tecnovite prepared to harvest for us for their last time.

Until that moment I had never stopped to consider what a

bottle of wine consisted of, beyond the liquid inside it. Suddenly, there were a multitude of decisions facing us: the type of bottle – 400 grammes weight, 600 or more? Normal height or a centimetre taller? Green glass or brown? Should the cork be 45 millimetres long, 50 or more? Bleached white, natural or in-between? (Plastic or composite never entered the frame.) How about the capsule, its length, colour and quality? (Lead was outlawed but there were some pretty good imitations.) And finally the label: Jon's design was fine, but so much text was needed to meet EU, Italian and US government criteria that artistic liberty was severely compromised.

But such concerns were trivial compared with the problem now looming. Here we were, racing headlong to bring in another year's tonnage of grapes and we had nowhere to put them as the winery was already full! It had been another hot summer with hardly any rain. Picking was going to be a week or two ahead of normal, possibly just after the third week of September. We had to empty the vats and barrels and get bottling – and quick.

21 September, 1998. The truck was a normal, undistinguished vehicle when it rolled to a stop in front of the winery but in the time it took to press a few buttons it had undergone a transfor-mation. Steel legs shot out, panels appeared, platforms folded down, the sides collapsed and awnings went up. The whole body of the vehicle was exposed as a self-contained factory assembly line worthy of Charlie Chaplin in *Modern Times*: a relentless machine into which we poured our precious juice at the front and by some process of cogs, wheels, conveyor belts, corking plungers and other gadgets, fully finished bottles clinked out at the back. They lined up in position, chinking merrily and jostling like little soldiers on parade on a turntable from which they were whisked off by hand and stuck in cartons with our name on the side.

Jon came down from London for the occasion, having sent me precise instructions on how the printing should be done and even provided artwork at his expense. We were further fortunate in having the support of François Couturier, a stalwart French friend from Colorado who volunteered to stay on for six weeks and see us through the winemaking after harvest. Pier-Francesco, the son of our *agriturismo* chum Sylvie from Radda, came along to give us the benefit of his bottling experience. Another key player was Ada, the cook from our favourite restaurant Il Pestello, who was well into her seventies and drove the oldest Topolino we had ever seen. She measured 135 centimetres and was known to all as 'The Volcano' – whether because she worked the barbecue or worked so fast we couldn't tell, but after a full day's work with us she went off uncomplainingly to do a full night's work at the grill.

In all, we roped in a dozen-strong team to handle the operation, opening cartons, handing up empty bottles, handing down full ones, sealing the cartons with hot wax pistols, stacking the wine on palettes. Anelio, Franca and Fabiola were tireless at the core of this band of happy workers and fortunately we had more than a few recruits from among the guests – two of whom later told us they decided on the assembly line to get married. I'm not sure if that was after the 15,000th bottle that day or the 17,000th. We went at it from 8 a.m. to 7 p.m. with one break for lunch, a picnic under the oak trees which Mira and Fabiola prepared.

Bottles, corks, capsules, labels – plus cartons, palettes, sticks for the glue guns, appellation stickers that came too long and had to be cut down, and a supply of consortium logos showing a Black Rooster, an ancient image symbolising the peace reached between the two Tuscan republics of Florence and Siena. Everything had to be chosen carefully and ordered in advance to be ready for Bottling Day, then checked and re-checked to make sure there were no mistakes. Artwork had to be corrected. Printers had to be chased. The carton man had to be reminded we needed special inserts to separate the bottles, which were going into the boxes horizontally and not standing up. Samples of the wine to be bottled had to be tested and approved by the authorities. Mira had to organise the shopping for lunch as well as its preparation. Only then could we bottle our wine unfiltered, unfined, to Alberto's instructions, in order to capture our *terroir* to the full. (It's a funny word without easy explanation: the summation of elements particular to your own special spot on earth; the composition of land, soil, exposure to the elements.)

It is small wonder that we started to suffer from Pre-Bottling Tension and one day three years later this was to reach its peak during bottling when Mira took the Toyota over a cliff. It happened as she was returning to the truck for the now-traditional picnic. Her *pappa al pomodoro*, a hot Tuscan soup of tomatoes and basil, was already on the trestle table alongside a vast amount of hams and vegetable pies, salads, mountains of bread and fruit when she realised she had forgotten serving spoons. She rushed home in the jeep to get them but when she came back, in her anxiety she forgot something else too: the need to take an automatic gearbox from Drive to Park when stopping a car. The jeep went sailing over the edge of our bottling area, watched by myself and the entire team. It landed 4 metres below us, caught nose-down in the branches of a resilient young oak tree that acted as a safety net. We did not immediately realise that she had had the presence of mind to leap out (with the spoons) in the nick of time. So for the moment the shock felt by all was palpable: I know my own heart was in my mouth. Then she appeared, shaken but not stirred, and served lunch to the hushed, hungry and awed audience. We left the topic of conversation dangling for four hours, very much the off-road vehicle, while we finished the bottling. Then, by great good fortune our guardian angel Renato happened by and saw us struggling to tow it up over the jagged rocks. Like a monkey, he leaped down and sawed the tree, so freeing the wreck which we lowered gently to the ground and pulled out by tractor. The Toyota's engine started first time but we could see it needed surgery beyond a simple nose job to be put right.

Bottling the wine was one thing; we then had to ship it. When the time came to send our first consignment to the Wine Society in 1999 a haulage company in Dover contacted us to make sure all our paperwork was in order and said their lorry would be with us in three days' time. Fine – but a couple of hours before it was due we got a call from the driver telling us it was a TIR juggernaut, totally unsuited to travel on our bumpy, potholed and narrow country lane, so in a panic we made rapid alternative arrangements. In relays, using the Renault, Fabiola's car and the tractor (these were pre-Toyota days) we managed to get about 200 cases to the road menders' hut on the main road where there was an apron of tarmac large enough for it to park. Our truck was late arriving, however; I sat for three hours waiting for it on the mountain of white boxes, and in that time I think everyone we knew in Chianti must have passed by, waving and no doubt thinking 'Poor old Tony and Mira; they're having to flog their plonk by the roadside in order to survive.'

I could have withstood all that. What I couldn't stand was the awful stench coming from the side of the hut where it seemed someone had mysteriously dumped a pile of pig dung or some other evil-smelling substance that was threatening to make Jon's labels curl off the bottles. I felt nauseous. So much for *terroir*; I was terror-struck. If that disgusting odour could penetrate the cartons and interfere with the perception of hints of liquorice, black cherry, vanilla, raspberry and blackcurrant we hoped consumers would be able to detect within, we were sunk.

That very day, thousands of miles away across the Atlantic, the famous American wine expert Robert Parker Jnr was uncorking a bottle of Collelungo's best effort. He poured. He swirled. He sniffed. He tasted, made the usual strange noises wine gurus are wont to do, and he spat. Our newly appointed wine importer who had managed to introduce the 1997 Riserva to the great man sat across the table, immobile, afraid to speak. How was the wine? All our hopes of selling to North American customers were riding on his judgment, for 'Parker' has attained deific status among US consumers. In the business it is well known that his tastes and opinion can make or break any winery, young or old. *Well, how was it?* Steven Berardi asked. Mr Parker would not tell. It would be months before we were to get an answer. The suspense was like waiting for exam results.

Hedging our bets, we decided we had to make plans for an export programme anyway, given the amount of bureaucracy involved and the time things take in Italy. In anticipation of our assault on America I had to visit old Antonio, the *vigile*, again in his castle cell and present our very first samples in order to forward them to a laboratory for a permit that said our wines were safe to export to the USA and Japan. This seemed a little excessive as the very same lab had already been to us and picked up samples for the Chamber of Commerce to approve it for bottling and release for local and European consumption. My hands shook as I passed over our precious nectar together with a sheaf of paperwork. Antonio proceeded to the window sill of his stone cubicle and to my astonishment I saw him light a Bunsen burner on its lip, melt a stick of red sealing wax and drizzle it over our wine until it had completely covered the corks of our three sample bottles. Before the wax could set he tied a string around their necks and added a little lead seal like a medal. That done, he brought out a fountain pen and recorded the momentous event in meticulous caligraphy in three separate registers that each had to be rubber-stamped three times. The ritual seemed medieval, a kind of benediction, and left a big impression on me – but to him it was as mundane as making a cup of coffee.

I hurried home that evening because we had a big event planned: it was time to thank our loyal band of friends for their help with the *vendemmia* and the bottling work. A traditional *dopo-vendemmia* dinner was in order and with all that it entailed we had engaged the oldest trattoria in the village, La Torre, to help with the catering. It was some banquet. For antipasti we had a selection of *crostini* (bread topped with liver, artichokes, tomatoes or mushrooms) and *sformatini* (soufflé-style vegetables and herbs), polenta fritters and cold cuts including wild boar sausage. Next there was a selection of three pastas topped with either a wild boar ragout, *porcini* mushrooms or hare sauce. The main course was *bistecca alla fiorentina*, roast pigeon and veal. *Pannacotta* (literally, cooked cream) followed, along with *Torta della Nonna* (a tart with pine nuts, to Grandma's recipe) and of course, *gelato*. The wine flowed as the stories of the harvest, Francesco and his snails, the snakes, the sulphite crisis and all the old favourites were passed around the table and they laughed good-naturedly at our Italian mistakes.

Over the years we pressed on with the vine work, grubbing up old roots and replanting with Sangiovese stock of the right quality. As an experiment we tried grafting, turning existing white rootstock into red with a snick of the knife and a bandage to hold the graft together – a specialised technique very few people have the skill to perform successfully, but we found Signor Cimati, an Alberto contact, more than adept. He must have been over 70 and thought nothing of driving 200 kilometres to us to work overnight and sleep in a cot we slung up in the winery. The job involved taking a cutting of a good Sangiovese branch when the moon was waning in winter, refrigerating it and grafting it onto the white vine in spring when the moon was waxing and the sap rising. Amazingly, it worked.

Gradually we were working our way through Alberto's regeneration programme at a rate of about 10 per cent per year. At the same time we were caring for the baby vines and managing the regular chores of spraying, ploughing and fertilising thanks to Anelio, with the aid of two other stalwart pensioners, Marino and Duilio, who had joined our little family. But suddenly, in the area where we had obtained permits to create a brand new plantation, we had a problem.

We had hired the services of Salvatore, a cheery southerner with a giant excavator – alarmingly, a Caterpillar – to clear an old olive grove which had not survived the great 1985 frost that killed 80 per cent of Tuscany's olive trees and had lain abandoned ever since. Alberto had spotted this piece of land and greatly surprised us by saying it would make a fantastic vineyard, possibly the ideal site where our Super Tuscan grapes could be cultivated. Just like our previous experience with Valerio, it took Salvatore and a mate working another great digging behemoth months to get it anywhere near readiness for planting. It was another huge expense and worry.

Not unexpectedly, the permits were granted on condition that we removed the rocks we excavated rather than tip them on the property. Also, that we inform the forest police of the start of work and its likely completion date. Quite so, we said. Renato helped us find a contractor who was eager to take the rocks away for a riverside embankment job he was working on, further up the Arno valley. And Mira called the marshal of the forest rangers, who had already received a carton of wine from us as a Christmas present, to tell him of our intentions. 'OK', he said. 'Thank you for letting me know.'

Unlike the juggernaut with its delicate cargo of wine, the haulage contractor's huge trucks were designed to move rocks, so we had no worries about them crossing the property and down the unused track which led from the winery through the woods to the new field. This quickly became a road by default, but we were not unduly concerned as it was on our own land and when the work was finished we knew it would soon revert to its former condition as nature crept back. On the very last day of work, however, Salvatore called us in a panic on his mobile. 'The police are here and have ordered me to stop work. You'd better come quick,' he said.

Eight forest rangers, led by the marshal, were examining the track with tape measures and theodolites, taking photographs and filling pages of notes like detectives at a crime scene. Which it was, according to them: we were guilty of making an illegal road.

'But how else were we expected to get rid of the rocks?' we asked the marshal. 'We did as we were told and informed you of the work.'

'You needed a permit to make a road. You should have known. You have been denounced and there's nothing I can do about it now.'

Was it Mafalda again? We pondered on this for days.

We couldn't believe it when the rangers taped up the track with scene-of-crime tape, blocking both ends of a 500-metre length with makeshift barriers and notices saying KEEP OUT. They had confiscated this area of our land and a few days later we received a short note from the courts holding us responsible for this penal act.

It took over a year to unravel that one. We paid a large fine and our guilt was only mitigated by getting the chief of the local hunters, a buddy of our buddies Renato and Roberto, to sign an affidavit that there had always been a passage there in the first place. That cost us dearly; the quid pro quo meant we now had to be even nicer to the men with guns.

Cavolo!

33

Unfiltered, Unfined

❦

WE had been up and running for four years and the exigencies of Italian rural life were still causing us problems (not least of which was abiding by conflicting and curious rules – bedroom size, headroom, sanitary facilities, disabled access – set by four different authorities). However, we were pretending not to notice the often crackpot and dysfunctional system that kept the country going, and seemed to be muddling along quite nicely when suddenly a problem landed in our laps which we simply could not ignore. Alone among the 20 regions of Italy where *agriturismo* was by then flourishing, Tuscany had unilaterally decided – without any consultation of interested parties – that the activity was not regimented enough. It decided to impose a grading system on farms like ours, star-rating each *agriturismo* according to the quality of its facilities for the benefit of tourists. Nothing inherently wrong in that, we said, we're all in favour of consumer choice and anything to make life easier is to be welcomed. But the flaw in the plan was twofold: the grading was on a self-assessment basis, and the job of verification fell to – you guessed it – the local *vigile*, Antonio.

Poor Antonio! He was not a big fellow physically and I could see him floundering in a sea of paper and struggling to maintain his composure when I joined a line outside his office along with our rivals, friends and competitors to collect the self-assessment form. It ran to over 50 pages and contained hundreds of questions devised by some genius in the regional authority who, it soon became apparent, had never set foot on a farm in his life.

Instead of stars, we were to be awarded ears of wheat which had to be displayed in a ranking of one to five to symbolise degrees of rustic rectitude. The whole thing was like some nightmarish board game whereby points could be totted up in order to win an ear. But it was a game played with de-merits as well as merits. We gained one for having a swimming pool and two if guests were personally welcomed by the owner, but lost two for not accepting pets, for instance. (Accepting pets? On a farm? Was he joking? What about the possibility of our having our own dogs or poultry, nay child, that might be savaged by some touring Rottweiler?) What we needed to pull off the maximum, five-ear trick was a combination of trekking circuits (horse, bike or foot: score two for each); cookery courses for our guests; wine and olive-oil tastings; and diplomas proving our prowess in foreign languages (I was disqualified because English came naturally. Mira had never sat a language test.) Success was assured, though, if we had air conditioning, phones and minibars in all bedrooms.

It was about here that we lost the plot completely. *Agriturismo* was based on the concept of people staying on working farms, not dolled-up tourist attractions. We were supposed to generate more income from *agri* than *turismo* and in our case the business of making Chianti Classico kept us fully occupied. Who, then, was supposed to be looking after the vineyards and winery while all these delightfully desirable tutorials on wine, oil and food were going on? And besides, the real questions were not being addressed: did all the featured attractions actually work? Were the apartments clean, comfortable and well equipped? All this was quite beyond Antonio's remit and policing capability.

We massaged a few points, argued the toss here and there, and wound up with four ears to our credit. But it was a tense period and I still wonder if anyone has extracted any joy from the system or how long it will take for the ears to wither. As I write, no other region has adopted the grading system. No guarantees are offered the visitor, anywhere, that all the properties being offered under the name of *agriturismo* are up to scratch in terms of decorative order, comfort or functionality. Typically, a farmhouse may contain one apartment that was created in 1980, another from 1990 and a third from 2000. And don't you just know which one features in the brochure.

We were well into the swing of things on the tourism side, aided by the continuous rise of Tuscany as a star destination and the strong pound and dollar which meant visitors were getting really good value for money. We were further pushed along the road by some flattering articles, most notably a magnificent review of our guest accommodations by Michèle Shah in *Wine Spectator* magazine in America – our ideal target market.

Our road confiscation caused great merriment among the guests. Maybe they thought we would be led off in handcuffs at any moment; that would certainly have given them something to write home about, as well as a bit of extra housekeeping work.

We had a couple of VIPs staying with us at the time: one was the Governor General of one of the smaller Channel islands and the other a rather well-known QC – no, not John Mortimer

– who was most interested to hear of the taxi girl's murder in the village. 'I did a murder in Exeter once!' he boomed (and went on to explain to everyone's relief that he had been a stipendiary magistrate on the West Country circuit). This gentleman came with his wife and humidor containing a month's supply of fine cigars and entertained us every night with courtroom stories that grew more hilarious by the minute. We often had to break away reluctantly from our bar at around 10 p.m., knowing that the party of which he was the life and soul would probably go on past midnight – OK for everyone on holiday but not those who had to be up by 7 a.m. Our learned friend would even be abandoned by his wife soon after that, for she knew where things were leading. The poor man suffered from gout and could not walk far without the aid of a stick, and she confessed to us that she wondered sometimes how he managed to find his way back to their apartment in the dark unaided. Almost all the time.

One night when the moon was full and shining so brightly it seemed like daylight she awoke at 3 a.m. and discovered he had still not come home. Worried, she put on a dressing gown, went outside and started retracing her steps back towards the bar. Which is how she found her beloved barrister, flat on his back in a ditch, clutching a bottle of our best 1997 Chianti Classico and gazing fixedly at the moon. She decided to leave him there, he seemed so comfortable.

The only other celebrities who came to stay were musicians: the guitarist John Fillmore, the jazz vocalist Ann Hampton Callaway and a singer, introduced to us simply as Getta-san, who apparently was so well known in Tokyo that he was a legend in his own karaoke class, a bit of a Japanese Cliff Richard. We never heard Getta-san sing until after he'd left, having very kindly presented us with the latest CD of his work with his group, 'Dark Ducks'. They turned out to have a mellifluous style rather like an Oriental barber-shop quartet, singing songs like *Red Sails in the Sunset* in Japanese, and I was tempted to serenade our next Croquet party with their crooning but Mira talked me out of it; the culture shock could have been too much. It was more prudent to stick to the Three Tenors.

We had started a little system involving bread rolls which proved very popular. By now Fabiola had taken over from her mother and had become our housekeeper, an indispensable Girl Friday in the running of Collelungo. She lived near the village bakery and was happy to call in on her way to work at 8 a.m. to pick up orders that we asked guests to write in an exercise book by 8 p.m. the previous evening. We would then phone the order to her. On arrival in the morning she would place the rolls, fresh and warm, in a basket by the bread oven for collection.

The system worked without a hitch until we came up against a couple from Chicago who told us a sorry tale. They had completely misunderstood our method of working. Not realising we meant *our* bread oven, like the Germans at the Rain Festival before them they had wandered off into the village in search of 'the' bread oven – i.e. the bakery. The village was shut, it being 2.30 p.m. and siesta time, and they could not find the bakery but persisted despite not having a word of Italian between them. They knocked on the grain silo office door, where a puzzled English-speaking executive tried to give them directions they failed to understand. So he stuck them in his car and drove them to the bakery which, naturally, was also shut. These Yanks may be ingenuous but they certainly are persistent. After waiting about half an hour with nothing happening they were pleased to see a young man ride up on his Vespa, park it alongside the roll-down steel shutter at the front of the bakery and take out a key. They pounced.

'Where's the exercise book?' they asked the startled lad.

'What book?' he replied in good English.

'The one where we have to write our names down for rolls at Collelungo.'

'I know nothing about that,' he said. 'My dad's the baker and in 25 years I've never heard of such a thing, but maybe he's got some new system going. Would you like to come in?'

Which is how a tired baker and his wife, sitting watching *Wheel of Fortune* in their living room one afternoon, met a lovely couple of Midwesterners and were able to enlighten them a little about local customs.

The Whittakers' clients had a rental car per couple as part of their holiday package, and this led to some interesting moments. One elderly pair had already frightened me by returning to base only moments after leaving, on my reassurance that 'driving on the wrong side' was really a piece of cake and Italian drivers were not all as demonic as they seemed. They reappeared white-faced and jabbering about some Italian who came up behind them on our white road, flashing his lights and blaring his horn, 'trying to overtake!' He turned out to be the Hertz man, who had left his mobile phone in their car.

Having overcome their shock, the next day they collared me again and told me about the unusual rattle they kept hearing from the dashboard. I said something rude about rented cars and told them not to worry, but if it really bothered them they should take it up with Mr Hertz. They struggled on, but whenever I saw them they referred to this strange noise. In the end I promised to mention it to the agent when he came to pick up his car at the end of the rental. Which I did. His reaction was like mine. However, when I saw him the following week he was a changed man. Driving back to base he also heard this strange rattle coming from the air duct in front of the steering wheel.

By chance he was passing the Peugeot agency where the Hertz cars were garaged, and he pulled in. A mechanic lifted the bonnet, disconnected a couple of air hoses . . . and discovered a live snake trying to wriggle itself free of the dashboard grille. It was about a foot long, black, possibly a descendant of those themselves who descended from the skies. We assumed it must have crawled up a tyre in our parking area, found a cosy home in the wheel arch and then squeezed into the duct as the English couple moved off.

I won't say we had problems with our guests; there were no awkward customers and Mira and I quickly recognised the roles we were destined to play – she, the calm one, Sybil, always happy under stress and working the calculator; me, Basil, the one inclined to panic when left up-front and not working with spanner and screwdriver, drill and paintbrush. Very little could faze her, whereas to me each day the absence of a serious crisis seemed almost too good to be true. We were like the swan serenely crossing the lake: an observer would see only gliding movement and not the method of propulsion, the little webbed feet paddling furiously below.

We had two wedding parties, which were fun: the first couple, Californians looking like *Great Gatsby* characters, simply booked themselves a date at the register office in Florence and only told us about it the evening before the big day. We insisted everyone should join us for a small reception we sprang on them for their return. The second group was from the UK and was much more organised, consisting of around 20 friends from all over Britain. They booked the English church in Siena for their venue.

By the time we were into our third year as rustic hoteliers the notion of Tuscany as a top romantic destination had really taken off. In Castellina meanwhile life was changing. New *agriturismi*, new hotels, new restaurants and new shops had all opened, bringing an air of prosperity to the old place. The Internet had revolutionised our life too. Emails were occupying too much of my time, I thought, and I was becoming rather blasé about cyberspace when all of a sudden one day I opened our mailbox and read:

Dear Sirs,
I am hoping that you may help me in a SCHEME. What I mean is that I am planning on proposing to Christine taking my hand in marriage. This is a VERY HUGE step for me. This is both of our first time and hope our only time in marriage (if she accepts to marry me).

We are planning to travel to Venice for two days and I may want to ask her at that time, but I am afraid in loosing the ring in a gondola. I have in mind to possibly ask her then.

My second idea (this is where you come in) is to have you place the ring in a bottle of your magnificent wine. When we come to the final glass of wine, I will pour Christine the last of your grapes into her glass hoping the ring will fall into it.

Would you be willing to help me out? I look forward in your response.

Best regards,
Lorenzo

We replied, pointing out the negative aspects of the wine idea, namely – 1) our wine might have some sediment, being unfiltered and unfined, therefore the last dregs were hardly the thing fine dreams were made of; 2) more practically, we asked, have YOU tried to fit a ring into the neck of a bottle? It won't go, unless your bride-to-be is a Size Six disadvantaged person. Maybe a decanter might be a better bet . . .

Hello Tony and Mira,
Thank you for replying back so quickly.
   The decanter is a great idea. I will let you know from Venice what I shall do. In the mean time no matter which way I go purposing [*sic*] to Christine in Venice or Collelungo, it would be an honor for me in having you look for a decanter and having your 1997 Riserva Chianti Classico ready for us upon our arrival.
   I hope I am not burdening you too much. Thank you so much in making our stay a wonderful memory.
   Sincerely,
   Lorenzo

We bought Lorenzo his decanter along with a bouquet of flowers and sure enough, he popped the question. Only by now Lorenzo the Magnificent's love story had gone the rounds and Franca and Fabiola were not the only ones wondering what would happen once I had presented the wine to them on a silver salver. What would be his paramour's reaction? The question was resolved the next day when we and all the other guests saw her wearing a flashing diamond as evidence of the moment Christine said 'Yes'.

I am outside on a beautiful autumn day, inspecting the Toyota which has just come back from the bodyshop. The garage has done a marvellous job of the repairs, but the battery was disconnected for so long the radio has lost all its station pre-sets so I am having to retune it manually. Suddenly I hear an emotionally charged American voice, fragments of a scratchy commentary, coming through the mush of pop music and DJ chatter – a sound like Orson Welles reading H.G. Wells's *The War of the Worlds*, the radio play that caused panic in America in 1938 when Martians were thought to have landed in New Jersey. I retune again. Something about twin towers . . . plane crashes . . . New York and Washington under terrorist attack. How preposterous. How utterly outrageous. How dare they broadcast this kind of sensationalist junk?

On 11 September, 2001, we must have been hosting at least two dozen American guests, some British and some German (Lufthansa pilots, as it turned out). It was 3 p.m. Many of the visitors were by the pool when the news broke and made their way incredulously into the *salone* to follow the full horror on satellite TV. Others who were out on excursions came home happy and smiling only to find everyone openly weeping, and a bulletin board hastily constructed by yours truly on which I posted Associated Press and Reuters dispatches. One moment I shall never forget was when the phone rang as I was glued to our television – the second tower was collapsing before the eyes of the world – and I found myself talking to a girl in an office in midtown Manhattan, only a few blocks away. 'Please tell Mom and Pop I'm OK,' she cried as I heard the sirens coming down the phone before the line cut dead. I searched high and low for them but they were on a day trip to Florence. The awful business of telling our guests about Princess Diana had been nothing compared with the difficulty of the moment when they returned.

Like everyone, we were traumatised. The enormity of the tragedy would not go away but its emotional impact was only part of the problem; we had practical issues to face as well. Airlines were in chaos and guests were stuck, unable to fly home. Several were so worried about their safety they said they would prefer to stay in Italy anyway. There were cancellations and refunds to make for those left high and dry on the other side of the Atlantic, deprived of flights. We struck up a long conversation by email with many New Yorkers – notably a fireman and his family whose vacation we rolled over to the following year. Other stalwarts said they were coming anyway, once flights had resumed. It must have been hell, for they too thought they'd be safer in Italy.

For weeks, as the aftershock continued to reverberate our inbox piled up with emails from the most unexpected quarters, not always making grim reading. A retired judge wrote, postponing his holiday and telling us of the silver lining 9/11 had for the burghers of Baltimore. It had scuppered the plans of a local restaurateur for a diner called The Crash, with a DC-3 sticking out of the roof and guests obliged to enter through a foyer filled with faux wreckage. I supplied another moment of unintentional humour when I apologised to our guests for the poor quality of the TV picture they were getting on the satellite. 'A mouse ate the cable,' I announced with a shrug. 'Come on Tony, that was the story last year!' said the voice of Randy Schum from the back of the group. We installed a new dish.

Huge events such as September 11, a royal death or an earthquake shook our foundations both literally and metaphorically, but nothing could stop the momentum of the agricultural calendar and the fact that we were heading for harvest time once again. Life went on. The grapes were ripening, and would soon be ready for picking. It was a subdued occasion, all the same.

We were now dedicated to our new goal of winemaking, and our lives turned on Collelungo, shutting out anything that would distract us. What was happening beyond the little world of Chianti – in Siena, say, or Florence – was of distant interest. We had our grapes, wine and guests to look after and could not cope with anything that did not bear relevance to the job at hand. The bank business was still at an impasse.

Being so absorbed with navel-gazing we hardly noticed other fashions changing as in the world of telecoms, for instance. We first became aware of it during our rebuilding work, when we were startled by a ringing raincoat or toolkit. Often, Italian guests would arrive, leap out of their cars and instinctively reach for their phones while still in the car park. On one occasion four Neapolitans arrived and did just that, brandishing four different phones and heading off in different directions to see where they could get the best reception. I came back from the village one day in late summer when the vines were lush and fully grown and saw a man in swimming trunks in the middle of the vineyard happily chatting away, apparently to himself. Walking a few paces towards the house I heard another voice from the same general direction and saw a woman in a bikini, three lines of foliage down from the man, also on her '*telefonino*'. I still don't know whether it was a particularly good corner for GSM connections or a secret assignation. I'd like to think the latter, for we saw them holding hands by the pool two days later.

Our Italian guests provided continual entertainment. There was Dottore Siliquini from Turin who brought his guitar and a girlfriend, a charming girl with a skipping rope who made the floor shake. They presented us with a rosebush which is blooming gorgeously as I write, though sadly we understand their romance has perished. There was Signora Signorini from Empoli – 45 minutes down the road – who came to visit Siena for the Palio, bringing a male friend and a TV set which they watched from morning to night. There was Mario Rossi and a group of cyclists from Treviso, consuming tiramisu for breakfast and *prosecco* and grappa for most of the rest of the day and night. They explained in foghorn voices that where they came from it was so wet and misty in winter they were obliged to drink to keep the blood circulating.

Other guests? One Californian couple proudly wrote to us in advance to tell us they liked 'life in the slow lane' and 'just wanted to graze'. They hadn't been with us more than a few minutes before they went off to Portofino – a good five hours' round trip. When they left us they were planning a side excursion from Rome to Pompeii before flying back to the States. Probably taking in Venice as they went.

34

Lost Souls

As far as I know we never actually lost any of our customers but we came close. Various factors were to blame, not least the inventiveness of the Italian state railways which bestowed on Castellina a station which did not exist. In a masterstroke of initiative it featured the full name, Castellina in Chianti, in all its timetables and this came to haunt us like a true phantom when guests who could not face driving in Italy insisted on trying to reach us by ghost train. It was down to me to dissuade them, my word against that of the State. Alas, I said, the true station was 10 kilometres away with no connecting bus. Anyone wanting to come to Collelungo from there either had to thumb a lift for those 10 kilometres or hope the one taxi in the vicinity would turn up. And then what would they do, stuck in the countryside without their own wheels? For eating, we had no restaurant as each apartment had its own kitchen. At the very least they would need to shop for food. With the best will in the world, we had no spare time to help and although they could walk to the village from Collelungo in 40 minutes I could not guarantee the clemency of the weather nor moonlight to guide their way on night sorties. There weren't that many trains anyway and those that ran were not particularly useful. The Siena–Florence train made infrequent stops at Castellina *Scalo* – the name means 'halt'– and went round the houses to make the connection. The Bluebell Line probably sees more activity.

Some left behind the arrival maps that I sent to their homes. That didn't faze one couple who rented a late-model Mercedes in Rome and simply drove north, plotting their way by a satellite navigation system, delighted to have found Castellina in the computer program and genuinely surprised that Collelungo did not appear there as well. They seemed disappointed that they had to wind down their window in the village and ask the way for the last kilometre or two.

We were expecting one man, a professor from Vermont, who did not show up at the anticipated moment. A day passed without a call. Two days, and still no news. Because I had taken the booking I knew he was travelling alone and that his wife would be anxious, back home (people tend to tell you their life stories over the Internet). But what should I do? If I alerted her she might panic. If I called the US embassy or police what would I say? I decided to email her in the gentlest of terms so as not to cause alarm, asking if he had changed his mind or could have got his dates confused. No, no, she said, I should not concern myself. He was the independent type who marched to his own music and would definitely show up. This was reassuring, but he had only booked a four-night stay and now we were on Day Three of it. Mira and I were turning in for the night when our phone rang and our friend Mimma from the neighbouring farm asked: 'Are you expecting an American? I've just pulled one out of our ditch with the tractor.' Beguiled by some symphonic variation, the learned prof. had obviously been overwhelmed by Tuscany's charms and had been drifting about the Chianti countryside all this time, finally mistaking Mimma's turn-off for ours. In pitch darkness he had driven a kilometre and a half through vineyards, up and down gulleys and over rutted paths until his front wheels fell into a deep storm conduit next to her swimming pool and he had found his journey's end.

Two sisters from New York got the day wrong by 24 hours and won our vote as Calamity Janes. We wouldn't have minded so much if the day in question hadn't been New Year's Eve and we hadn't been expecting 14 at table for a special dinner Mira had taken a lot of trouble to plan. They phoned that morning from Rome, apologising for not arriving the previous night; they were jet-lagged, they said, and hadn't realised their overnight flight would land a calendar day later. They had missed a day with their bookings for Rome and Avis. I said OK, no problem. If they left straight away they should be with us within three hours; try to make it in daylight.

It was dark by 4.30 p.m. and there was still no sign of the ladies. At 5 the phone rang. 'We're lost,' said a metallic voice, the mobile connection breaking up badly. 'We think we're in Tuscany. We're at a crossroads with a sign saying Santa Maria to the left and Firenze to the right. Which way should we turn?' *Mamma Mia!* There are four columns of Santa Marias in the gazetteer. Eventually, three or four calls later, the pair made it to Collelungo.

It was 7 p.m. and I was happy to see their rented Ford sweep right up to the top of the steps in front of the office. They were in their early thirties and in excited nasal accents started to recount their adventures as I showed them their apartment, named after the Giraffe *contrada*. 'Save it for dinner!' I shouted as I left them to help with preparations for the feast. Ten minutes later all hell broke loose. There was such shrieking I thought someone was being murdered. Black water was spewing from the radiator in Giraffe's bedroom, had already covered its white flokati rug and was now creeping up the leg of the younger sister's jeans. In her panic the elder of the two had fled Giraffe in a white mink coat and nothing else, screaming for help and looking for me – and by mistake barged into Tortoise next door to the office, coming face-to-face with a startled guest at exactly the moment he exited the shower in his birthday suit. That accounted for the second shriek I'd heard.

'It just came off in my hand!' said the first sister, visibly shaken and pointing to the inlet valve on the radiator while holding out its screw cap for me to see. They had used the wrong control, trying to turn up the heat. The valve was about 9 centimetres above floor level, 5 of which were now awash and I was on my hands and knees for a fair while before I could get the screw aligned correctly against the force of the jet to stem the incoming flow. Happy New Year! More fun followed as we started our emergency clean-up. The second sister came perilously close to running their car down the steps as she tried to put it away for the night. Not being accustomed to manual transmission she had trouble engaging reverse gear and kept slipping forward on the 45-degree slope.

We decided we'd had enough of winter visitors. Thereafter we would open from Easter until the start of November, and even then our primary concern was to keep guests warm at the start and end of each season. For fuel we had to rely on a 2,000-litre liquid-petroleum gas tank that would have needed replenishing once a week at a cost of £1,000 a pop had we left the central-heating boiler on all the time. Most guests understood: at home they too turned off the heating after midnight and during the warmest hours of the day. For extra comfort we put halogen space heaters in all the apartments, which were kept beautifully cool in summer by the same thick stone walls that now made them terribly difficult to heat. Besides, each one had its own fireplace or parlour stove and we encouraged guests to practise the techniques of fire-building they had no doubt last used when they were Scouts and Guides. It was so romantic, we said, and most guests agreed. Those who didn't included a crotchety oncologist from Florida who almost set fire to the property by leaving all four gas burners turned up, full-flame, on his cooker with nothing (such as a pan of boiling water) separating them from the wooden hood above. Trying to generate more heat, no doubt to bring it up to Miami standards.

I must include an Australian visitor, Stan Dumbrell, in this last category too. While Stan proved the perfect guest and would not dream of pyromania, he and his wife were forever remarking on how cold it could be in April. They swaddled themselves in extra clothes, lit their stove, lit their halogen heater, lit the extra gas heater we pressed on them, switched on their electric blankets and settled in resignedly like Arctic explorers for a month's stay in an apartment called Forest. All was redeemed when they awoke one morning and saw snow, for the very first time in their lives. The expression on their faces was priceless.

One man's ceiling is another man's floor. We once had a bunch of Canadians, supposedly hearty people used to tundra conditions, who walked out on us after doing the gas-cooker trick (complete with oven accompaniment). I was heartened when I realised that the people telling me about their moonlight flit – their next-door neighbours, again an Australian couple – were barefoot and wearing kit that would have been suitable for Bondi Beach.

And apart from our residents we had visiting outsiders to

contend with. Articles were appearing all over the world, vaunt-
ing the joys of Tuscany and encouraging tourists to turn up at
country farmhouses for a free tasting and a tour of the winery.
The implication was that if they followed the Black Rooster sign
they would be welcomed with open arms at any time of day; it
was free entertainment and the smart thing to do. Unfortunately,
it did not work that way for us. Although we wanted to be
friendly and sell wine there was no way we could afford the
time – and after a few tries we had to give up. It was frustrat-
ing, spending time with Americans who liked to chat and asked,
when the moment of truth came, 'Is your wine available in the
United States?' When we proudly said 'Yessir!!' the answer was
invariably, 'Great! We'll be sure to look out for it then. No need
to buy it here!' An Englishman took the biscuit (along with the
crackers we supplied for the tasting) when he said: 'I like your
wine very much and I have a proposition for you.'

'Yes?' said Mira, always open to a deal.

'I have a lovely bottle of Californian wine here,' he said,
reaching into his rucksack and bringing out a well-travelled
Cabernet. 'How about doing a swap?'

Mira declined, but for days afterwards kept saying she wished
she'd thought to ask him for a tasting of his wine before saying
no.

Basically, we sold wine but couldn't offer tastings. Instead,
we suggested passers-by should try our wine at the local restaurants and then come back for their supplies. One rainy afternoon two cars stopped in front of the office and about eight
Israelis descended. Mira headed them off at the door, where a
bizarre bit of dialogue ensued. A man spoke to Mira in English,
saying they had come for a winery tour. Mira replied diplomatically: 'I'm so sorry, during August we are short of staff and
we have cancelled our winery tours.'

From the back, his wife shouted in Hebrew: 'What did she say?'

'She said she has no staff available for a tour.'

'Then ask her if we can taste some wine!' said the woman.

He repeated the question in English for Mira's benefit, little knowing that she spoke fluent Hebrew.

'I'm so sorry,' said Mira, 'because we are so short of staff we have also cancelled the wine tastings.'

'What did she say?' shouted the woman in Hebrew.

'They've also cancelled the wine tastings.'

'Then ask her if we can buy a bottle.'

He repeated the question in English and Mira told him the price would be 14,000 lire.

'What did she say?' shouted the woman in Hebrew.

'What did *she* say?' I asked Mira in English.

The man told his wife the price of the wine, which caused an intake of breath. Then, to show that we were not in the presence of amateurs, she said to her husband: 'Ask her, does it have the chicken on it?'

At this point their teenage son, who had been following the drama, turned to her and said in Hebrew: 'Ma, they all have the chicken on it here.'

They said they would prefer to taste it in a restaurant after all, so it was back to life as usual, dealing with emails, making bookings, drawing maps for people, answering tourism questions, running to the post office (we had no deliveries) and making sure Mira was all right with her own problems and chores.

We had no hard and fast rules but our division of labour was quite remarkably calibrated and self-levelling. We had come to realise that the years we had spent working together in such close proximity had brought about the kind of profound relationship few couples could hope to achieve no matter how mature their marriage. We were appreciative of each other's strengths while recognising their weaknesses. Fortunately, it seemed that these were complementary in a roundabout way and we could laugh at it as long as we didn't look down from the high wire we were treading. She, the former travel agent, left everything to do with bookings and dealing face-to-face with customers (which she was good at) to me, who had nowhere near the same kind of patience or way with people but did enjoy writing and working the computer. In truth I would have preferred to be out driving the tractor and having fun with Anelio, but she was Earth Mother who had bagged the wine portfolio after my disastrous flirtation with sulphites. She was a kibbutznik *manquée* anyway, and given half a chance she'd be in the tractor seat when she wasn't with Manuela and the grapes or (mercifully) dealing with the books and Italian problems and other such time-consuming jobs. There were agricultural matters, gardening, staff business, bureaucracy, financial affairs, consultants, salesmen and all manner of other paperwork to deal with.

For my part I had an undercurrent of unscheduled work constantly demanding my attention too. The questions, from virtual customers on the computer and real ones ambushing me wherever I happened to be, meant my day was never short on humour or surprise. 'Hey Tony, we see all these signs for Pee-No-Kio everywhere. What is it?' asked a lady from California. And I had to explain that Pinocchio was a puppet, the creation of a Tuscan writer who took the name of his village, Collodi, and was as familiar to Italians as Mark Twain is to Americans. And I've already told you about the emails. One fellow even wrote asking: 'We're planning to cross into Italy from France. Will we have any problems? Do they drive on the same side of the road?' This time I cast both caution and client to the wind. 'No problem,' I replied, 'unless you plan to cross the Alps barefoot at night using the contraband trails. Yes, they drive the same way: straight down the middle.' You see what I mean about my great way with people?

When I could get away from emails I turned into Collelungo Repair Man, our very own Caped Crusader running around lighting fires for people, bleeding radiators, purging air from the boiler system, replacing dead light bulbs, repairing flyscreens that jumped their tracks and chasing the odd lizard that had scared the daylights out of people by getting into their apartments. When well-meaning guests told me I should organise my days better I simply nodded and agreed, not wanting to disillusion them.

Ah, indeed *la dolce vita*! I returned to my chores. The best part was fixing the 17 toilet seats that took turns to work their way loose or come adrift or break with mystifying frequency. One week I lost three in a row (not literally, you understand). Hardly had I repaired No. 3 when a couple of new guests turned up early and wanted to settle in. Hubby was USN (Retd.) but clung to his rank of Rear Admiral and must have tipped the scales at an equally elevated level: his deadweight tonnage was more battleship than destroyer. The seat gave way the moment he put his intimidating posterior on it and I was out the door again on Operation Loo Quest, targeting Tutto Mercato in Poggibonsi and in particular Umberto, who could usually be relied on in such moments of crisis. It was quite incomprehensible; I lost count of the number of seats I had to attend to in any one season and wondered what it was that made our lavs so vulnerable. Why had we been so singularly cursed in this way? Then some French guests arrived and in conversation I discovered they themselves happened to be in the hotel business. I found the right moment and mentioned it casually, as one does, kindred spirits and all. 'Oh, we had the same problem,' said Alain with a shrug. 'I was fed up with it too but got rid of it long ago.'

'Yes?' I said. 'Help, tell me what you did.'

'It was simple. I took out the seats and now people have to make do with, how do you say it, the porcelain?'

More than one guest asked if the property had been in the family a long time, I suspect rather hoping to be able to write home about being billeted with aristocracy, and this gave rise to mischievous thoughts about a coat of arms. As a sales aid it would certainly help and would not be difficult to procure: in the back streets of Naples there are purveyors of crests, escutcheons and heraldic devices of dubious origin who'll make one up for you faster than you can say '*Torna Sorrento*'. I could even see it in my mind's eye, complete with the motto *Nulla Tenente* – a pretty armorial bearing with crossed spanner and screwdriver, a bunch of grapes and toilet lids rampant (three in a row). Now that's what I call a family seat.

35

A Dazzling Chianti

WE had to wait two years from that first bottling to hear what
Robert Parker had to say about our wine, and when he handed
down his tablets from the mountaintop we were ecstatic. The
Press had been hailing 1997 as 'the vintage of the century'
for Chianti Classico. Mr Parker agreed, describing our wine
as:

> A thrilling new discovery . . . something that could easily
> pass for a fine *premier cru* Volnay. Extraordinarily well-
> delineated, full-bodied, and layered, with a sensationally
> deep mid-palate and a gorgeously proportioned finish. A
> dazzling Chianti. Impressive!

On Parker's rating system of points out of 100, I quote,

> 90-100 is equivalent to an A and is given only for outstand-
> ing or special effort. There are very few wines that actually

make it into this top category because there are not many great wines.

Our Riserva (the one I'd ruined) scored 93. Our regular 1997 Chianti Classico scored 87 – 'equivalent to a B in school and such a wine, particularly in the 85–89 range, is very, very good'.

Soon afterwards in England, *Decanter* magazine ran an article which began:

'Englishman buys abandoned farm in Chianti': not exactly a stop-Press headline. After all, foreigners have been buying up property in Tuscany ever since those who had to try to make a living from the land left in droves during the late 1960s and early 1970s. And many of the new residents have been tempted to have a bash at winemaking.

Read 'Foreign owner breaks 90-point barrier in Parker with first vintage,' however, and you're bound to sit up and take notice. It is remarkable to see how many of the buzz wines of the moment in Chianti are made on estates owned by non-Italians. And it is even more remarkable how quickly many of the latest generation of immigrés-owners have made it to the top. Perhaps most remarkable of all, though, is that many of today's high flyers arrived in Tuscany with no intention of making wine.

It was great PR, but worrying nonetheless: Benito and our lawyer had told us to keep a low profile because of the Monte dei Paschi threat which was still hanging over us. (It was because of this that we had to turn down a TV company's approach to feature in a documentary.) However, this was diametrically at odds with our desire to promote the product. And once the wine became available we found ourselves passengers on a roller-coaster of publicity which was far beyond control. As word got out that Alberto had created a new star the accolades started coming from all sorts of unexpected corners. A Grand Prix d'Honneur from the Hamburg Wine Salon. Two silver awards from the Mundus Vini wine show, also in Germany. '*Coup de coeur*' ranking twice in *In Vino Veritas* magazine (Belgium). Special mention twice in *Falstaff* (Austria) and once in *Capital* (Germany). Voted second-top Italian wine by Le Grand Jury Européen (beaten by a Barolo) in Las Vegas. Selected amongst the top 100 wines of the world by German sommeliers in *Der Feinschmecker*. And finally, in 2002, *Decanter* awarded us five stars, top ranking, and Parker again gave us 93 points. *Harpers*, *Alles Über Wein* and *A la Carte* also chimed in with nice mentions.

The big American guns set their sights on us. We went to top position in *Wine Spectator* more than once, scoring 88 and 90 points out of 100 in a blind tasting, and James Suckling, European Editor, reported: 'Clever wine-making here. A new producer to watch.' The *Wall Street Journal* even included us in seven top Chianti Classicos it placed on its 'Dow Jones Chianti Index', describing our 1998 vintage as: 'Fruity and fun, with big, plummy tastes.' We had our share of attention from Fleet Street: Joanna Simon in *The Sunday Times* ('top-notch'), Anthony Rose in the *Independent* ('a characterful beauty'), and Jancis Robinson in the *Financial Times* ('excellent'). When the two Italian wine bibles, *Gambero Rosso* and *Veronelli*, joined in the onslaught, I finally conceded. We were awash in a sea of purple prose for purple plonk. It was aristocratic, captivating, classy, creamy, dazzling, elegant, exuberant, outstanding, powerful, silky, spicy, succulent, subtle, sumptuous, toasty and voluptuous. It was redolent with hints of bitter chocolate, kirsch, oak, plum, raspberry and resin.

We only had one word for that. *Cavolo!*

All of this was very gratifying of course, but it was even more warming to see how our new friends and guests were beating the drum for us on both sides of the Atlantic. Our US lawyer, Randy Schum, and his wife Buffy even went to the length of organising professional tastings for us and sent us regular reports of how Collelungo sales were doing at Sam's of Chicago, a hugely important retailer.

It was an agreeable distraction. But our bank worries were like a Sword of Damocles. Every few months we would hear that our case had been adjourned, for reasons of the judge wanting more evidence; the lawyers going on strike; the judges going on strike; 'our' judge resigning; the new judge needing to start all over again from the beginning; the August recess. And so it went.

When we read that five of the seven judges on the local court circuit had resigned, for reasons unspecified, and the backlog of cases was stretching 10 years we really did despair. Every so often we had asked our lawyer to come to an amicable resolution with the bank. He had worked relentlessly at it but his approaches were either left unanswered or rebuffed out of hand. Now it seemed a good moment for one last push to try again to bring matters to closure.

36

Bin Ends

❧❧

TWELVE years after we first set eyes on CO LE NGO we finally realised our dream. Over that period we had built the apartments; made the winery (and recently had to extend it); created new vineyards; replanted old vineyards; planted more than 50 cypresses along the approach road; acquired a tractor and attachments to include a stone crusher (Anelio's pride and joy); bought a jeep and even a second-hand fork-lift for the winery. Lastly, at considerable risk of incurring the wrath of the mayor, we had made a *Fondo Chiuso* and fenced in our 30 acres of cultivations. This gave Anelio more work: he had to patrol it constantly to repair the amazing number of breaches caused by tunnelling porcupines, wild boar, and hunters with pliers. The ring fence was only legally enforceable if it was unbroken and we knew not all hunters were as respectful of private property as our Castellina friends. The one thing missing in all this was the original object of our desires: a place of our own that we could call home.

Until that moment we had been living in the same apartment that Massimo had cobbled together for us, never doing much to it to make it more comfortable, always thinking we could be moving the following year. But with each new project and purchase the house plan lost its place in the list of priorities; the lessons from the Monte dei Paschi fiasco were very well learned and we were being ultra-cautious. Each phase had to be funded from cash-flow and profits: we literally ploughed everything back. Our own requirements were small, never having time to go out shopping nor feeling the need to wear smart clothes. Even the Renault had passed its 13th birthday.

Then, in spring 2001, the last Big Blu scaffolding came down to reveal a house that had emerged from the ruins of an old stone barn, standing by itself on the top of the hill. Our dream home was almost ready, but we had to move quickly because the season was in full swing. The old apartment needed painting and we had the decorators in, with four Texans booked to take up occupancy there within a week.

It was a happy moment. The old place looked massive without all our clutter, and we were touched that our guests Monte and Cathryn Bricker from Portland, Oregon, who had become old friends over the years, insisted on helping us move. Typical of their generosity, they even presented us with a painting which showed the Black Rooster of Chianti Classico in human form wearing a morning suit and waving a Collelungo label. We celebrated the move (and the ladies' birthdays) with a meal of quail and fresh salmon accompanied by a Sassicaia and Solaia (both 1997), kindly supplied by Monte.

Another landmark in the history of Collelungo came when Fabiola, our faithful friend, daughter of Franca but by then also a genuine part of our family, at last tied the knot with her school-days' sweetheart, Vito. Their engagement had lasted 10 years while they saved enough money to buy an apartment to live in, to furnish it and to have a grand wedding. It was a stylish affair; she looked like the princess she wanted to be for the day in a gown that cost five million lire (by then equivalent to £2,000). A lovely ceremony in a small private chapel was followed by the most moving reception we have ever attended. Anelio looked spiffing in his Sunday best and enjoyed dancing with the bride. It surprised us to see what a great dancer he was.

The Carabinieri never did get round to arresting The Pilferer for the murder of that taxi girl even if, indeed, he had ever been a suspect (we never did get to know the truth). Before they could make any move he surrendered himself to a far more proficient and inescapable force in circumstances that gave the local bar busybodies abundant scope for speculation.

One summer's night, a year after the body had been found in the tombs, he donned his crash helmet, fired up his fiercely powerful Motoguzzi motorbike (which he rode at weekends as a diversion from his pick-up) and came head to head with the Grim Reaper in the form of an Iveco truck on the winding road that leads to Massa Marittima.

Suicide or accident? The way the villagers told it, the man was travelling at a preposterous speed when he entered the tunnel on the state highway just after Costalpino. The tunnel was badly lit, in common with all Italian road tunnels. It went into a bend after a couple of hundred metres, so a lone biker on a two-lane road, travelling fast, would inevitably have leaned into the curve, thereby crossing the white line as he did so (assuming there was a white line; a risky hypothesis). That there was a 38-tonne lorry hauling a container of shoes to be flogged off cheaply in the Cascine market in Florence the next day, also crossing the same presumed white line at the same time in the opposite direction, was the stuff of destiny.

We felt sad about the poor old Pilferer. In the ongoing saga of everyday Tuscan folk the whole incident was perceived to be a small chapter, best forgotten for the sake of everyone's peace of mind. The murder remained an unsolved mystery, case closed.

Life in Clochemerle-in-Chianti has resumed its languorous, predictable routine. There are national public holidays: Epiphany, National Day, Liberation Day, Easter, *Ferragosto*, All Saints' Day and the Day of the Dead, one day later, when everyone saunters off to the graveyard with bunches of chrysanths that have miraculously doubled in price in the preceding days; as well as Christmas and New Year. We enjoy local holidays too as the seasons change, chief among which is our village's big showpiece celebration that draws visitors every August: a watermelon festival.

The theme is a mystery: watermelons aren't even grown in Castellina, but local mythology holds the *cocomero* to be as representative of our village as the Black Rooster. Doubly puzzling, there is never much watermelon in evidence; instead, suspicious-looking gypsies selling sweets, nougat and dried fruit vie all day to hasten our dental decay. The Piazza del Comune, venue for the evening's entertainment, rings to band music when we can elect Miss Watermelon, enjoy The Great Furbo's magic tricks and eat Chinese delicacies courtesy of the Golden City Takeaway of Poggibonsi. If we are very lucky some ancient agricultural machinery might be trundled out and we'll be treated to a threshing display. On such occasions the crowd will gasp as a team of old-timers dressed as Chianti Hillbillies toss pitchforks of wheat into the wooden contraption with its flailing wheels, cogs and drive-belts, as grain emerges from one end and stalks fly out the other. *Hay presto!* (as the tabloids might headline it). The wheat has been separated from the chaff. As newly enrolled horny-handed son and daughter of toil, Mira and I especially appreciate this. It is odd to think that two generations earlier it would have been the combine harvester that drew the crowds and inspired a similarly amazed reaction.

From April until December food festivals are held in villages throughout the area, dedicated to anything from wild boar, frogs, tripe and beans to pasta, cheese, figs, honey, *bruschetta*, chestnuts, mushrooms, truffles and oil. Any excuse to party is good enough for Tuscans, but the highlights are the Friendship Festival run by the Christian Democrats, and the Unity Festival run by the Communists. More regular entertainment is assured in summer in the form of the *ballo liscio*, literally a 'smooth dance' of waltzes, polkas, quicksteps and tangos, held every Saturday night – with no age barrier, as we can see from the tiny tots solemnly dancing like adults in one corner. Everyone is one big happy family.

Similar crowds are drawn to the Cinema Under the Stars when rows of municipal plastic seats are set out in the piazza and a film is shown, free of charge, at night in the open air. It is beamed onto a bit of the 14th-century ramparts from the back of a van by a visiting projectionist who is extremely fond of his wine, so picture clarity is not always guaranteed any more than is continuity of programme. We turned up four times to see *Babe*, hoping to witness a pig talking Italian, but were thwarted on each occasion. Another time, the projectionist decided the film was out of focus and instead of adjusting his lens took it upon himself to reposition the van. At least he didn't start the engine. As the warm-up movie, a Popeye cartoon, continued to roll he put his shoulder to the vehicle and pushed it backwards. Predictably, the beam started to wander. Olive Oyle threw a tin of spinach just as a lady was opening her apartment window within the ramparts and caught it full-square in the face.

The choir give several concerts, appearing in their smart new costumes which everyone has commented on approvingly. A special musical event was staged to celebrate the restoration of the Via delle Volte, the Street of the Vaults, an ancient way which runs like a tunnel through the ramparts and is starting to attract commerce. That such an important gem should have lain dormant so long has always amazed us. Work on building the great dome of Florence cathedral was stopped so that this defensive work could be completed by the same team of 15th-century builders employed by Brunelleschi, the master architect. Since then it has gone unappreciated but for those villagers who used it as a shelter during the war in the same way Londoners used the Tube.

Of course there are the region's wine festivals – in May at Castellina, in June in Radda and in September at Panzano and Greve – at which visitors are encouraged to buy a glass for a modest sum and circulate around the stalls of local Chianti Classico producers, tasting as much as they like over three days, swilling, drinking, spitting and chatting with enthusiasm. They can keep the glass, engraved with the name of the village to remind them where they got their hangover. We mostly abstain, having a few other matters to attend to.

Sometimes a funfair or travelling circus comes and sets itself up in the public car park, with dodgems, a wretched dromedary, a llama with creeping alopecia, and a whole snakepit full of wriggling reptiles which seem to hold particular fascination for Italians. But these are foreign imports from Milan and Rome. Home-grown events are what draw the big crowds, as when, soon after the circus left town, I saw a new village show being advertised as a *Gymkhana di Ape*. I had the uneasy feeling that animal exploitation acts had reached their nadir. A gymkhana for *apes*?

I need not have worried. Far from being a sporting event for primates it was a rally for aficionados of the kind of curious little three-wheeled vehicle that The Pilferer used to drive. Like the scent of garlic, it is adept at permeating every nook and cranny of Italy. Tuscans especially have a great affection for the machine called an Ape, made by Piaggio, not far from Pisa. (Its name, pronounced 'Appy', means Bee and it is the cousin of the Vespa, or Wasp. Both make the same buzzing sound.)

Small things happen to prevent our daily schedule becoming too humdrum: a stray cat here, a lost pet there, a poisoned dog or two. There are mini-scorpions in the pool, mini-scorpions in the apartments, mini-scorpions in the glass of water by my bedside, even a mini-scorpion in Mira's shoe once (discovered 20 minutes *after* she put it on). We have been attacked by a swarm of bees. We have discovered wood-boring beetles munching their way through our main beams; another memorable moment. Mira's gardening work has borne fruit: she has managed to cultivate Tom Thumb tomatoes, wood strawberries, mint, basil, rosemary and sage on the terraces around the apartments for guests to pick along with the walnuts, plums, figs, nectarines and apples that grow quite prolifically now. Several guests have taken pity on Mira when they've seen her weeding and offered to help – one even going to the extreme length of sending her a patented weeding tool from the States when she got home. She has found a new vocation: snail killer. Francesco's monster molluscs have descendants, voraciously chewing all the leaves and flowers they can find. Surreptitiously, she started banging her heel down on them when she thought no one was looking – only to be spotted by Cathryn, a dentist by profession, who has taken over the west side while Mira concentrates on the east. Benito has been fined 600,000 lire and had his driving licence suspended for a month, having been clocked doing nearly 70mph in a speed trap in the historic centre of Florence. ('I go speedy,' says our accountant, who claims he was still in second gear when nabbed.)

One winter's day Mira fell and twisted her ankle, just crumpling before my eyes. She'd done this several times before, tripping up and down our steps, so we were both accustomed to it and although she was in more pain than usual we thought she would be all right. The next morning, however, the pain had become intense and the ankle so swollen she could not wear tights. It was impossible for her to put her shoe on. 'Right my lass, it's off to hospital for you,' I said, bundling her into the Toyota and paying a visit to Anelio to tell him we would be away for a couple of hours.

'What have you done?' he asked. And on hearing the story he said: '*Cavolo!*' Then he added: '*Senta* – listen – before the hospital why not go and see The Manipulator first?'

'The *who?*'

'The man we all go to when we have something wrong with our bones. It may well save you months in plaster.'

The idea of having Mira laid up, immobile, for several months hardly bore thinking about, so we said: 'Why not? Let's try him first.'

The Manipulator, it transpired, was a local witch doctor who had been a shepherd all his life. After his mother died when he was 13 he found he had inherited her skills and was able to set the bones of sheep that had dislocated their limbs. He progressed to humans and had entered local folklore as a great healer.

The mercury was showing zero Celsius as we left Collelungo. By the time we got down into the valley where he lived it was minus 6 and a bank of frost was suspended off the ground like dry ice on a West End stage. We found our man at 8 o'clock in the morning at a solitary house in the middle of a field, miles from anywhere. The encounter was amazing: there he was, outside, clearing his field of rocks by hand, an old man – 82, he told us. He put Mira on a seat in his kitchen and started to feel her ankle. 'Congratulations!' he said after a few moments. 'You're dislocated in three places.' He rolled up his sleeves and manipulated the bones back into position, in that freezing room with no anaesthetic, with me holding her down screaming in agony. 'All done!' he said a minute later, and then brought out flour and eggs, made a dough and slapped it on the offending ankle. 'Try not to move for three days,' he said. And with a simple bandage that was it.

Within a matter of days Mira was able to walk again normally and was so overjoyed by this miracle that she unwisely decided to remove the entire poultice prematurely. That's my girl. Four months later the ankle was still giving her twinges when the season started again. By May we were both wondering if she should have had it X-rayed, and right then our American lawyer, Number One wine fan and top Collelungo cheerleader Randy Schum hove in sight with his wife and two neighbours from Edwardsville, Ill., Dr Jose Ramon and his wife Eva. Dr Ramon, a Cuban exile, turned out to be an orthopaedist. He looked at the foot, said words to the effect that it appeared a bit worn but was probably all right. But to be on the safe side why didn't we have an X-ray taken and send him a J-PEG? And so it was that Mira's ankle was diagnosed 4,000 miles away thanks to the wonders of the Internet. She was in the clear.

More Croquet parties arrive, needing assurance that driving

on the 'wrong side' (ha, ha!) of the road is not a major problem. More Americans come, needing to know that a shift stick is something that helps you to change gear, preferably with the coordinated action of a clutch. We have trouble with air-conditioning. Our fresh mountain air is not enough for some people who cannot bear to be without a cooling system and fail to understand why a/c is not available. We are also always at odds with our American cousins over king-size and queen-size beds as opposed to plain old double beds. There are more enquiries via email, getting more bizarre by the day: questions about the kind of coffee-maker we supply and the type of coffee; questions about room dimensions in feet and inches; questions about 'factory outlets' and our proximity to Gucci and Prada. Several Americans are evidently taking the whole business of visiting Italy so seriously that they are studying the language at home and insist on communicating their new-found skills. I realise their Italian is even worse than mine but so as not to disappoint them I reply in kind, hoping they won't be able to spot my bloopers.

Suddenly, a blow: I have lost the faithful Renault. Over the years I've grown very attached to the old girl, but she finally gave up the ghost as she clocked up 315,000 kilometres. I was driving the superstrada between Florence and Siena, doing rather more than the official limit of 55mph, when the engine caught fire. I hastily pulled over and found an exit after another three minutes (there was no hard shoulder). Flames started licking the bonnet. I had a sickening choice: all I had in the way of liquid to douse the flames were two bottles of precious 1997 Riserva (Parker, 93 points); it was either save them or save the old banger.

By our sixth year in business we are enjoying a full house for nearly 90 per cent of the season which lasts seven months from Easter until Hallowe'en. We are on our third Guest Book, and estimating that some 600–700 visitors are staying at Collelungo every year. We have some lovely comments and notes. One sweet couple from Michigan, visiting for the third time, left a particularly poignant tribute for all to see.

'It is so idyllic here,' they wrote. 'You never fail to disappoint.'

Idyllic maybe, but the bank business was still there, nagging at us. What good was a successful wine and a happy band of tourists when the bank could step in at any minute and whisk the whole thing from under our noses? Our lawyer, Benito's friend, had warned us years earlier that we risked what he called 'working for the bank'; now our dossier at his office was well over a foot thick after all these years and we were still in a state of limbo on the case. I stood outside the magnificent headquarters of the Monte dei Paschi in Piazza Salimbeni one winter's day and determined we really had to do something to bring matters to a close. I felt very small and powerless in front of that huge edifice, that seat of power and patronage that controlled the destiny of so many lives.

It was shortly before Christmas when the posters went up and we read in big black type:

To all citizens!!!
Solidarity with our mayor!!!

A crisis meeting for all the villagers had been convened to hear some shocking news. It appeared that our Nike-wearing louvred-shutter expert, he whom Faraoni had threatened with denunciation for abuse of power, had been arbitrarily suspended from office for issuing building permits illegally. We were dumbfounded. Had our surveyor, that effete little dandy, finally exacted his revenge after a long-running vendetta we knew nothing about? Had he talked the all-powerful Caterpillar *contrada* into delivering the *coup de grâce* to settle that ancient score on his behalf?

This was an emergency call from Refounded Communists, the ones who pinched our oak tree logo, enjoining the entire populace to rally around our brave First Citizen whose moral rectitude, honesty and integrity were, as everyone knew, totally above reproach. Not to mention his impeccable political attitude towards Milanese industrialists (and by implication others who parachuted into his kingdom) who threatened to destroy the villagers' heritage and trespass rights by erecting gates and fences.

It was bitterly cold, threatening to snow, when the solidarity meeting took place three nights later on Christmas Eve. The venue was an underground smoke-filled room stuffed with back-lit figures in overcoats and trilbies like extras on a Hitchcock set. I spotted Renato and Roberto and a good section of building hands from Big Blu who we'd become pally with. There was Alessandro the pharmacist and Edouardo the haberdasher, the leading tenor from the Castellina chorale and many other choristers too. In short, virtually *le tout* Castellina. I had not seen so many glum faces since the last union meeting I'd been to at *The Sunday Times*. Much of the debate passed me by in a howl of hyperbole and microphone feedback, but a handbill signed by the mayor himself gave general details of the charges, his protests of innocence, and his dismay at being described by the investigating magistrate as a person who 'demonstrates an extreme propensity for breaking the law' (as the lovely Italian had it). This alone, he said, was worse than a guilty judgment for the blackening of his name, the social ostracism it would bring, and the slight on his personal ethics.

We are still awaiting the outcome of the case. Life carried on under a 'regent' commissioner imposed on us by the *provincia* until a new election could be held, and now we have a new mayor. But it does not seem to have made one bit of difference. The place is just as inefficient as ever. The only change we have noticed is that the price of dry cleaning has gone up.

There has been one unfortunate sequel, I am sad to report. Antonio the *vigile* was suspended from duty. Not for negligence or dereliction: far from it! Manfully, he seemed to withstand the temptation of the many bribes and favours he must have been offered in the daily execution of his chores. All the bureaucracy must have become a bit too much for him, though, because what happened next seems totally out of character. He punched someone in the town hall and was sent away in disgrace, to be replaced after a contest involving exams, and the inevitable accusations of favouritism and nepotism such events attract in a small village. Nobody knows where the stressed-out ex-*vigile* is today but I rather hope he is lying down in a field somewhere, surrounded by ears of wheat, drinking a bottle of a certain red wine and giggling demoniacally about crazy foreigners and even crazier locals.

We were just welcoming some new arrivals when the phone rang one day in the summer of 2002. It was Fabrizio, the village barman. 'Signor Tony, I want you to be the first to know,' he said excitedly. 'It's Mafalda. They have come and shut her down. She has gone.'

It appeared the denouncing season was in full swing and someone had put the finger on Mafalda too. Was there any connection with the article I posted on the Internet? We would never know. Fabrizio said he suspected someone had an old score to settle and used the publicity we had provoked to get their revenge. It was a double whammy: a classic pincer movement conducted simultaneously by the Guardia di Finanza, tipped off about her outrageous accountancy practices, and the health people, alerted by the tourist authority. The upshot was that Mafalda had fled 'back to Calabria' and the Villa and its restaurant were sealed shut. So Mafalda had not even been local. *Cavolo!*

Well, well. Things could not have been stranger. Or could they? The next day our lawyer called. 'You're not going to believe this,' he said. 'The Monte dei Paschi have agreed to settle.'

Twelve years on, we were finally going to be able to walk proudly through their gilded front doors, cut a deal and walk out smiling, having put the mountain of litigation behind us. Only it was not quite like that. A flunkey met us on the steps and directed us to a little side street in the Caterpillar *contrada* behind the Piazza Salimbeni. Together with Benito and the lawyer we were ushered into a semi-underground back room, with little light and even less ventilation, where metal tables stacked high with copies of our legal brief were awaiting our signature. We were finally done.

Epilogue

As 2002 dawned and we began our 14th year in the vineyards we little realised it would turn out to be our last. Although the property was definitely not on the market, that year, quite out of the blue, we received an offer for Collelungo from a young Italian couple and it brought us up short. The years were advancing and we had no children to whom we could pass on the business; indeed, the only child around was the business itself. Could we bear to part with it, our baby that had taken over our lives?

We thought back on how we started, to all the good things that had happened and some of the not-so-good; of dreams fulfilled and lessons learned; of hopes and disappointments and the reality that in the process of 'our Italian job' we ourselves had become *pensionati*. A couple of old *contadini*, to be correct.

Perhaps the time had come to move on.

We had probably achieved our life's work here and certainly felt hugely enriched by the experience. Leaving it would be a wrench: we had come to spend longer at Collelungo than anywhere else so it was no wonder we felt at home, integrated into the heart-beat of the village. This was where we had experienced some of our best moments as well as some of our most agonising.

Our whole attitude had changed and become proprietorial. Newly arrived 'immigrants' now found us giving them the same advice we got from Bruno so long ago: 'Don't you come here with your foreign ways and expectations.' Funnily, we had even come to support the rigidity of the planning laws (a sure sign we were cracking up). Well, they had managed to preserve the Chianti that we all sought: a homogenous landscape for a homo-genous people.

In our own small way it seemed we too had an effect on those around us:

- Guests who stayed in the *agriturismo*, Robert and Sigrid Longo, were inspired to buy their own abandoned farmhouse and now hope to plant vineyards and make their own top wine.
- Our great friend Laura di Battista had also been renting out her vineyards at her *agriturismo* for years, and was stirred to build a winery herself. Now her son Iacopo has found his mission in life making the award-winning wine Podalirio.
- Mimma and Franco Ferrando, our friends and neighbours, had previously been satisfied tending their 1,000 olive trees. Now they too have planted a hectare or two of vines.
- Paolo is now a senior enologist and is making some of Italy's top wines. Alberto has become a business tycoon; his budding consultancy has blossomed internationally.
- Anelio says he has learned as much from Mira as she has from him. He even prunes some fruit trees to feast the eyes rather than the palate.
- And Fabiola says we have changed her young life in count-less small ways.

What we cherish above all is the shift in attitude of the villagers. These are wonderful, warm-hearted people descended from generations of Castellinese who came to appreciate that we had no intention of plundering their heritage. Quite the opposite: we lived and worked alongside them, supporting the local traders, artisans and restaurants, and encouraged our substantial number of guests to do the same. We printed a little booklet full of hints and addresses to help visitors enjoy their holiday better. It was a very proud moment when the restaurateurs and food shops reciprocated by asking if they could add Collelungo to their wine lists.

Our quest had begun on a long, cold hill in Tuscany one winter's day when everything seemed possible and we had boundless optimism spiced by what now seems like romantic naivety. It reached its zenith in New York City on a cold March morning in 2002.

The venue was the Four Seasons Restaurant in midtown Manhattan. Mira had been chosen as one of only a handful of Chianti Classico producers to speak at a day-long symposium to promote the wine in the United States. It was a singular honour, especially for a non-Italian.

'The vineyards called out to me,' she told a packed Press conference, actually speaking for both of us. 'I grew passionate about it and got into winemaking as if it were second nature. Our farm was a dying ruin when we arrived. What drove me on was an ambition to bring the vineyards back to life and build a winery so the vines could speak with their own voice for the very first time in 600 years.'

Nobody listening and applauding her sentiments could have realised the full story that her little speech disguised.

Castellina today still bears all the hallmarks of the charming hilltop place I describe, though change and EU regulation have overtaken the village and certain elements such as the petrol stations (and sadly the *Vespasiano*) are no more. At time of writing, Collelungo is still a going concern.

We are taking away some golden memories and the knowledge that whatever happens to the old place now, nothing can change the fact that we revived the farm and gave it a new soul. In the full spectrum of time our presence may be viewed as having been as short-lived as the fireflies', but we changed its destiny and wrote one very small part of Chianti history.

We are not going far away. Just over the long hill.

Chianti, Autumn 2003

Acknowledgements

A number of people have been helpful to me in writing this book but it would not have been possible without the stalwart support of my wife whose powers of recall and persistence never fail to amaze me. I would like to express particular gratitude, also, to the following: my friends and former *Sunday Times* colleagues Paul Eddy and Sara Walden for their patience and incisive comments; Celia Haddon, another true friend from *Daily Mail* days; Jon Cousins, who arrived as a guest and remains a great buddy; my agent Doreen Montgomery for never losing faith; my editor Oliver Johnson for his expert advice; former Collelungo client and author Paul Kilduff for his encouragement; Robert Parker, for the use of his reviews from *The Wine Advocate*; Tim Parks for graciously granting me permission to quote from *Italian Neighbours*; the *Consorzio del Marchio Storico Chianti Classico*; and Tony Rae of the Manchester Italian Association for enlightening me about Ancoats and the origins of our community of ice-cream makers. Thanks also to Emily

Sweet, Vikram and Michèle Shah and our lifelong friend Valerie Waters for her invaluable help at Collelungo. My special thanks go to all the gentle people of Castellina, some of whose names I have changed to protect their privacy. I have taken some non-pivotal events out of sequence and disguised some other names of individuals and companies, but this remains a true story.